THE EXPRESSIONIST REVOLUTION IN GERMAN ART 1871—1933

1978 Leicestershire Museums Publication No. 13

Leicestershire Museums, Art Galleries and Records Service
Printed by William Caple & Company Ltd., Leicester

Colour photography by Iona Cruickshank.

ISBN 0 · 85022 017 3 (cloth)

ISBN 0 · 85022 023 8 (paper)

THE EXPRESSIONIST REVOLUTION IN GERMAN ART 1871—1933

A catalogue to the 19th and 20th century German Paintings, Drawings, Prints and Sculpture in the permanent collection of Leicestershire Museums and Art Gallery.

Barry Herbert and Alisdair Hinshelwood

Leicestershire Museums
1978

In the Twentieth Century we shall live amongst strange faces, new pictures and unheard sounds. Many who are not filled with an inner passion will withdraw to the remnants of their memories. Woe to the demagogues who try to drag them out. Everything has its season and the world has time.[1]

Franz Marc *Aphorism* 25

[1] Written at the Front in early 1915. Quoted by Hans Konrad Roethel in *Modern German Painting,* 1958, p. 79.

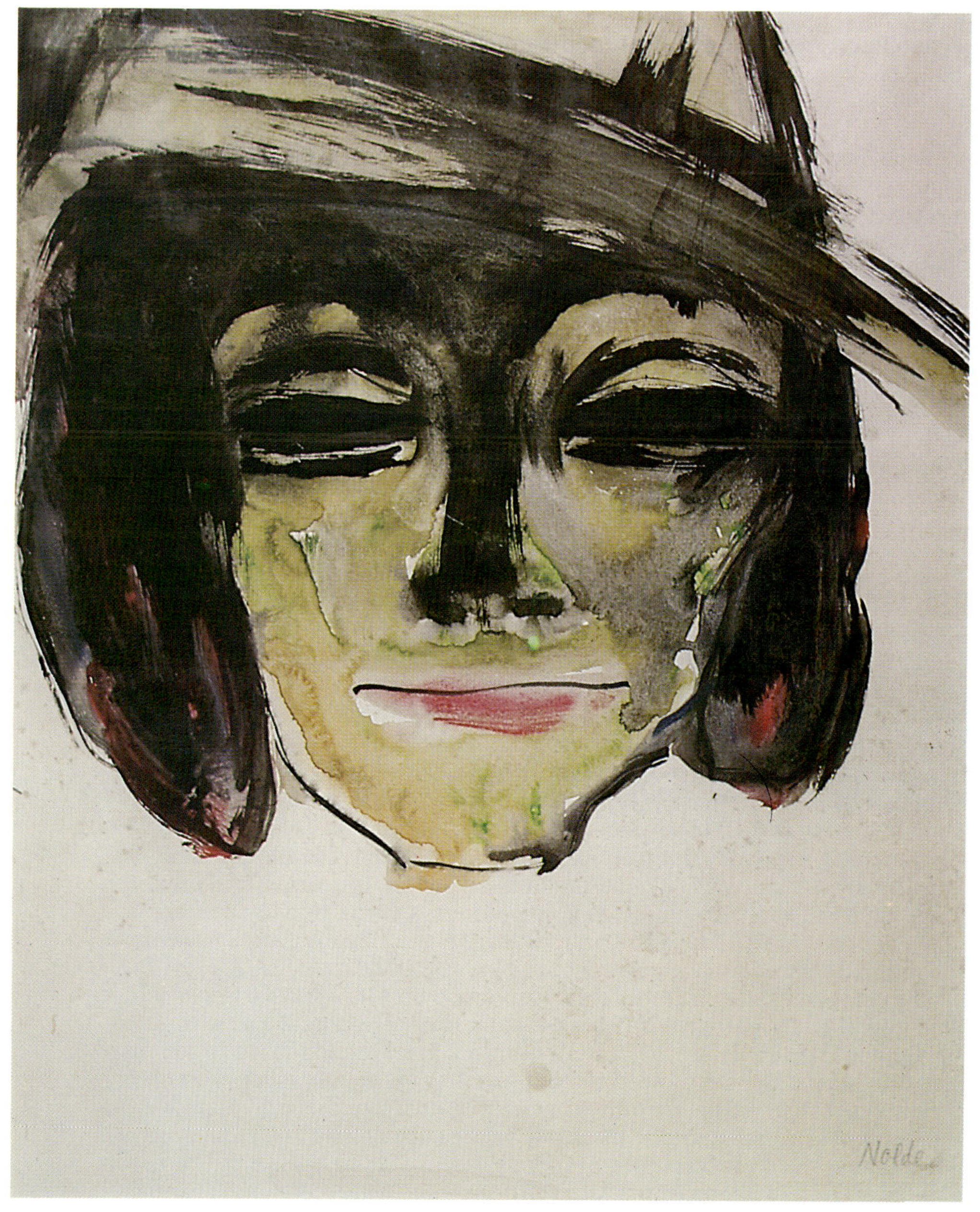

52 **NOLDE**
Kopf mit rot-schwarzem Haar c.1910

Foreword

When Franz Marc's **Rote Frau** and Lyonel Feininger's **Hinter der Stadtkirche** were acquired for Leicester Museum and Art Gallery's permanent collection in 1944, German Expressionism had made little impact beyond an immediate circle of admirers and collectors and was hardly known outside Germany. In Germany it had been proscribed as decadent by the National Socialists in 1933 and was the subject of one of Hitler's most hysterical public outbursts in 1937. Since then the important role played by Expressionism in the development of non-descriptive art forms in the 20th century evolution of European art has been fully recognised and the Expressionist artists occupy a place in the mainstream of modern art alongside their better known French counterparts – the Fauves and Cubists.

The origin of Leicestershire Museums and Art Galleries' collection of Expressionist art arose from the appointment of the late Hans Hess as the Museum's Assistant Keeper of Art in 1944. Alfred Hess, his father, had been one of the chief collectors of Expressionist painting under the Weimar Republic and the family home at Erfurt was visited by many of the most advanced painters and musicians of the day, as the family visitors' book shows by its remarkable number of free sketches. Three of the German works in Leicestershire's permanent collection – the Feininger oil mentioned above and two watercolours, Nolde's **Kopf mit rot-schwarzem Haar** and Pechstein's **Die Brücke in Erfurt** originally belonged to the Hess family.

This most auspicious and, at the time, nationally unprecedented establishment of an Expressionist collection at Leicester was subsequently developed and its range widened to include the immediately preceding generation of German Impressionists and the later New Objectivity artists. Although the collection is still far from comprehensive – there is, for instance, no example of the work of Paul Klee, August Macke, Paula Modersohn-Becker or Gabriele Münter – it remains what is probably the largest public representation of Expressionism in the United Kingdom. This fact in itself was considered to be sufficient justification for publishing a catalogue devoted exclusively to this area of the permanent collection. It is also hoped that the catalogue will serve to bring to the attention of a wider public on every level an aspect of modern European art that has, to an unfortunately large extent, been neglected and overlooked by our public galleries.

The catalogue entries, introductory essays and time-chart have been written and compiled by Barry Herbert and Alisdair Hinshelwood of Leicestershire Museums and Art Galleries' Fine Art Section. They are indebted to the many people listed in the acknowledgments who have willingly given of their specialised knowledge and time in order to help make the individual entries on each work as complete as possible. Without their help the catalogue would not exist. A special debt of gratitude must be expressed to Professor Dr. Hans-Jurgen Imiela of the Kunsthistorisches Institut der Universitaet, Mainz, who generously gave permission for his research material on Max Slevogt to be included here. Any mistakes and oversights remain the responsibility of the compilers.

Acknowledgments

The following is a list of scholars, museums, art dealers and private people
who have in one way or another helped to make the production of this
catalogue possible and whose assistance has been most warmly appreciated.

Stedelijk Museum, Amsterdam
Brücke Museum, Berlin
Nationalgalerie, Berlin
Schloss Charlottenburg, Berlin
Kunstmuseum, Bern
Dr. Gustav Delbanco
Mrs. Herta Emery
Fischer Fine Art Ltd., London
Elaine Frost
Mrs. S. W. H. Goddard
Goethe Institut, London
Professor Dr. Hans-Jurgen Imiela
Dr. Gunter Kruger
Evelyn Lehmann
Museum der Bildenden Kunste, Leipzig
Marlborough Fine Art Ltd., London
Munch Museum, Oslo
Josephine Parry
Jonathan Rashleigh Phipps
Dr. Peter Plesch
Dr. B. Roland
Roland, Browse and Delbanco
Dr. Rainer Schoch
Jeffrey Solomon
Staatsgalerie, Stuttgart
The Tate Gallery

Contents

Introduction

The aim of the generation of young artists responsible for the revival of the spirit of German art prior to 1914 was to replace the outmoded conventions of traditional art forms and, in particular, the autonomy of Impressionism with their own progressive work which, to quote Franz Marc in *Der Blaue Reiter Almanac* would 'create symbols for their own time which could take their place on the altars of the future spiritual religion, symbols behind which the technical heritage cannot be seen'.[1] This expression of a new consciousness extended not only to the artists' role in creating modern art forms but also to their equally passionate concern for individual human existence and the need for a new world. Their hatred for what they recognised to be a fatal decline in German cultural and moral standards, its materialism, empty intellectualism and nostalgia was as great as their rejection of an art routine, dominated in turn by the Academies and the various Secessions which isolated the artist and his work from the realities of everyday life.

[1] 'The German Savages', by Franz Marc in *Der Blaue Reiter*, 1912, p.7.

The German Empire

Germany did not exist as a unified state until 1871. Previously it had been a loose federation of four kingdoms, six grand-duchies, five duchies, seven principalities and three free towns. This new German Empire was not the Germany we see on the map today but included much of Poland, part of Denmark and Alsace-Lorraine, which had been given up by the French in 1871 following the Franco-Prussian War.

The new Germany was dominated by Prussia which constituted two-thirds of the total land area and population and whose King became Kaiser Wilhelm I. Although a new system of government was required to cope with a country undertaking rapid industrial expansion and thereby undergoing equally rapid social change, the Empire retained a system dominated by the aristocracy and landowners. The government now consisted of the Reichstag, a body of elected members, and the Bundesrat, a council of representatives from all the states. The Reichstag had no real legislative power as the Bundesrat, acting in an advisory capacity to the Kaiser, was answerable only to him and, more importantly, so was the military. Wilhelm I's government was dominated by the Prussian Chancellor, Otto von Bismarck.

By 1879 Germany's industrial growth rate was greater than Britain's and second only to that of America. Despite a comparatively late industrial development, its advanced industrial plant design achieved rapid ascendancy and, in addition, Germany backed new and vital industries such as the production of chemicals and electricity. Not only was its plant superior but its whole industrial structure of production, banking, distribution and retailing was more efficient. Despite the advantages brought by this rapid advance, it created many tensions in German society with an increasing number of industrialists and an urban working class.

The middle class, previously so secure, was now caught between the workers and big business and, to maintain their position, allied themselves with Imperial authority and values. In doing this they adopted prevailing Prussian standards in a desire to strengthen Germany's new national unity against changes within society. Duty towards the state, when assumed as a safeguard of social status and national stability, easily developed into a blind acceptance of a rigid and authoritarian social order.

The increasing conservatism of German society was reflected in the arts. A passive academic tradition developed, reliant on the past and unable to forge its own identity. These circles, constrained by the meaningless academicism favoured by the Imperial authorities and producing superficial and sentimental paraphrases of obsolete ideas, were to force younger artists into finding new forms of expression.

> 'The creative man honours the past by leaving it in peace and not by living in it. It was the tragedy of our fathers that they, like the alchemists, wanted to make gold out of venerable dust. In doing so they lost their fortune. They ran the gamut of past cultures and lost the ability to create their own.'
>
> Franz Marc *Aphorism* 39

A National Cultural Identity

The separation and independence of the German states prior to 1871 had a considerable influence upon the development of German culture. In the numerous provincial capitals the arts and sciences developed independently until the emergence of Berlin as a capital city and cultural centre. The lack of unity within Germany led many artists to look to Rome or Paris for a cultural tradition in which to work, thereby failing to utilise and recreate Germany's own identity.

However, some artists, particularly in Dresden, did attempt to reassert the Northern European tradition. The most notable of these artists was Caspar David Friedrich 1774-1840 who rejected neo-Classicism and was a relentless opponent of the 'Nazarenes' who, in an attempt to introduce a spiritual quality into their works, reverted to the styles of Italian and German artists prior to the high Renaissance. Friedrich and other German Romantics rejected the influence of Italianate landscape painting, replacing it with a representation of their own native landscape, often imbued with deep religious feeling and a philosophic expression of human vanity and isolation. The landscape of Germany became a symbol, the manifestation of God, but this development was frowned upon by the more conservative. In 1809 the critic Ramdohr wrote in the *Zeitschrift für die elegante Welt:*

> 'it is truly presumption when landscape painting tries to slink into church and crawl on to the altar'.[1]

The Romantics attempted to express that which they felt lay beyond mere appearances but without constant reference to the over-used symbols and allegories of classical mythology and traditional religious representation.

> 'Close your bodily eye so that you may see your picture first with the spiritual eye. Then bring to the light of day that which you have seen in the darkness, so that it may react upon others from the outside inwards.'[2]

Caspar David Friedrich

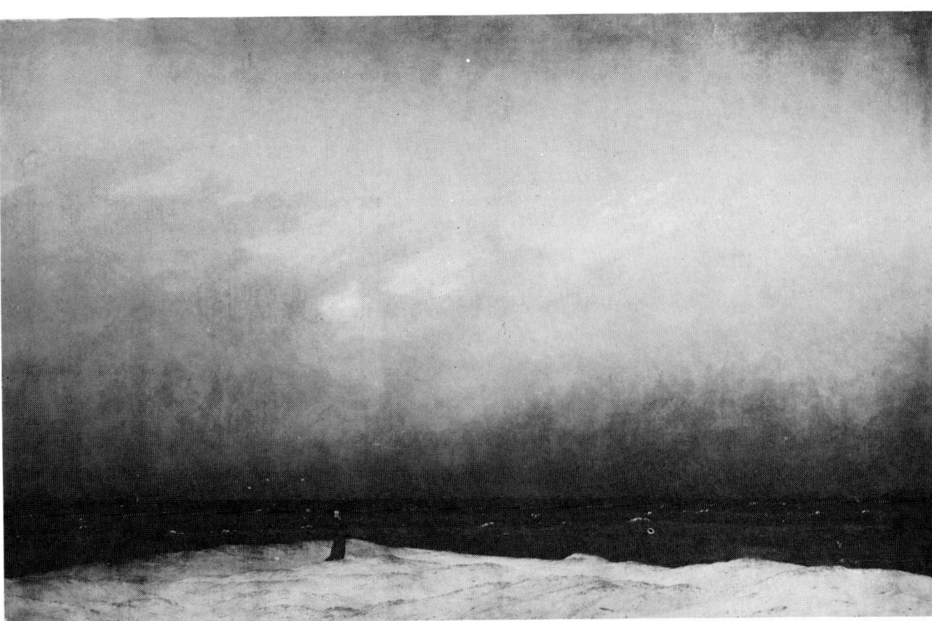

FRIEDRICH
Mönch am Meer 1809
Monk by the Seashore
Oil on canvas 110×171
Reproduced by kind permission of the Staatliche Schlösser und Gärten, Schloss Charlottenburg, Berlin.

With the Wars of Liberation following the Napoleonic invasion, many hoped for a unification of Germany and interest grew in its mediaeval heritage. However, unification did not occur but mediaevalism became an active part of German culture, particularly in a revival of Gothic architecture. Amongst earlier German painters to whom 19th century artists now turned were Albrecht Dürer 1471-1526 and Hans Holbein 1497-1543, whose woodcuts were particularly influential on the visual imagery of artists such as Alfred Rethel 1816-59, as in Plate Six of his series **Another Dance of Death** 1849.

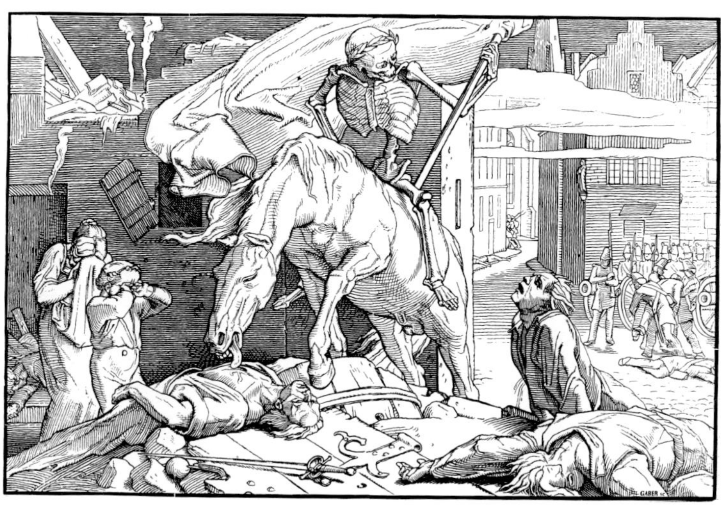

57d **RETHEL**
Plate six from **Auch ein Todtentanz**
1849

This positive re-emergence of an independent German spirit in early 19th century art was, however, rapidly transformed into a sterile academic style associated with political and religious conservatism. Friedrich was virtually forgotten within his own lifetime and was not acknowledged until the 1890's and the *Berlin Centenary Show* of 1906 when it could be seen how close in spirit he was to the new generation of truly North European artists such as Munch and Hodler.

> 'I am not so weak as to submit to the demands of an age when they go against my convictions. I spin a cocoon around myself: let others do the same. I shall leave it to time to show what will come of it: a brilliant butterfly or a maggot.'[3]

Caspar David Friedrich

Throughout the second half of the 19th century German artists continued to look to other cultural traditions and made no attempt to create their own. In 1844, in his book *Critical Approaches,* the critic Theodor Vischer wrote:

> 'We paint gods and Madonnas, heroes and peasants, in the same way as we build in the Byzantine, Florentine, Renaissance and rococo styles, without having any style we can call our own. We paint everything in the world catalogue; we are jacks of all trades and masters of none ... The artist stands pondering and wondering what to choose from all the wares that have ever been available.'

[1] Quoted by Ulrich Finke in *German Painting from Romanticism to Expressionism,* 1974, p.24.
[2] Quoted in *Caspar David Friedrich* 1774-1840, Exhibition Catalogue, The Tate Gallery, London 1972, pp.14 and 103.
[3] H. V. Einern, *Caspar David Friedrich,* Berlin 1938. Quoted in *Caspar David Friedrich* 1774-1840, Exhibition Catalogue, The Tate Gallery, London, p.44.

New Directions

In September 1858 Gustave Courbet 1819-1877, the French Social-Realist painter, visited Frankfurt, where four years before several of his paintings had caused a public outcry. His work was a major influence on artists of the younger generation in Germany, particularly his masterpiece **The Stonebreakers** 1850 which was exhibited in Munich in 1869, along with works by his contemporaries such as Corot, Millet and Manet.

Hans Thoma 1839-1924, who had seen Courbet's work in Paris in 1868, expressed the enthusiasm inspired in the young German artists when he said:

> 'Seeing his pictures, I had the impression that I might have painted them myself: I felt free of the shackles of the Academy and I was filled with confidence that I too could do something worthwhile.'

More so even than in France, the relaxation in the choice of subject-matter instigated by Courbet's influence, received a hostile and uncomprehending reception amongst the conservative German middle-classes. Realist painting in Germany was seen as an overt attack on the structure of society. As the critic Karl von Lützow observed in the *Zeitschrift für bildende Kunst* 1869/70; 'the social question sweeps in through the wide open gates of art'.

Alongside these new elements from France, there emerged within Germany a Naturalist movement which, whilst preserving academic concepts of subject matter and technique, introduced a subjective attitude into its work that was to have considerable influence on later developments. The most important exponents of this school were Arnold Böcklin 1827-1893, Hans von Marées 1837-1887 and Max Klinger 1857-1920. The symbolic significance of their chosen subject – often of a religious or allegorical nature – introduced a highly personal iconography into German painting and a heightened interpretation of old ideas.

Adolph von Menzel 1815-1905, whose early training had been in contemporary history painting, was the leading German painter of his generation. Three visits to Paris in 1855, 1867 and 1868 introduced him to the work of French Realism and Impressionism. Although he extracted from the Impressionists those elements that appealed to his personal style, Menzel was essentially critical of their technical merits, a personal attitude which reflected the general hostility and official rejection of any form of foreign contemporary painting. In the 1880's and 90's, Hugo von Tschudi, Director of the National Gallery in Berlin, personally purchased works by the French Impressionists as the state would not support their purchase for a public collection. He subsequently presented his collection to the Bayerische Staats-gemaldesammlungen in Munich. In 1889 official sponsorship was withheld from artists wishing to contribute works to the Paris World Exhibition. Max Liebermann, however, encouraged Berlin artists to submit their work independently.

BÖCKLIN
Toteninsel 1886
Isle of the Dead
Oil on panel 80×150
Reproduced by kind permission of the Museum der bildenden Kunste zu Leipzig.

MAREES
Die Ruderer 1873
The Oarsmen
Oil on canvas 136×167
Reproduced by kind permission of the Staatliche Museen Preussicher Kulturbesitz, Berlin.

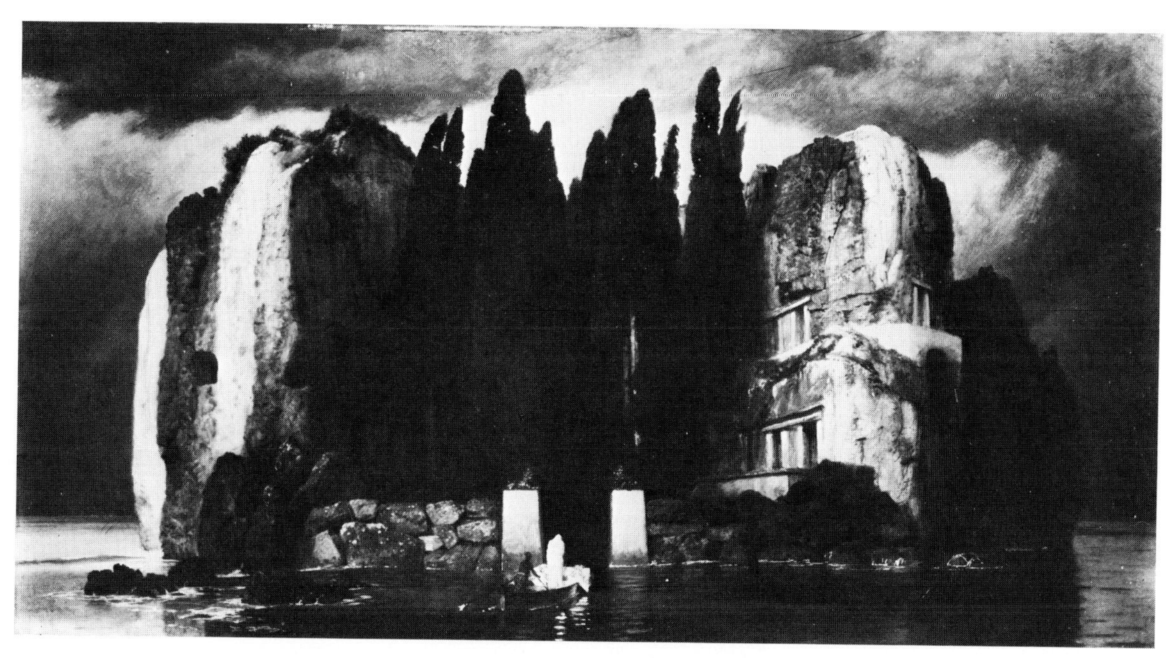

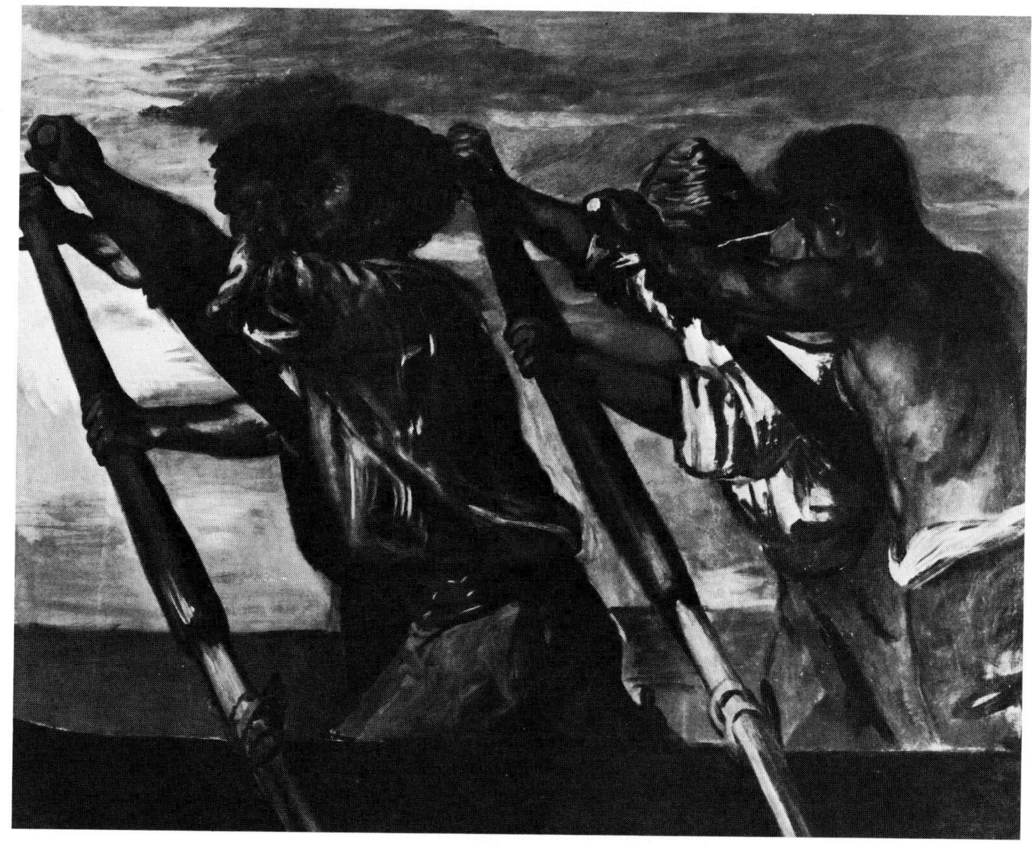

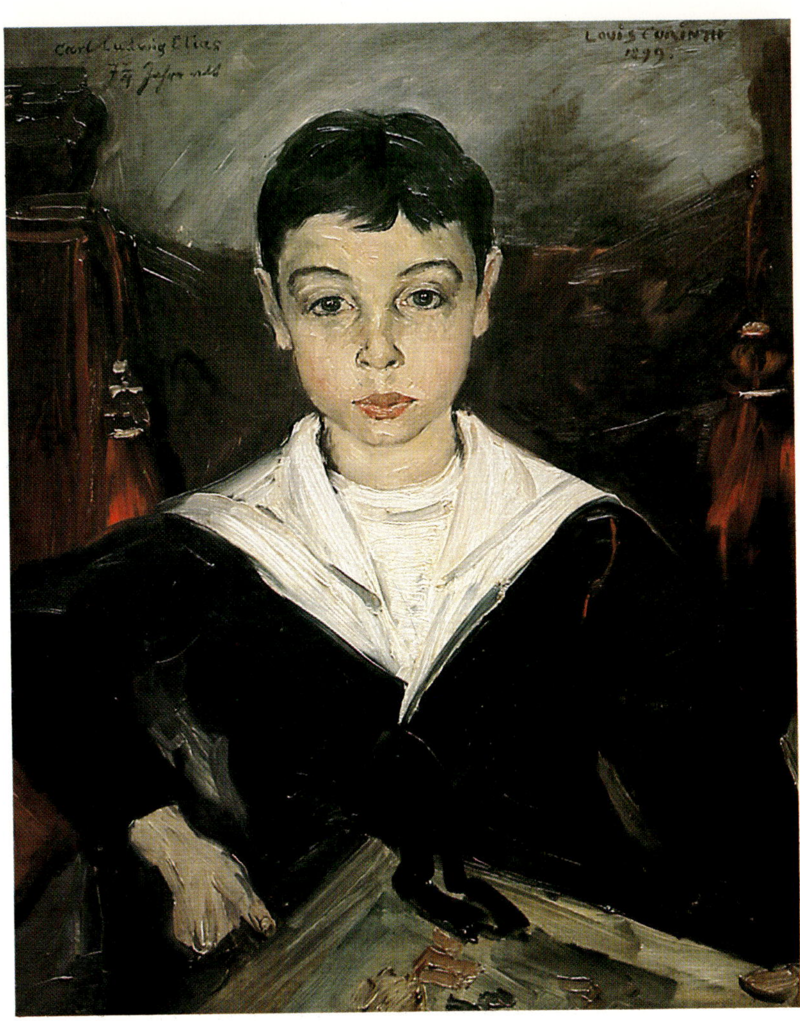

6 **CORINTH**
Bildnis Carl Ludwig Elias 7¼ 1899
Carl Ludwig Elias was the son of Dr.
Julius Elias, the distinguished art critic
and translator who did much to promote
a true understanding of French
Impressionism in Germany and was on
personal terms with most of the leading
artists of his time. When the Nazis came
to power in Germany, Carl Ludwig Elias,
who had been a lawyer in Berlin,
emigrated to Norway where he was
granted asylum and citizenship. He was
subsequently captured by the Nazis and
died in a concentration camp. Corinth
was the most significant member of the
group of German artists who
experimented with French Impressionism
at the end of the 19th century and utilised
it in a characteristically German manner
stressing inner meanings where the
French concerned themselves more with
momentary effects.

Secession

Max Liebermann 1847-1935, with Lovis Corinth 1858-1925 and Max Slevogt 1886-1932 formed the Triumvirate of German Impressionists and were the immediate forerunners of Expressionism. In 1892 a group of young artists, including Corinth, formed the Munich Secession, a breakaway movement opposed to academic domination of the arts. In the same year Liebermann and Ludwig von Hofmann 1861-1941 formed Gruppe XI in Berlin which was the origin of the Berlin Secession, whose first exhibition was held in 1898. The independent action of these young artists was initiated by the abrupt closure of an exhibition of fifty paintings by the Norwegian artist Edvard Munch in Berlin in 1892. Munch had been invited to exhibit by the Berlin Artists' Association but conservative elements within this body forced it to close immediately.

At the same time as the Secessionists established their independence, various liberal and satirical magazines were appearing in Berlin and Munich. The most important of these new publications were *Pan,* Berlin 1894 and *Jugend* and *Simplicissimus,* Munich 1896. Amongst the contributors who gave their support to the Secession were Maximilian Harden 1861-1927, Julius Meier-Graefe 1867-1935, and Bruno 1872-1940 and Paul Cassirer 1871-1926 who, through their publishing house and gallery respectively, supported the contemporary movement.

The Secession exhibitions included the work of foreign contemporaries, especially the French Impressionists and Post-Impressionists. Van Gogh's work was first shown in Berlin at the Secession exhibition of 1903. Progressive attitudes generally came under constant attack from the Imperial establishment which succeeded in casting political suspicion on the work of young artists especially where it was concerned in drawing attention to social injustice as exemplified in the graphic work of Käthe Kollwitz 1867-1945. The visual arts were not the only subject of Imperial criticism. The Empress Auguste Victoria attacked Richard Strauss's *Salome* 1905 and *Der Rosenkavalier* 1911 as being immoral.

An intellectual climate was forming, however, with which young and progressive artists and writers in Germany could identify. A deepening belief in an intuitive and emotional response to life and a condemnation and rejection of materialism was influenced and consolidated by a growing interest in the philosophy of Nietzsche and the Frenchman Henri Bergson 1859-1941 and the paintings of van Gogh, Gauguin, Munch and Hodler.

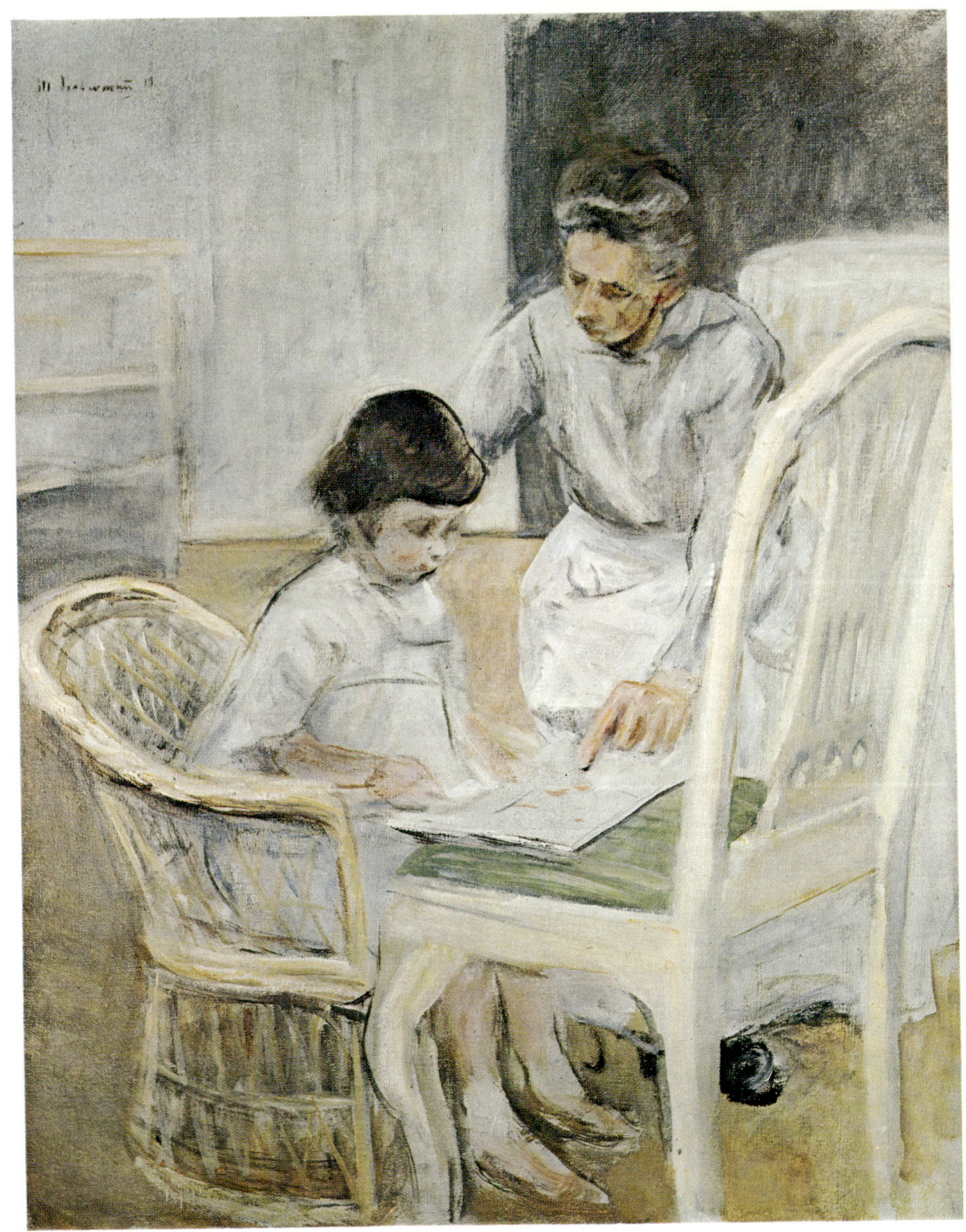

40 LIEBERMANN
**Die Enkelin des Künstlers mit ihrem
Kindermädchen 1919**
Liebermann's reputation as one of the
foremost representatives of German
Impressionism, along with Lovis Corinth
and Max Slevogt, established him as the
dominant figure in the Berlin art world for
several decades. His approach to life was
unsentimental and objective and
succeeded in establishing within German
Art the modern trends that had been
developed in other parts of Europe.

Precursors of Expressionism
Paul Gauguin 1848-1903

Gauguin belonged to the generation of late 19th century French artists who rejected Impressionism's analytical and illusionistic view of the world. His colour symbolism was adopted by the Expressionists and his decorative autonomy of form was the starting point of Kandinsky's more extreme abstract statements. Syntheticism, the new visual language developed by Paul Gauguin, allowed the artist to present his subjective vision of the world when it was considered more important to depict the essence of a subject rather than to document its external appearance.

Gauguin's artistic evolution was influenced by the artefacts of primitive cultures and the quality of their way of life with which he identified in Brittany and Tahiti. His belief in the value of a natural and primitive way of life served as a precedent to several Expressionist artists, most notably Nolde and Pechstein.

Gauguin's first successful attempt at interpreting a totally subjective and symbolic image was **Vision after the Sermon** 1888 (now in the National Gallery, Edinburgh) which he described as the 'synthesis of a form and a colour achieved by omitting everything except the keynote'.

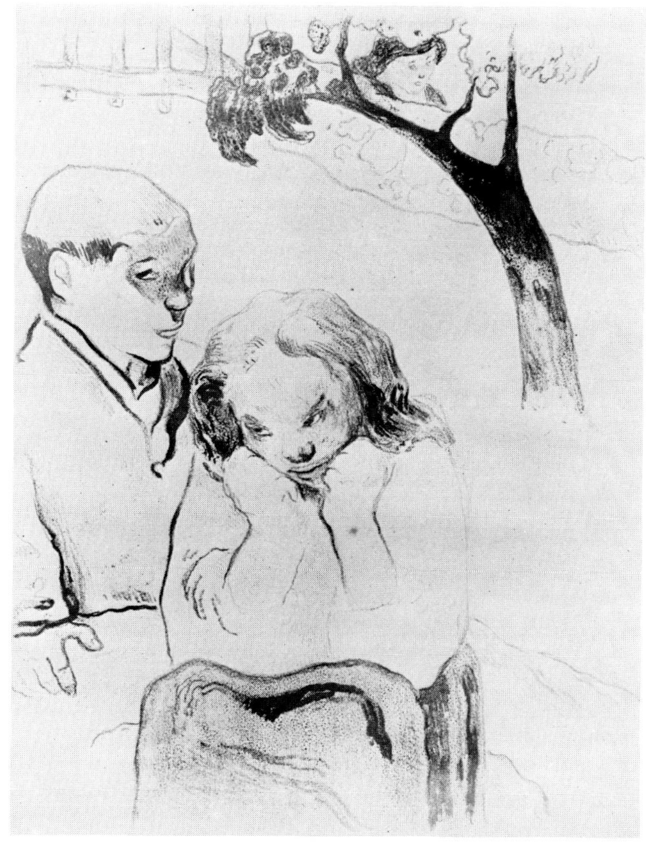

GAUGUIN
Misères Humaines 1889
Zinc lithograph 30·5 × 22·75

Vincent van Gogh 1853-90

The publication of van Gogh's letters and the exhibition of his paintings in Germany, beginning in 1903, were important to the development of Expressionism. In his feeling for nature as a vast and powerful force in which he could lose himself, van Gogh established a precedent for the Expressionists. A primary feature of his painting was the expressive use of pure colour which, like Gauguin, he adopted from Japanese prints. His frenzied brush strokes and distorted forms were equally influential on Expressionist technique.

Van Gogh's mysticism exerted a powerful influence over the lives of many Expressionist artists, including Kirchner, Nolde and Meidner, who consciously identified with his isolation and his dependence on introspection for the ability to create.

Van Gogh's consciousness of his mission in life and the exceptional control which he exerted over his destiny are clearly expressed in his letters to his brother Theo. In terms of the cultural predicament of his time he passionately resisted the fragmentation of the artistic personality and the increasing social disorder and decadence. Like many 19th century thinkers concerned by the loss of tradition, van Gogh sought to restore the values of an earlier age which would once again unify art and society, culture and religion without abandoning the present. His articulate writing, commitment to work and his beliefs, the dynamic energy and arbitrary colours of his paintings made van Gogh one of the most powerful influences on the early development of the Expressionist style.

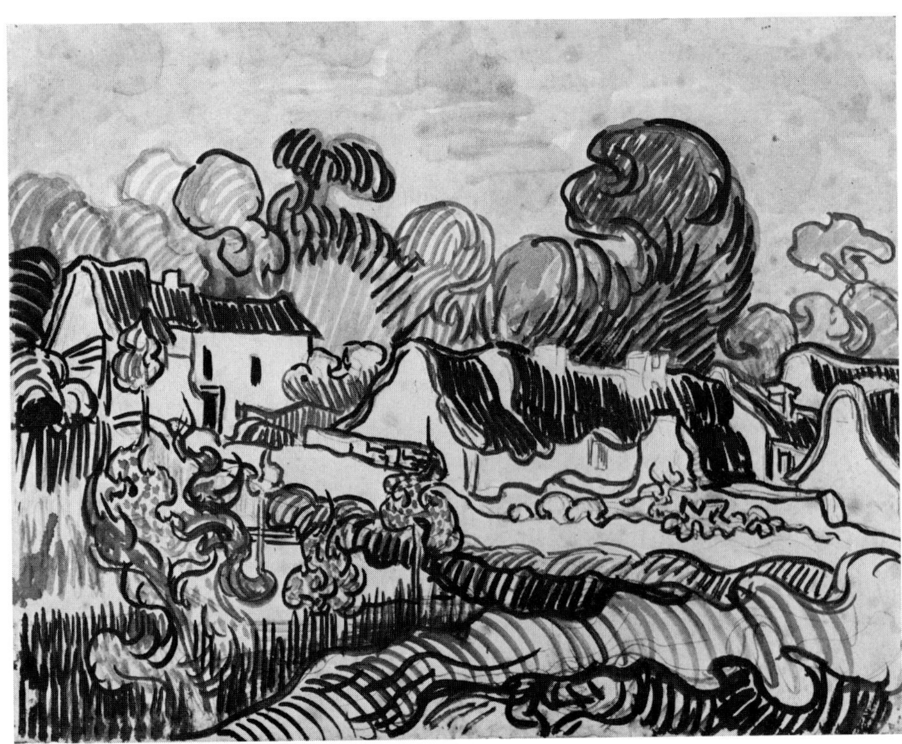

VAN GOGH
Landscape with Houses and Trees
1890
Watercolour and black crayon 45 × 54·5
Reproduced by kind permission of the Stedelijk Museum, Amsterdam.

Ferdinand Hodler 1853-1918

Hodler was isolated for most of his life in his native Switzerland and his
paintings developed in a highly individual manner. Like the Parisian
Rosicrucian artists, whom he most closely resembled, his work was mystical
and emotional but charged with a unique feeling for the earth that appealed
most readily to the Germans.

Hodler expressed man's deep-rooted preoccupations with the subconscious
or spiritual life which, combined with the complex linear rhythms and abstract
space of his 'Parallelism' technique, influenced the pre-war generation of
young artists in Austria and Germany.

Towards the end of his life Hodler sought different ways in which he could be
absorbed by nature, finding in the Swiss lake and mountain scenery a perfect
symbol of his need. In 1904 his importance in the development of modern
trends was finally acknowledged when the main room of the Vienna
Secession exhibition was devoted to his work.

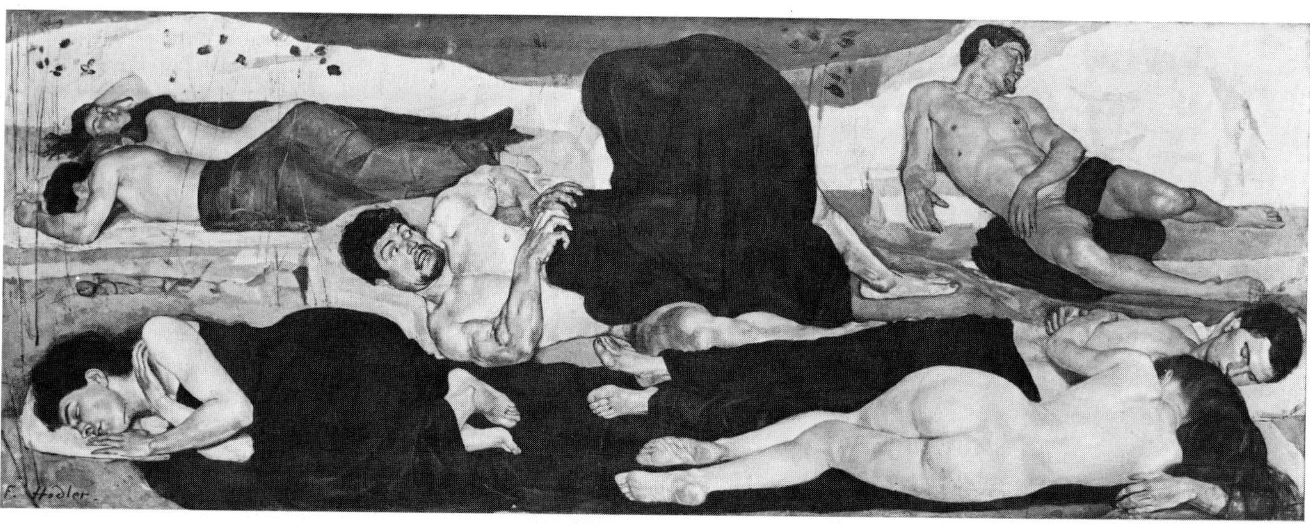

HODLER
Die Nacht 1890
Night
Oil on canvas 116×299
Reproduced by kind permission of the
Kunstmuseum, Bern.

Edvard Munch 1863-1944

Munch's influence on the work of the German Expressionists was direct, creating not only a conducive spiritual climate in which the movement could develop but also affecting their choice of subject matter and technique. Geographically and psychologically Munch epitomised the outsider, a voluntary exile from his native Norway, and, with his penetrating insight into the dark nature of man's mind, showing an intense degree of introspection. The recurring themes of his work – illness, sex, depression and death – anticipated the discoveries of psycho-analysis and shared many affinities with the plays of his compatriot, Henrik Ibsen and the Swedish writer August Strindberg, with whom he associated in Berlin's Bohemia in the 1890's.
At a time when the influence of Paris as the art centre of the world was possibly greater than it had ever been before, Munch was a living example to many young German painters that it was possible to be original elsewhere than in the French capital. The exhibition of his work in Berlin in 1892 and its premature closure caused a split in official art circles which ultimately led to the foundation of the Berlin Secession. The artists of **Die Brücke**, particularly Kirchner, were most influenced by his example, although Munch always maintained a cool if polite distance from their activities. Unlike the Expressionists, he did not make concessions to the brutalisation of form in order to convey a desperate view of the human condition, although such things as his use of exaggerated perspective were successfully borrowed by them to heighten the emotional content of their work.

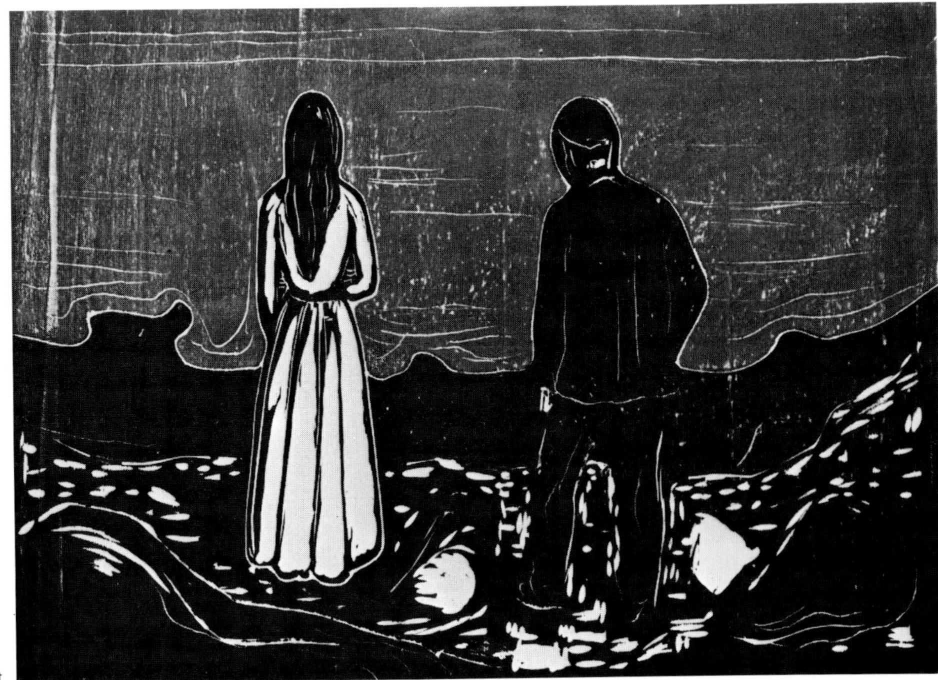

MUNCH
The Lonely Ones 1899
Colour woodcut 39·5 × 53
Reproduced by kind permission of the Oslo
Kommunes Kunstsamlinger, Munch-Museet.

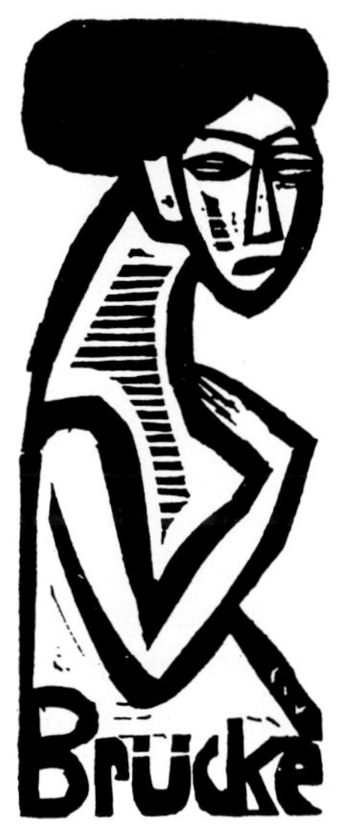

Die Brücke

The Secession's decisive move away from conservative academicism in the visual arts enabled young artists to see work by many foreign painters who were to influence their own future development, such as the Post-Impressionists, the Nabis and Munch. Most of the artists instrumental in setting up the Secession, however, were already established and respected figures and it was left to a group of young, impassioned artists working outside the official auspices of the Secession to set in motion the first major progressive development in German art in the 20th century.

The formation of the group known as **Die Brücke** (The Bridge) took place in Dresden in 1905 and consisted of four enthusiastic students of architecture from the Technical College whose dissatisfaction with a society coarsened and dehumanised by modern technology and materialism impelled them to try and create a new world and a new art. Their dedicated belief in their own ability to do this was founded to a large extent on youthful optimism and energy which was stimulated by their admiration for the humanistic writings of Nietzsche, one of whose texts gave the group its name and their disappointment in contemporary standards of German painting.

The spiritual and dynamic leader of **Die Brücke** was Ernst Ludwig Kirchner 1880-1938, who was the only member of the group to have received formal art training, a short period between 1903 and 1904 spent in the private art school of Debschutz and Obrist in Munich. Otherwise, they were all self-taught, encouraging and stimulating one another in their work and experiments in oils and watercolours, the various graphic media and the applied arts in their first communal studio on the Berlinerstrasse. Kirchner's fellow members were Fritz Bleyl 1880-1966, Erich Heckel 1883-1970 and Karl Schmidt-Rottluff 1884-1976. Bleyl was to leave the group because of economic necessity in 1908 to take up a career as an architect; the others devoted their lives to art.

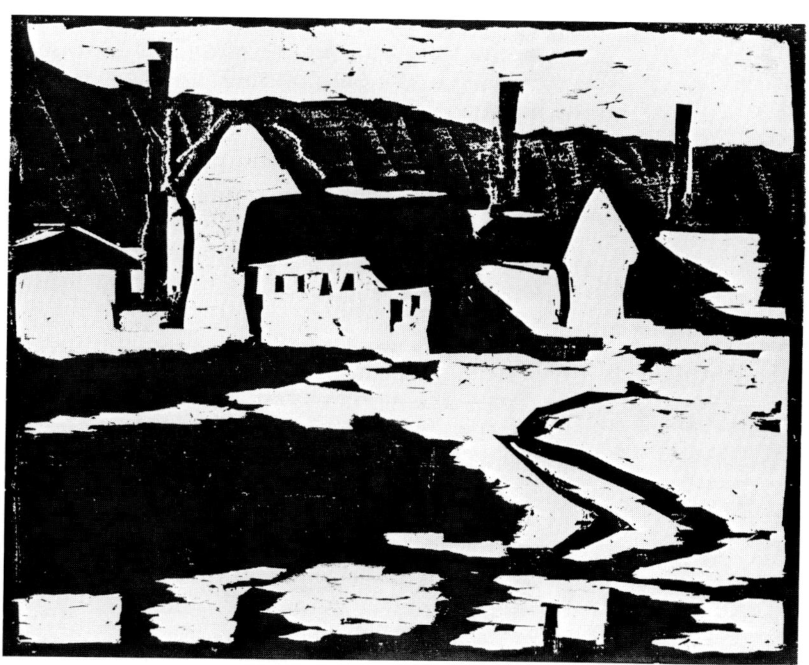

63 SCHMIDT-ROTTLUFF
Häuser am Wasser 1910

The sources of their inspiration were widespread and multifarious. Believing as they did in the original importance of the mediaeval German mind, they turned to the work of the old German masters including Dürer's woodcuts and the emotional, tortured paintings of Cranach and Grünewald. Added stimulants were discovered in the primitive sculptures of the African and Oceanic races to be seen in the local Museum of Ethnography. Their belief in the importance of these objects as genuine art forms was verified by the life and work of Paul Gauguin, whilst their spiritual unrest and social isolation found a mentor in van Gogh.

Both Gauguin and van Gogh influenced the stylistic technique of **Die Brücke** in addition to enhancing their belief in life's fundamental values by their own example. The new psychological content of Munch's work was important but less relevant to **Die Brücke's** needs than his revitalisation of the woodcut and lithograph as a means of visual expression. The decorative qualities of the Nabis's paintings and Felix Vallotton's strong revival of the woodcut were also absorbed into the young German artists' visual language. The pervasive influence of the Jugendstil movement's cursive line and strongly defined juxtaposition of flat colours is a predominant feature throughout the work of all these artists.

From the beginning the group placed as much emphasis on attracting a sympathetic public as it did on drawing to itself 'all revolutionary and radical elements' of the art world. In 1906 they were joined briefly by Emil Nolde 1867-1956, a contact from which all benefited artistically. Max Pechstein 1881-1955 also became a member in 1906 and later succeeded in popularising the movement in Berlin before any of the original founders' work was accepted. The last important member to join the group was Otto Mueller 1874-1930 in 1910, the year before Kirchner, Heckel and Schmidt-Rottluff moved to Berlin. **Die Brücke** had a small but active number of private subscribers who became known as the 'passive members'. They included art specialists and collectors such as Gustav Schiefler and Rosa Schapire but also ordinary professional people who were enthusiastic and could give practical help, such as Seifert, whose lighting factory showroom provided the premises for the first two Brücke exhibitions in 1906. Much time and effort was devoted to the promotion of this side of the group's activities: an annual portfolio containing original graphics, an annual report and a membership card were produced between 1906 and 1912. Exhibitions were also arranged, though with little success. Each artist divided his time between Dresden and one of the North Sea resorts to which they retreated during the summer months.

By 1911 each member of the group had made his way to Berlin and in 1913 **Die Brücke** was dissolved by mutual consent following disagreement with Kirchner's account of their history in his *Chronicle of Die Brücke.* By this time the group's communal way of life, the sharing of studios, models and materials and the group 'style' had given way to individual artistic development and the pursuit of personal careers. The last occasion on which they exhibited as a group was at the Cologne Sonderbund of 1912. For eight years **Die Brücke** had been the true focal point of German Expressionism and was the most thoroughly national of the three revolutionary movements which dominated Germany at the beginning of the 20th century.

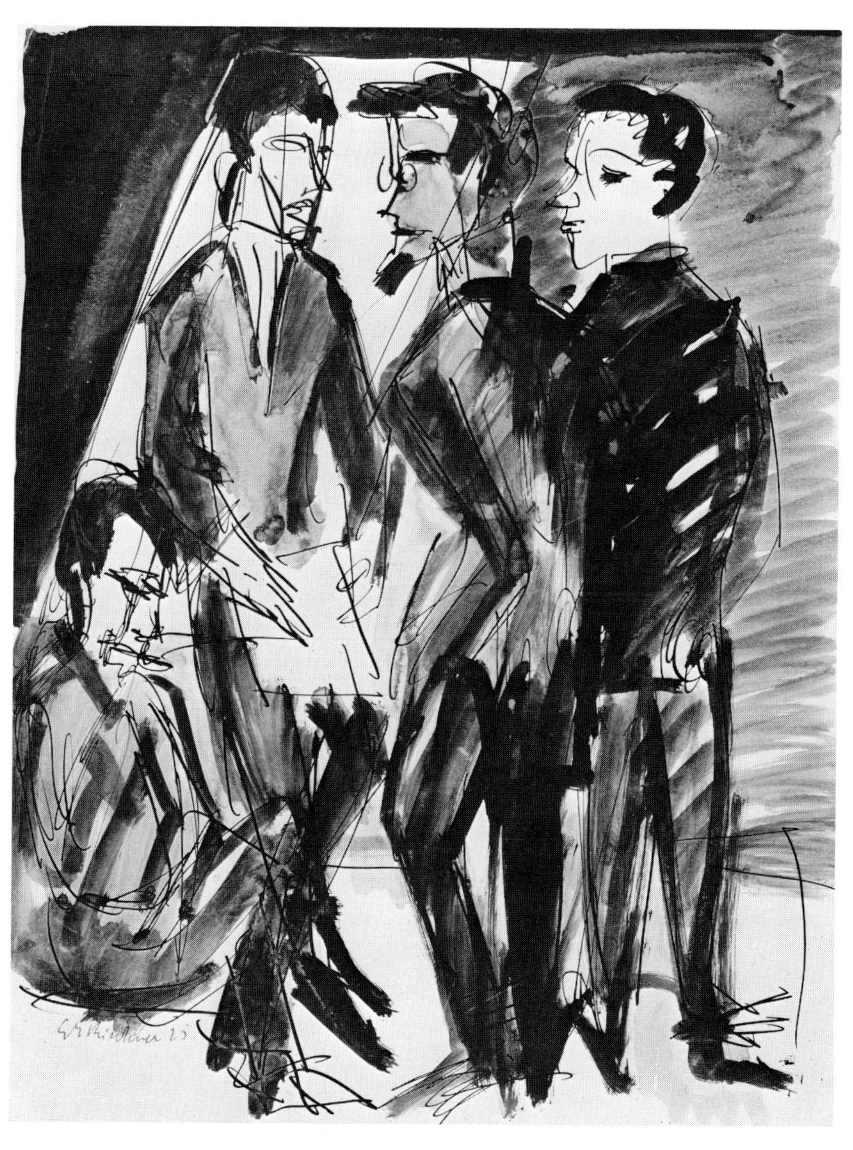

KIRCHNER
Die Maler der Brücke
The Painters of Die Brücke
Pen, ink and wash 48×36·25
Reproduced by kind permission of the
Staatsgalerie, Stuttgart.
One of three drawings related to the 1926
painting *A Group of Artists* in the Wallraf-
Richartz-Museum, Cologne. Kirchner has
chosen to represent the Brücke
membership as it stood in 1913 when the
group was dissolved. From left to right it
shows Otto Mueller seated, Kirchner
holding the *Chronicle of the Brücke*
which was repudiated by the others,
Schmidt-Rottluff advancing towards him
and Heckel. In the painting Heckel is
interposed between Schmidt-Rottluff and
Kirchner in his usual role of mediator.

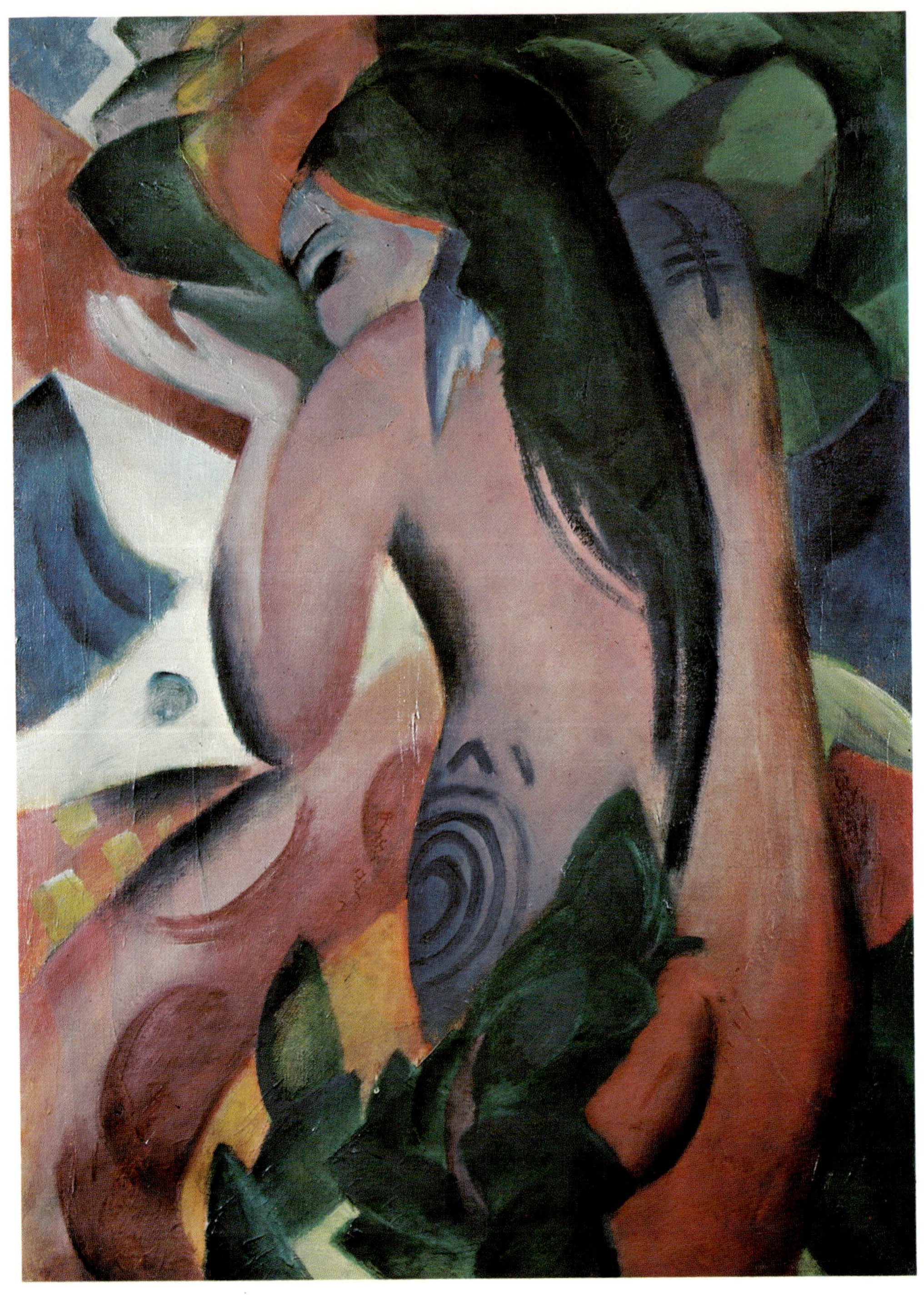

44 **MARC**
Rote Frau 1912

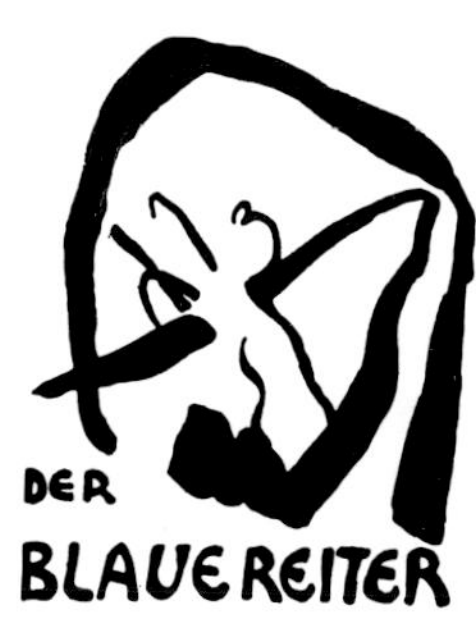

Der Blaue Reiter

Munich before the war was a city composed of rural and cosmopolitan elements, whose lively atmosphere attracted many foreign artists. Dresden had become the centre for **Die Brücke**, an essentially nationalistic group but Munich brought together a far more international group of artists. In 1896 Alexej von Jawlensky 1864-1941 came to Munich from St. Petersburg, accompanied by Marianne von Werefkin 1860-1938. A year later they were followed by Wassily Kandinsky 1866-1944 who came from Moscow. In 1898 Paul Klee 1879-1940 came from Munchenbuchsee in Switzerland and Alfred Kubin 1877-1959, originally from Leitmeritz in Bohemia.

In 1909 Kandinsky and Jawlensky, neither of whom had received any formal artistic training in Russia, after studying at the studio of Anton Azbé, where they had met, formed **Neue Künstlervereinigung München** (New Artists' Union), which also included Werefkin, Gabriele Münter 1877-1962, Adolf Erbsloh 1881-1947 and Alexander Kanoldt 1881-1939. The exhibition arranged in the same year demonstrated their positive rejection of the Secessionist's impressionism and the exhibition held in 1910 included works by the following invited artists: Braque, van Dongen, Picasso, Rouault and Vlaminck. Kandinsky and Jawlensky had already worked in Paris and were familiar with current artistic activity. An internal dispute prior to the Union's third exhibition planned for 1911 led to a split within the group.

The splinter group composed of Kandinsky, Münter and Kubin, at this point joined by Franz Marc 1880-1916, formed the basis of the new group which became known as **Der Blaue Reiter** (The Blue Rider). This was a very loose association and had no clearly defined programme. The principal outside influences at work on the group were the Orphism of Robert Delaunay 1885-1941 and the Fauvism of Henri Matisse 1869-1954.

Within the group the dominant figures were Kandinsky and Marc who edited the *Blaue Reiter Almanac* of 1912 which included articles on art theory and culture contributed by the editors as well as Delaunay, August Macke 1887-1914, the composer-painter Arnold Schönberg 1874-1951 and others. Particular reference is made in the Almanac to the importance of Bavarian glass painting, the form of which particularly affected Kandinsky, Jawlensky and Klee.

By 1912 Kandinsky had already produced his series of drawings, **Improvisations,** that clearly illustrate his search to create an abstract language for painting entirely his own. Although partially recognisable motifs in the form of horsemen, cupolas, women, swords and spears, derived from myth and legend appear, they are largely concealed in his movement towards non-representational painting.

In *Über das Geistige in der Kunst* 1910 (Concerning the Spiritual in Art)
Kandinsky wrote:
> 'Only just now awakening after years of materialism our soul is infected
> with the despair born of unbelief, lack of purpose and aim. The
> nightmare of materialism, which turned life into an evil, senseless game,
> is not yet passed: it still darkens the awakening soul'.

This conviction in the creation of a new art form born out of a conscious
return to an innocent and unspoilt awareness of life's fundamental principles
is also reflected in the work of Marc, whose development was cut short by his
death in action in 1916. Animals were the symbol of Marc's optimistic belief
in the possibility of a return to an earthly paradise:
> 'The impious people around me, above all the men, do not arouse my
> real feelings, whilst the animal's innocent attitude towards life evokes all
> that is good in me.'[1]

Men and women appear infrequently in his later paintings, and when
included, are carefully integrated into the landscape.
Marc's *Aphorisms* 1915 express in very precise terms the ideas to which he
and his contemporaries attempted to give visual form:
> 'Everything has its shell and kernel, semblance and being, mask and
> truth. The fact that we only grope at the shell instead of seeing into the
> being of things, that we are so blinded by the mask of things, that we
> cannot find the truth – how does that refute the inner definiteness of
> things?'[2]

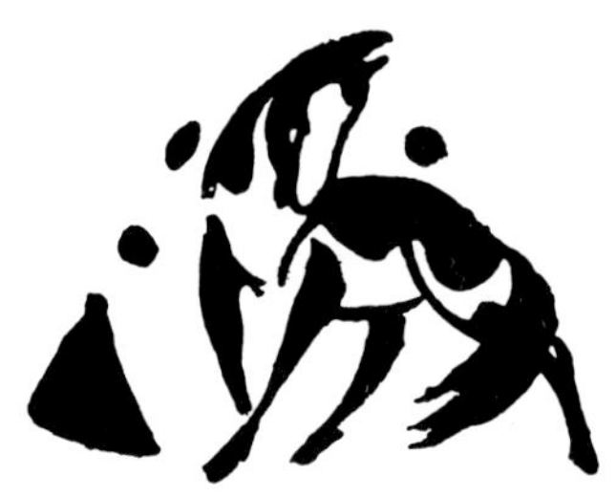

[1] Quoted by Hans Konrad Roethel in *Modern German Painting*, 1958, p.39.
[2] *Ibid.*, p.79. *Aphorism* 1. Written at the Front.

45   **MEIDNER**
Apocalyptische Vision 1912
During the years prior to the First World
War, the Expressionist innovators in
Berlin were well served by Meidner's
prophetic and visionary painting of which
his apocalyptic landscapes were most
important. Their stridency, violent
distortions of form, abrupt perspective
and livid colour suggest a deeply felt
anticipation of the impending war. The
influence of van Gogh and Cézanne is
unmistakable.

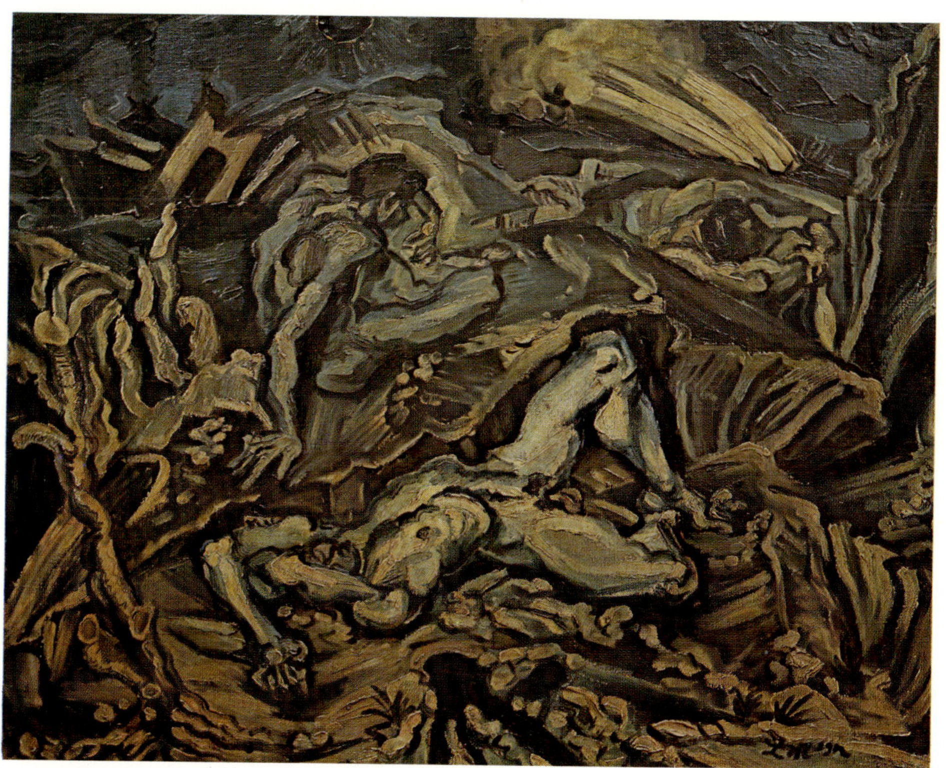

War and Revolution

In 1913 when the outbreak of hostilities was merely a matter of time, various
artists, particularly Marc and Ludwig Meidner 1884-1966, produced works
anticipating the approaching holocaust. The war completed the disintegration
of Expressionism as a united cultural movement. Marc and Macke, amongst
others, were killed in action, Kandinsky and Jawlensky were forced to leave
Germany as aliens and Kirchner emigrated to Switzerland following a nervous
breakdown whilst undergoing military training. However, the war and the
ensuing bloody political and social turmoil forced artists either to retreat from
involvement with contemporary events or to express an increased critical
awareness of the social and political situation.

Before the war some artists had felt that 'Art' was too detached from the reality of everyday life, an attitude which was strengthened by the experience of war and revolution. These artists, particularly George Grosz 1893-1959, John Heartfield 1891-1968 and others involved with the Berlin Dada movement, became increasingly political and both Heartfield and Grosz were active members of the left-wing Sparticist movement. Grosz, in reference to his painting **Dedicated to Oskar Panizza** 1917-18 (Staatsgalerie, Stuttgart), wrote:

'In 1917 . . . I began to draw what moved me in little satirical drawings. Art for Art's sake seemed nonsense to me . . . I wanted to protest against this world of mutual destruction . . . everything in me was darkly protesting. I had seen heroism . . . but it appeared to me blind. I saw misery, want, stupor, hunger, cowardice, ghastliness. Then I painted a big picture: in a sinister street at night a hellish procession of dehumanised figures rolls on, faces, representing Alcohol, Syphilis, Pestilence. One figure blows the trumpet, and one shouts "hurrah!", parrot fashion. Over this crowd rides Death on a black coffin – direct as a symbol, the boneman. The picture was related to my ancestors, the mediaeval masters, Bosch and Breughel. They too, lived in the twilight of a new epoch and formed its expression . . . Against Mankind gone mad, I painted this protest.'[1]

Curriculum Vitae inscribed 'Notes for the trial 3 December 1930'.

The war, with its enormous death toll, and Germany's defeat and acceptance of ignominious terms of surrender, caused the breakdown in leadership which resulted in the revolution of November 1918. Many Germans, with the monarchy discredited, saw the opportunity to create a truly democratic system but, due to internal disagreement, this never took shape. The declaration by the Social Democrats of the Weimar Republic on 19th November 1918 was as much aimed at keeping from power the Sparticists who, under Karl Liebknecht, were about to declare a Soviet Republic, as to take over the control of the country from the Imperial court. This confrontation between the Social Democrats and the Sparticists not only delayed the rational formulation of a new system of government but made it possible for the right-wing factions to quietly regain their control. Whilst the bloody street fighting between the two parties of the left raged through Berlin and other cities, the forces of the right moved in. Rosa Luxemburg and Karl Liebknecht, the Sparticist leaders, were murdered on 15th January 1919 and on 21st February so also was Kurt Eisner, Prime Minister of Bavaria. Following Eisner's murder, a Bavarian Soviet Republic was declared but was brutally put down during April and May by regular and Freikorps troops.

'The paradox of a republican – Social Democratic government allowing itself and the capitalists' safes to be defended by hired unemployed and by royalist officers, is simply too insane.'[2]

Count Kessler *Tagebücher* 1918-37, p.117, 1961.

[1] Translated and quoted by Hans Hess in *George Grosz,* 1974, p.80.
[2] Quoted by Peter Gay in *Weimar Culture* 1968 (Pelican Edition 1974, p.21).

Although not dedicated to any particular party, many artists felt the impulse to be involved in the social change which seemed so likely following the war and, with musicians and people from the theatre, they formed the **Novembergruppe,** which included Pechstein, César Klein, Hans Richter, Mueller and Campendonk. The group was a cultural focal point embracing all the arts and maintained contact with artistic development in France. In 1919 they formed the Workers' Council for Art which wished to involve the arts increasingly in the life of the people. However, before long it was apparent that the only real support for their work came from the very middle classes they denigrated; members of the Council included Lyonel Feininger, Walter Gropius, Paul Cassirer, Meidner, Heckel, Nolde, Rohlfs and Schmidt-Rottluff. By 1924 disillusionment had already set in as the general social climate of Germany swung to the right. The hope that a new democratic Germany would emerge from the revolution was gone.

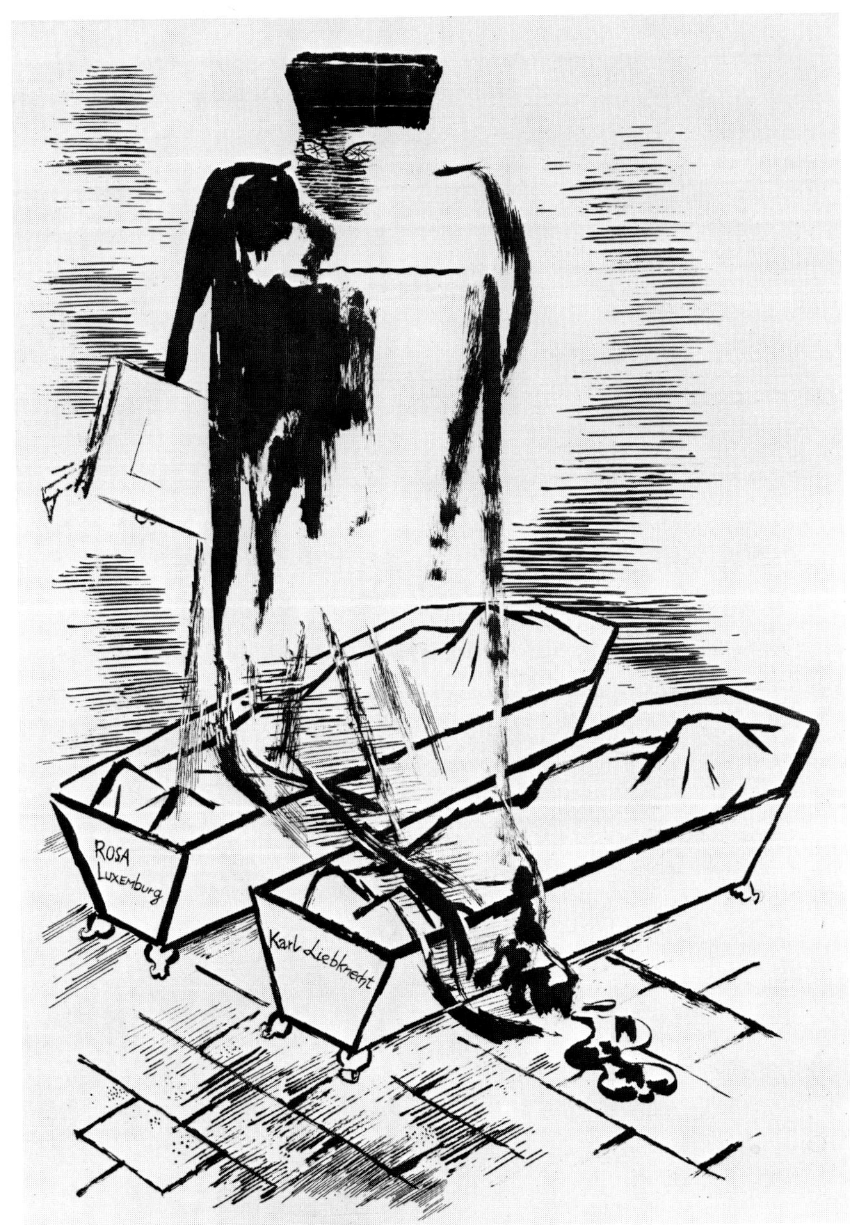

15 **GROSZ**
**Zur Erinnerung an Rosa Luxemburg
und Karl Liebknecht c.1919**
Rosa Luxemburg and Karl Liebknecht,
two of the primary leaders of the
revolutionary Sparticist movement, were
brutally murdered by government troops
on the 15th January 1919. Many left-
wing supporters in the arts were aroused
by the savagery of this act to
commemorate the subject in their work.
Grosz has represented German Law as a
bloody ghost rising above the open
coffins of the murdered pair.

Disillusionment: The Weimar Republic

The Social Democrats, fearing a left-wing take-over, did little to prevent the resurgence of those conservative and nationalistic elements which they had hoped to defeat with the formation of the Weimar Republic. Unwittingly, the government allowed the right to regain its credibility and finally gain a position where it could bring down the Republic.

Between 1918 and 1922 twenty-two assassinations were carried out by the left-wing, ten being punished by death. On the other hand, of the three hundred and fifty-four assassinations committed by the right-wing only one was rigorously punished, though not by death. The revolution and the Republic had failed to discredit the pre-war military-aristocratic-industrial alliance that had propelled Germany into the war and, by 1924, the military had regained favour and recaptured its old charisma. In 1934 the Social Democratic Party in *Politische Justiz* wrote in exile:

> 'That the German working class movement, disorientated during the war, should have taken over the old state apparatus practically unchanged, was its grave historical error.'[1]

The trial of Hitler and Ludendorff after the failure of their 'putsch' in 1923 became a political farce with their defence lawyer denigrating and haranguing the government. Hitler served less than a year of his five-year sentence and should have been deported as an alien but was allowed to remain as he 'thought' he was German.

The Weimar Republic's failure to solve Germany's social, political and economic problems except with increasing right-wing and nationalistic intervention, left many artists with the same sense of despair and cynicism concerning society that they had felt prior to 1914. The former members of **Die Brücke** and the other groups of the pre-war era were now accepted artists and many found teaching posts under the Republic. However, the artists whose work most clearly and directly demonstrated this disillusion were those who became known under the title **Neue Sachlichkeit** (New Objectivity) which was given to the first exhibition arranged by G. F. Hartlaub in Mannheim in 1923.

Hartlaub expressed their viewpoint:

> 'Cynicism and resignation are the negative side of Neue Sachlichkeit: the positive side expresses itself in the enthusiasm for immediate reality as a result of a desire to take things entirely objectively, on a material basis, without immediately investing them with ideal implications.'[2]

[1] H. and E. Hannover *Politische Justiz* 1918-33, 1966, p.34.
[2] Die Kunst, January 1931. Quoted by Bernard S. Myers in *Expressionism, A Generation in Revolt* 1963, p.224.

The most important exponents of this movement were George Grosz who, though he moved away from his more radical political position, continued to launch scathing attacks on the middle-class and their willingness to follow the propagandist slogans of the right, Karl Hofer 1878-1955, Otto Dix 1891-1969 and Max Beckmann 1884-1950. Their work uncompromisingly presented Germany's social condition, disregarding the superficial appearance of well-being and exposing the hypocrisy, violence and corruption.
In Beckmann's work the war produced an increased sense of horror and violence using grotesque figures in settings of distorted and claustrophobic perspective to describe his observation of and reaction to the society in which he lived. In 1918 he wrote:

> 'Just now, even more than before the war I feel the need to be in the cities among my fellow men. This is where our place is. We must take part in the whole misery that is to come. We must surrender our heart and our nerves to the dreadful screams of the poor disillusioned people.'[3]

In 1923 George Grosz's satirical and aggressive condemnation of Berlin middle-class society, **Ecce Homo,** published by Malik Verlag (owned by John Heartfield's brother Wieland Herzfelde), led to his prosecution by the police and confiscation of the book. Thirty of the plates were destroyed and Grosz was heavily fined for 'corrupting the inborn sense of shame and virtue innate in the German people', of whom the Austrian Stefan Zweig wrote in 1924:

> '... Amid the general collapse of values, a kind of insanity took hold of precisely those middle-class circles which had hitherto been unshakeable in their order. Young ladies proudly boasted they were perverted: to be suspected of virginity at sixteen would have been considered a disgrace in every school in Berlin.'[4]

The sense of unity increasingly desired by the German people was not provided by the Weimar Republic but they found it in the nationalism of the right.

> 'The German people was simply not ripe for parliamentary democracy, especially under the pressure of the Versailles peace. I said that to myself, under my breath from the beginning.'[5]

Friedrich Meinecke *Briefwechsel 7 May 1933.*

[3] Quoted by Peter Selz in *Max Beckmann* 1964, p.32.

[4] Die Welt von Gestern, p.287. Quoted by Peter Gay in *Weimar Culture* 1968 (Pelican Edition 1974, p.136).

[5] Friedrich Meinecke, *Briefwechsel* 7 May 1933, p.138. Quoted by Peter Gay in *Weimar Culture* 1968, p.36.

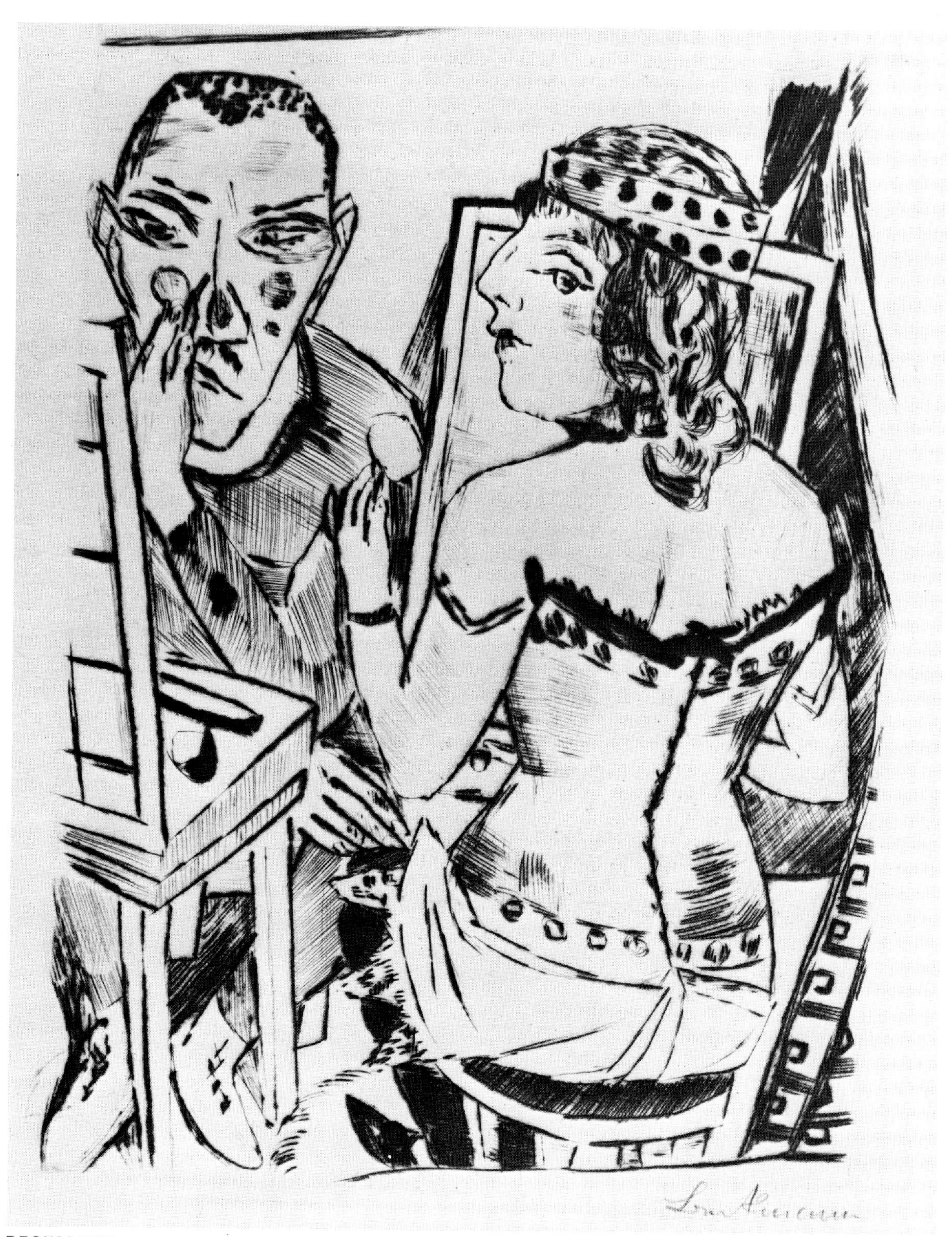

4 **BECKMANN**
Garderobe 1922

The Bauhaus

> 'The **Bauhaus** strives to co-ordinate all creative effort, to achieve, in a new architecture, the unification of all training in art and design. The ultimate, if distant, goal of the **Bauhaus** is the collective work of art – the Building – in which no barriers exist between the structural and the decorative arts.'
>
> From Walter Gropius *The Theory and Organisation of the Bauhaus* 1923.

The **Bauhaus** school of design, craftsmanship and architecture was founded by Walter Gropius 1883-1969 at Weimar in 1919 and was the most important development in the plastic arts in Germany between the two world wars. It was a school for the teaching of art and design and amongst the invited 'masters of form' brought in as teachers by Gropius were Kandinsky, Klee, Oskar Schlemmer 1888-1943, Lyonel Feininger 1871-1956 and Lazlo Moholy-Nagy 1895-1946.

> 'Architects, sculptors, painters, we must all turn to the crafts. Art is not a 'profession'. There is no essential difference between the artist and the craftsman. The artist is an exalted craftsman. In rare moments of inspiration, moments beyond the control of his will, the grace of heaven may cause his work to blossom into art. But proficiency in his craft is essential to every artist. Therein lies a source of creative imagination.'
>
> From the *First Proclamation of the Weimar Bauhaus* 1919.

Despite the basic soundness of its programme and Gropius's intentions in creating what amounted to a new guild of craftsmen-designers who were acquainted with the theoretical and practical work of all departments, the **Bauhaus** was openly disparaged and disapproved of by the conservative authorities.

From the hostile atmosphere of Weimar, the **Bauhaus** was moved to Dessau in 1925 and many of the familiar adjuncts of contemporary life appeared at this time – steel furniture, modern textiles, modern typography and layout. Gropius left the **Bauhaus** in 1926 in the face of growing difficulties and personal attacks. Although the school continued under two succeeding directors, it was eventually dissolved altogether in 1933 due to political pressure. The ideas propagated by the **Bauhaus** and its staff continued to exert widespread influence even after its closure.

In 1932 H. Pflug explained in the newspaper *Die Tat* why such animosity had been directed at the work of the **Bauhaus:**

> 'Those no longer able or not yet willing to change and learn, realised that the **Bauhaus** stood for a new life and a new style in a new time. Philistines and reactionaries rebelled. All the animosity they could not unload elsewhere was directed against the visible embodiment of what they feared.'

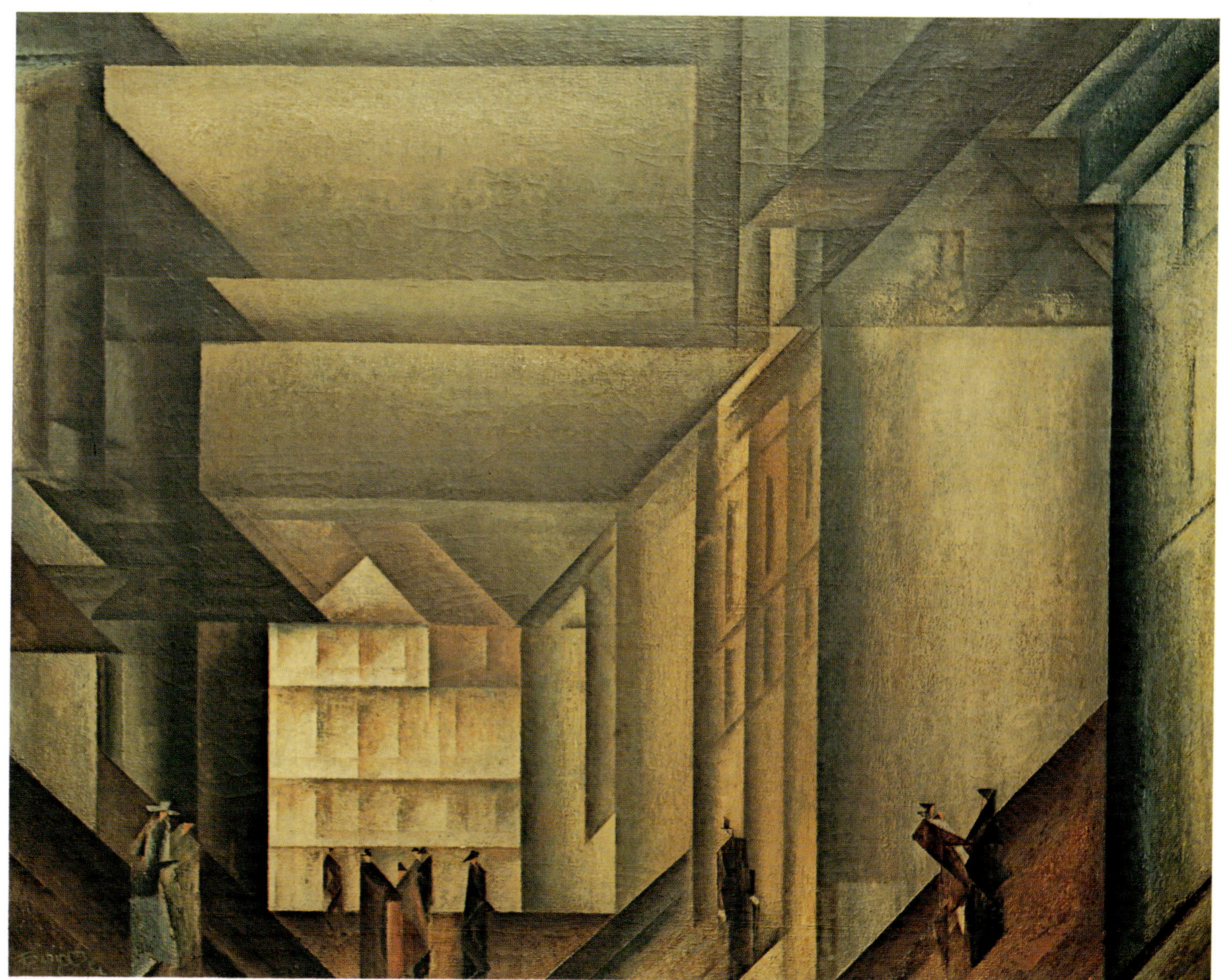

13 FEININGER
Hinter der Stadtkirche 1916
Feininger's principal motif was
architecture which he depicted in Cubist
terms using extremely precise linear
structures. The rigidity of these forms is
relieved by his use of rich colour,
reducing the corporeality of the pictorial
objects and giving the architectural motifs
a dream-like quality, not unlike the
designs effected by the contemporary
German cinema. The subject from which
this picture derived was the Stadtkirche
and adjoining square in Weimar.

National Socialism

By 1930 the dry realism of the art of the **New Objectivity** artists had begun to turn into a sentimental academicism, extolling the nationalistic virtues of the homeland. The advent of National Socialism, with its fascist doctrine, swept away all the new forms of modern German art in preference for a totalitarian art which, as displayed in exhibitions, served Hitler's Nazi propaganda programme as successfully as his military rallies. All the artists mentioned in the preceding sections were subject to persecution and harassment under the National Socialists. Many were forced to leave Germany in order to survive as working artists including George Grosz, Max Beckmann, Ludwig Meidner and Lyonel Feininger, the writers Thomas Mann, Herwarth Walden, Bertholt Brecht, the film directors Fritz Lang, Erich Pommer, Robert Siodmak, the composers Paul Hindemith and Arnold Schönberg. Of those artists who remained in Germany, Max Liebermann, Karl Schmidt-Rottluff, Ernst Barlach and Emil Nolde had their work withdrawn from public galleries and Max Pechstein was refused an exit visa. Nolde and Schmidt-Rottluff were actually forbidden to paint by the Nazi government. Following the famous Munich exhibition of 'degenerate art' held in 1937 in the **Haus der Kunst,** German museums were purged of all the works officially classified as 'degenerate' or 'Judo-Bolshevist'. As well as German Expressionist paintings, the same classification was applied to foreign works of art including the Impressionists, van Gogh, Gauguin and Picasso. From 1938 onwards this became official policy. As a result many works were destroyed and a significant number auctioned in Lucerne in June 1939.

In July 1937 Hitler opened the **House of German Art** in Munich with the words:

> 'Cubism, Dadaism, Futurism, Impressionism and the rest have nothing in common with our German people . . . they are . . . the artificial stammering of people whom God has denied the boon of genuine artistic talent and given instead the gift of prating and deception . . . . who . . . .'experience meadows blue, the sky green and clouds sulphur yellow. I do not wish to enter into an argument as to whether the gentlemen in question really do see and experience such things in this way or not, but I wish, in the name of the German people, to forbid such lamentable unfortunates, who plainly suffer from defective sight, to try and talk the world about them into accepting the results of their false observation as reality, or to represent them to it as "art".'

Of those artists who remained in Germany few survived the damaging effects of their oppression and enforced idleness and Expressionism could hardly be said to exist after World War II. Expressionist concepts as they had originally been understood and practised depended for their growth on those artists who had left Germany and carried their ideas with them into other European countries, such as Kirchner, Klee and Kokoschka in Switzerland, Kandinsky in France, and Beckmann and Feininger in America, where they provided a vital stimulus to the development of Abstract Expressionism and Surrealism.

Cover to the official exhibition catalogue of the *Grosse Deutsche Kunstausstellung* (Great German Art Exhibition) held in the *Haus der Deutschen Kunst,* Munich in 1937.

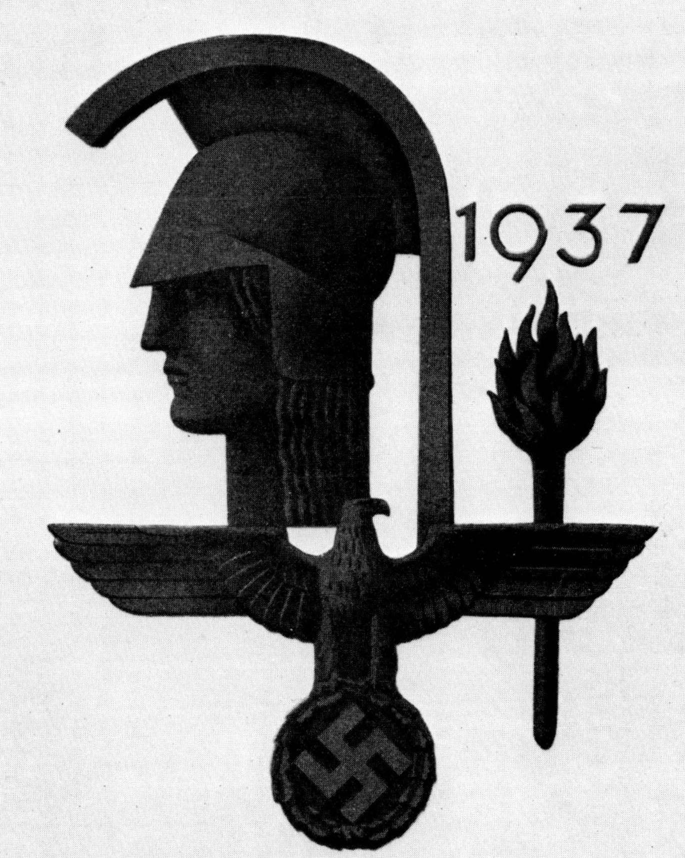

1937
GROSSE
DEUTSCHE
KUNSTAUSSTELLUNG
1937
IM HAUS DER DEUTSCHEN
KUNST ZU MÜNCHEN
OFFIZIELLER AUSSTELLUNGSKATALOG

Map of Germany since 1871.

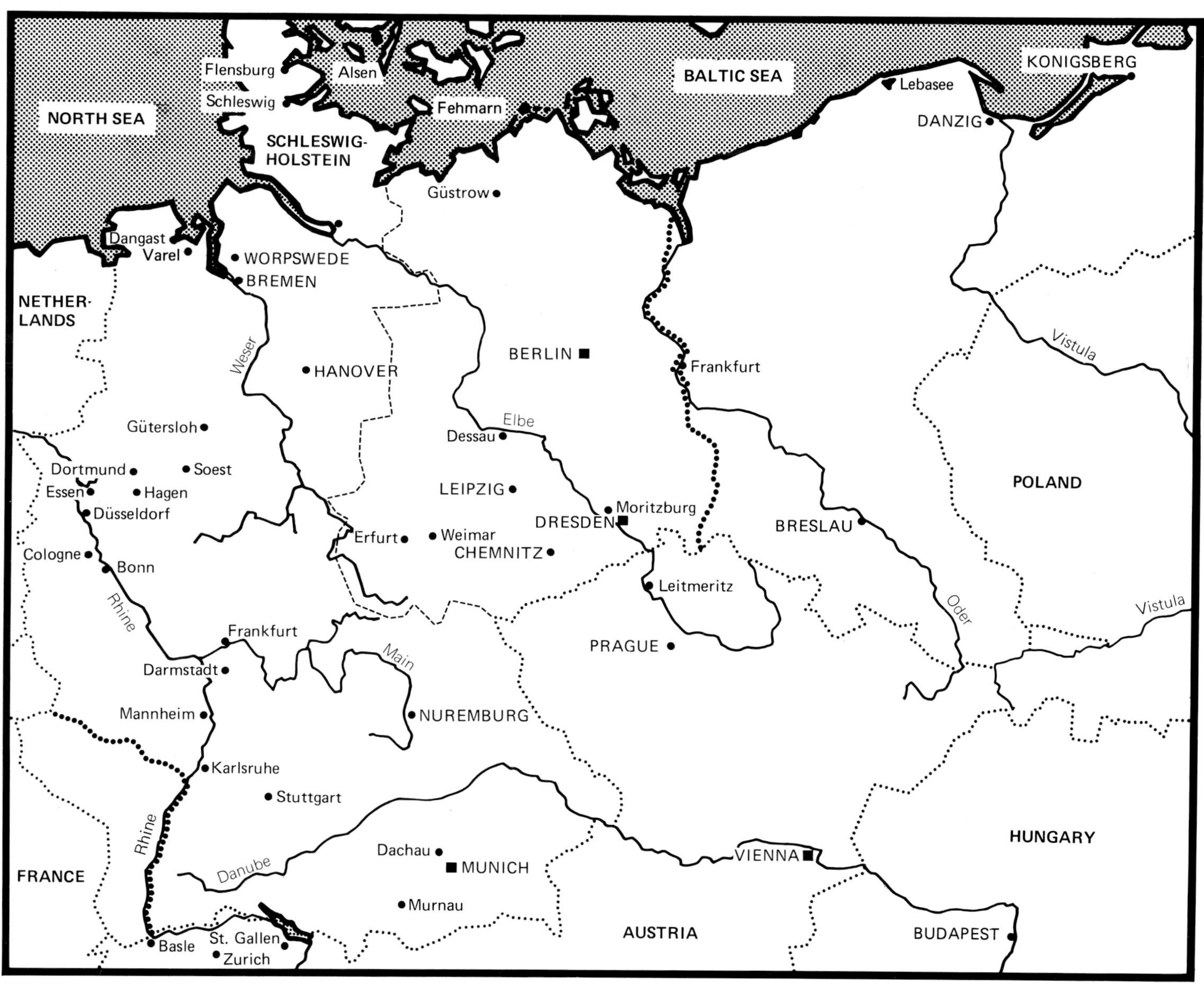

NORTH SEA
BALTIC SEA
KONIGSBERG
Flensburg
Alsen
Schleswig
Fehmarn
Lebasee
DANZIG
SCHLESWIG-
HOLSTEIN
Güstrow
Dangast
Varel
WORPSWEDE
BREMEN
NETHER-
LANDS
Weser
HANOVER
BERLIN
Frankfurt
Vistula
Gütersloh
Elbe
Dessau
Dortmund
Soest
POLAND
Essen
Hagen
LEIPZIG
Düsseldorf
DRESDEN
Moritzburg
Cologne
Bonn
Erfurt
Weimar
CHEMNITZ
BRESLAU
Rhine
Leitmeritz
Oder
Vistula
Frankfurt
Main
PRAGUE
Darmstadt
Mannheim
NUREMBURG
Karlsruhe
Rhine
Stuttgart
HUNGARY
Danube
Dachau
VIENNA
FRANCE
MUNICH
Murnau
AUSTRIA
BUDAPEST
Basle
St. Gallen
Zurich

Frontiers 1871
Revised frontiers of the 1918
Treaty of Versailles
East German Frontiers

**Chronological Table tracing the Development of German Impressionism and Expressionism
1871-1933**

1871	Paris commune; Courbet imprisoned for involvement with destruction of Vendôme Column. Birth of Kandinsky. Dostoievsky writes **The Devils.** Nietzsche teaching at Basle University.
1872	Death of Gautier. Courbet released.
1873	Death of Napoleon III. Courbet flees to Switzerland. Van Gogh an employee in London branch of Goupil and Co., art dealers.
1874	Death of Millet; Lautréamont. Birth of Schönberg; Churchill. Van Gogh in Paris. First group exhibition of Impressionists, Paris.
1875	Death of Corot. Birth of Ravel; Jung. Van Gogh an employee in the Paris branch of Goupil and Co.
1876	Birth of Vlaminck. Second group exhibition of Impressionists, Paris. Strindberg in Paris, admires Impressionist painters, particularly Manet and Monet.
1877	Death of Courbet. Birth of Kubin. Third group exhibition of Impressionists, Paris.
1878	Paris World Fair. Duret publishes **Les Impressionistes.** Death of Daubigny. Strindberg writes **The Red Room.** Hodler in Spain.
1879	Fourth group exhibition of Impressionists, Paris. Death of Daumier. Birth of Stalin; Trotsky. Nietzsche leaves Basle University.
1880	Death of Flaubert. Birth of Derain; Apollinaire. Fifth group exhibition of Impressionists, Paris. Dostoievsky writes **Brothers Karamazov.** Hodler experiences religious crisis.
1881	Tsar Alexander II assassinated. Death of Dostoievsky; Disraeli. Birth of Léger; Picasso; Bartok. Sixth group exhibition of Impressionists, Paris. Ibsen writes **Ghosts.**
1882	Death of Garibaldi; Darwin. Birth of Joyce; Braque; Stravinsky; Boccioni. Seventh group exhibition of Impressionists, Paris. Courbet Retrospective, Paris.
1883	Death of Marx; Manet; Turgenev. Birth of Mussolini; Kafka; Severini. Impressionist exhibitions in London and Rotterdam. Gauguin gives up bank job, moves to Rouen, then to Copenhagen; work exhibited in Copenhagen but closed by order of Danish Academy.
1884	Birth of Modigliani. Manet Memorial Exhibition in Paris. **Groupe des Artistes Indépendents** formed in Paris.
1885	Death of Hugo. Birth of Delaunay; D. H. Lawrence; Ezra Pound; Moholy-Nagy. Foundation of **Les XX** in Brussels. Gauguin returns to Paris; suffers illness; recuperates in Brittany. Munch aged 19 visits Paris. Zola's **Germinal** published. Marx's **Das Kapital Vol. II** published. Van Gogh paints **The Potato Eaters.**

RELATED SOCIAL AND CULTURAL EVENTS IN GERMANY	GERMAN IMPRESSIONIST AND EXPRESSIONIST ARTISTS
Foundation of German Empire; Prussian King becomes Kaiser Wilhelm I; Bismarck becomes Chancellor, Minister of Prussia and Foreign Affairs (double office held for next 20 years). Birth of Feininger (in New York); Heinrich Mann.	Leibl in Munich after living in Paris; meets Thoma and Trübner; working in close contact until 1873. Marées living in Berlin and Dresden (having travelled in Spain, France and Holland studying Velasquez, Barbizon School, Delacroix, Courbet, Rembrandt). Rohlfs student at Weimar Art School under Thumann, Schauss and Struys until 1881. Thoma meets Böcklin in Munich. Liebermann studying at Weimar Art School 1868-1872 under Pauwels and Thumann.
France pays war reparations to Germany. Triple Alliance drawn up with Austria and Russia. Nietzsche's **The Birth of Tragedy** published.	Liebermann moves to Düsseldorf; visits Paris and Holland.
Prussian Bank converted into the Imperial Bank.	Leibl leaves Munich; moves to Grasslfing near Dachau, remaining until 1874. Liebermann in Paris until 1878; influenced by Barbizon painters and Courbet.
Socialists win 9 seats in Reichstag. Birth of Hofmannsthal; Mueller; August Stramm.	Leibl moves to Unterschöndorf on the Ammersee until 1877. Marées living in Florence; friendly with Böcklin. Thoma visits Italy.
Birth of Thomas Mann; Rilke.	Liebermann living in Paris spends summers in Holland, influenced by Jongkind and Israels. Marées settles in Rome.
Bayreuth Festival inaugurated with first performance of **Der Ring des Nibelungen** by Wagner.	Corinth studying in Königsberg until 1880. Birth of Paula (Modersohn)-Becker. Von Uhde in Vienna.
Socialists win 12 seats in Reichstag and poll 500,000 votes. Birth of Hermann Hesse.	Thoma settles in Frankfurt until 1899.
Two attempts made on Wilhelm I's life; Bismarck moves against the Socialists. Birth of Döblin, co-founder of **Der Sturm; Hofer.**	Leibl moves to Berbling until 1881. Liebermann settles in Munich until 1884.
Anti-Semitic agitation instigated by Christian-Social movement. Birth of Einstein.	Von Uhde studying in Paris under Munkacsy.
Bismarck begins to lose power. Birth of Kirchner in Aschaffenburg; Marc in Munich; Bleyl. Ibsen, who has lived in Munich since 1875 moves to Italy.	Corinth at the Munich Academy. Von Uhde, on his return from Paris, meets Liebermann in Munich. Death of Feuerbach in Venice. Leibl moves to Aibling until 1892.
Alliance between Germany, Austro-Hungarian Empire and Russia renewed. Official unions formed. Insurance made compulsory for working men. Anti-Semitic agitation in Berlin, Breslau amd other Prussian cities. Birth of Stefan Zweig; Wilhelm Worringer; Lehmbruck in Duisburg-Meiderich.	Rohlfs leaves Weimar Art School.
Improving relations with Russia. Richard Strauss devotes himself to music and moves to Berlin.	
Alliance between Germany, Austro-Hungarian Empire and Italy to prevent Russian attack on Austria or French attack on Germany. Death of Wagner. Birth of Heckel near Chemnitz; Gropius. Impressionist exhibition in Berlin. Nietzsche starts to write **Thus spoke Zarathustra.**	Hofmann at Dresden Academy.
Secret treaty with Russia that each should remain neutral if either attacked. Colonial expansion, acquisition of Togoland; Cameroon; S.W. Africa; German New Guinea; Bismarck Archipelageo. Birth of Schmidt-Rottluff near Chemnitz; Meidner in Bernstadt; Beckmann in Leipzig; Oskar Loerke.	Corinth travels to Paris via Antwerp and studies at the Académie Julian, remaining until 1887. Liebermann moves to Berlin.
Bismarck passes bill to aid expansion of the merchant navy; increase in overseas trade and influence. Colonial acquisition of East Africa; Marshall Islands. Birth of Hindemith; Pabst. Ibsen returns to Munich; remains until 1891. Nietzsche completes **Thus spoke Zarathustra.**	Von Menzel has large exhibition in Paris. Slevogt at Munich Academy until 1889; short trip to Paris, studying at the Académie Julian.

1886	Death of Liszt. Birth of Kokoschka; Permeke. Final group exhibition of Impressionists, Paris. Rousseau exhibits at the *Salon des Indépendents,* Paris. **Symbolist Manifesto** published, Paris. Kandinsky studying law in Moscow. Van Gogh meets Gauguin, Paris. Gauguin in Pont-Aven; meets Bernard. Rimbaud's **Illuminations** published.
1887	Lenin's brother executed for an attempt on the Tsar's life. Birth of Le Corbusier; Chagall; Gris; Duchamp; Arp. Gauguin visits Martinique; meets van Gogh again in Paris. Strindberg writes **The Father.**
1888	Birth of T. S. Eliot; de Chirico. Strindberg writes **Miss Julie.** Gauguin paints **Jacob wrestling with the Angel.** Van Gogh in Arles, paints **The Night Cafe;** later joined by Gauguin.
1889	Birth of Hitler; Cocteau. Jawlensky, an army officer, studies painting at evening classes at St. Petersburg Academy. Kandinsky visits Syrien tribes in N.E. Russia; impressed by folk art and religion; visits Paris. Van Gogh at Saint-Rémy paints **Starry Night.** Gauguin returns to Pont-Aven. Paris World Fair; Eiffel Tower erected. Bergson writes **Time and Freedom.**
1890	Death of van Gogh. Birth of El Lissitsky; Schiele. Hodler paints **Nacht** (Night).
1891	Death of Seurat. Birth of Gaudier-Breszka. Gauguin in Tahiti. Jawlensky meets Marianne von Werefkin in Moscow.
1892	Death of Tennyson. Gauguin seriously ill in Tahiti. Hodler paints **Die Lebensmüden** (The World Weary).
1893	Death of Maupassant; Gounod; Tschaikovsky. Birth of Miro. Gauguin returns to France. Munch paints **The Cry.**
1894	Dreyfus affair in France. Hodler visits Antwerp.

RELATED SOCIAL AND CULTURAL EVENTS IN GERMANY	GERMAN IMPRESSIONIST AND EXPRESSIONIST ARTISTS
Germany increases ''peace-time'' armed forces to 468,409 men. Colonial acquisition of Solomon Islands as protectorate. Nietzsche's **Beyond Good and Evil** published. Birth of Gottfried Benn.	
Colonial acquisition of Kiao-Chow, China, as protectorate. Death of Krupp founder of the industrial empire. Birth of Schwitters; Georg Trakl; Georg Heym. Ibsen's **Ghosts** performed at Berlin Dramatic Society and Berlin Residenz Theater; **An Enemy of the People** première in Berlin; **Rosmersholm** world première in Augsburg, also staged in Berlin. Sudermann writes **Frau Sorge.**	Death of Marées in Rome. Corinth, on return from Paris, settles in Berlin. Nolde apprenticed to cabinet-maker and studying at School of Sauermann in Flensburg until 1898. Feininger arrives in Germany to study music but takes up painting.
Death of Wilhelm I; brother crowned Frederick III, but dies after 90 days; succeeded by his son, Wilhelm II. Military bill increases length of service from 12 to 18 years; another half a million men made available; £14m allowed for equipment. Bill passed restricting Sunday working and employment of women and juveniles. Nietzsche writes **Twilight of the Idols** and **The Anti-Christ.** Beginning of Nietzsche's mental disorder from which he never recovers. Death of Theodor Storm.	Corinth moves to Königsberg. Hofmann moves to Karlsruhe.
Law passed enforcing insurance against retirement; pensions at 70. Ibsen's **Lady from the Sea** premières in Christiana and Weimar; Ibsen week in Berlin, **Lady from the Sea, The Wild Duck, A Doll's House.** Hauptmann writes **Vor Sonnenaufgang.** Nietzsche's **Twilight of the Idols** published.	Rohlfs one-man exhibition in Weimar. Modersohn working in Worpswede near Bremen.
Wilhelm II dismisses Bismarck; assumes direction of foreign policy, abandons Bismarck's attempt to maintain the European balance of power; strengthens alliance with Austro-Hungarian Empire; new Chancellor, von Caprivi. Birth of Fritz Lang; Franz Werfel. Munch and Strindberg in Berlin.	Hofmann studying in Paris at the Académie Julian; returns to Berlin, in close contact with Liebermann, Klinger, Leistikow. Liebermann comes under the influence of Manet. Thoma (influenced by Courbet and the Barbizon School) has great success at the Munich Arts Club.
Renewal of alliance with Austro-Hungarian Empire and Italy. Birth of Dix; Ernst; Helmut Herzfelde (John Heartfield). Ibsen's **Hedda Gabler** world première in Munich. Wedekind writes **Frühlings Erwachen** (Spring Awakening). **Danton's Death** by Büchner printed in Berlin paper, editor given 4 months in prison.	Corinth in Munich; remains until 1900. Feininger studying in Berlin.
Von Caprivi signs commercial treaties with Austro-Hungarian Empire, Italy, Belgium and Switzerland. Munch invited to exhibit 50 works by the Berlin Artists' Association but the exhibition is immediately closed as a majority of the members thought it too modern. Hauptmann writes **Die Weber** (The Weavers).	Von Uhde leads the formation of the Munich Secession; first exhibition includes work by Corot, Courbet, Millet, Böcklin and Liebermann. In Berlin Liebermann and Hofmann form Gruppe XI which becomes the core of the Berlin Secession. Nolde drawing teacher at the Fachschule in St. Gallen, Switzerland, Feininger studying at the Colarossi School in Paris. Leibl moves to Kutterling; remains until his death in 1900. Paula Becker studies at London School of Arts.
Dual entente signed with France. Compulsory military service. Munch exhibition in Berlin independent of Berlin Artists' Association; shown in Breslau, Dresden, Munich; Munch settles in Berlin; remains until 1908. Strindberg in Berlin. Ibsen's **Master Builder** première in Berlin. Hauptmann's **Hanneles Himmelfahrt** (Hanneles' Journey to Heaven) staged. Birth of Grosz.	Böcklin moves to Italy. Feininger returns to Berlin; working as an illustrator and cartoonist.
Von Caprivi dismissed; new Chancellor Prince Chlodwig von Hohenlohe calls for return to conservatism; criminal code amended to allow 3 years imprisonment for attacks on religion, monarchy, marriage or family using ''abusive expression as to endanger public peace''. Rilke writes **Leben und Lieder.**	Kollwitz produces prints based on scenes from Zola's **Germinal.**

1895	Birth of Eluard. Hodler paints **Eurhythmie.** Munch paints **Puberty.**
1896	Death of Bruckner. Birth of Breton; Masson.
1897	Lenin exiled to Siberia until 1900. Klimt becomes president of the Vienna Secession. Matisse meets Pissarro. Gauguin paints **Where do we come from? What are we? Where are we going?** and **Nevermore.**
1898	Trotsky exiled to Siberia until 1902. Death of Beardsley; Moreau; Gladstone. Birth of Henry Moore; Magritte. Strindberg writes Parts I and II of **To Damascus.** First exhibition of the Vienna Secession.
1899	Stalin robs banks to raise party funds; imprisoned five times, escapes four. Kraus starts the magazine **Die Fackel** in Vienna. Matisse meets Derain; purchases Cézanne's **Three Bathers.**
1900	Lenin in Switzerland. Birth of Bunuel. Freud's **Interpretation of Dreams** published.
1901	Death of Queen Victoria; succeeded by Edward VII. Death of Toulouse-Lautrec. Birth of Dubuffet; Giacometti. Strindberg writes **Easter.**
1902	Britain forms alliance with Japan. Mussolini in Switzerland to avoid military service. Death of Zola.
1903	Death of Gauguin.

RELATED SOCIAL AND CULTURAL EVENTS IN GERMANY	GERMAN IMPRESSIONIST AND EXPRESSIONIST ARTISTS
Von Hohenlohe forced to withdraw bill forbidding ''public exhibition of pictures, statues or sale of writings which, without being actually obscene, might rudely offend the feeling of modesty''. Ibsen's **Little Eyolf** première in Berlin. Hauptmann's **Florian Geyer** published. Nietzsche's **The Anti-Christ** published. Magazine **Pan** founded in Berlin.	Formation of Worpswede Artists' Club. Rohlfs in Berlin. Barlach in Paris.
Slevogt collaborates on the magazines **Die Jugend** and **Simplicissimus** founded in Munich. Hauptmann writes **Die versunkene Glocke** (The Sunken Bell).	Jawlensky and Werefkin move to Munich; Jawlensky studies under Azbé. Kandinsky moves to Munich; studies under Azbé; meets Jawlensky. Hofer studying in Karlsruhe until 1900. Paula Becker studying at Women's Art College, Berlin. Mueller studying at Dresden Academy until 1898.
Bill passed to finance naval expansion, to be completed by 1904. Ibsen's **John Gabriel Borkmann** staged at Frankfurt-am-Main with two passages cut. Death of Brahms; Burckhardt. Birth of Goebbels.	Liebermann has one-man exhibition in Berlin; made a professor of Berlin Academy. Friendship develops between Jawlensky and Kandinsky. Klee in Munich; studies at the Knirr School; moves to the Academy under Stuck. Paula Becker in Worpswede, continuing studies at Berlin Art School.
Growing rivalry with Britain over colonial and maritime power. Hauptmann writes **Fuhrmann Henschel** (Fireman Henschel). Birth of Brecht.	Slevogt in Holland studying Rembrandt. Rohlfs meets Munch. Nolde studying in Munich. Kubin at the Munich Academy. Paula Becker visits Norway, then settles in Worpswede.
Colonial acquisition of Caroline, Palau and Mariana Islands as protectorates. Passive support of Boers. Wedekind imprisoned for one year.	Liebermann made a member of Prussian Academy, Berlin; President of Berlin Secession. Thoma appointed professor and Director of the gallery in Karlsruhe. Nolde living in Dachau; visits Paris; studies at the Académie Julian. Paula Becker's first exhibition in the Kunsthalle, Bremen.
Lenin in Germany. Death of Nietzsche. Birth of Krenek. Heinrich Mann writes **Im Schlaraffenland.**	Death of Leibl. Corinth and Slevogt move to Berlin. Rohlfs exhibits with the Berlin Secession. Hofer visits Paris. Kandinsky becomes President of the 'Phalanx Group' and teaches at their school for three years. Paula Becker meets Nolde; visits Paris; on return to Worpswede meets Rilke. Pechstein attends the Arts and Crafts School, Dresden. Beckmann enters the Weimar Academy. Marc enters the Munich Academy. Mueller living in the Riesengebirge mountains.
Schönberg Kappellmeister at the **Uberbrettl** artists' cabaret in Berlin. Thomas Mann writes **Buddenbrooks.**	Hauptmann and Paula Becker friends. Schmidt-Rottluff and Heckel at school together. Death of Böcklin in Italy. Paula Becker marries Otto Modersohn, taking the name of Modersohn-Becker. Rohlfs made Professor at the Folkswangschule in Hagen. Hofer working in Karlsruhe. Nolde travelling in Germany; visits Copenhagen. Klee visits Italy. Kirchner studying architecture at the Technische Hochschule, Dresden.
Germany refuses alliance with Britain. Birth of Leni Riefenstahl.	Kandinsky meets Gabriele Münter, a student at the 'Phalanx School'; remain together until 1916; Kandinsky shows with the Berlin Secession. Slevogt teaching at the Berlin Academy. Hofer studying at the Stuttgart Academy. Pechstein studying at Dresden Academy. Kirchner meets Bleyl in Dresden. Klee returns to Munich, then returns to his parents' home in Berne. Marc visits Italy, Paris and Provence. Kubin exhibits at the Cassirer Gallery.
Hauptmann writes **Rosa Bernd**. Rilke writes **Worpswede**. Thomas Mann writes **Tristan** and **Tonio Kröger**. Kubin illustrates Thomas Mann's **Tristan**.	Hofer in Rome until 1908. Modersohn and Modersohn-Becker in Paris. Hofmann invited to Weimar Art School. Beckmann visits Paris; impressed by exhibition of French primitives. Meidner studying at Breslau Academy. Jawlensky exhibits with Munich Secession. Klee painting little but reading Dostoievsky, Gogol, Byron, Baudelaire and studying Ensor, Redon, Blake and Goya.

1904 Anglo-French Alliance. Russia and Japan at war. Mussolini returns to Italy joining the Socialist party. Death of Chekhov. Birth of Dali. Strindberg writes Part III of **To Damascus.** Hodler given main room at Vienna Secession exhibition.

1905 Unsuccessful Bolshevik uprising in Russia; Lenin returns to Switzerland; Trotsky goes to America. Russia defeated by Japan. Kokoschka gains scholarship to Vienna School of Arts and Crafts. Matisse and the Fauves exhibit at the Salon d'Automne, Paris.

1906 British navy launches Dreadnoughts. Death of Ibsen; Cézanne.

1907 Alliance between France, England and Russia. Cézanne Memorial in Paris. Bergson publishes **Creative Evolution** in France. Picasso paints **Les Demoiselles d'Avignon.** Matisse paints **Nu Bleu.**

1908 Young Turks rebel; Russia intends to seize Dardanelles as Austria seizes Bosnia and Herzogovinia; Austria abandons Russia. Braque paints **Grand Nu.**

1909 Rodin organises von Marées commemorative exhibition in Parish. Birth of Francis Bacon. Kokoschka's plays **Murderer, Hope of Women** and **Sphinx and Straw Man** staged in Vienna; visits Munch in Switzerland. Marinetti publishes first **Futurist Manifesto** in **Le Figaro.** Diaghilev Ballet in Paris.

RELATED SOCIAL AND CULTURAL EVENTS IN GERMANY	GERMAN IMPRESSIONIST AND EXPRESSIONIST ARTISTS
234% increase in shipping tonnage since 1894. Foreign trade doubled in same period. Munch in Weimar. Hesse writes **Peter Camenzind.** Freud writes **Zur Psychopathologie des Alltagslebens.**	Jawlensky exhibits in Salon d'Automne, Paris and in St. Petersburg. Kandinsky exhibits in Salon d'Automne and Exposition Nationals des Beaux Arts, Paris. Phalanx exhibition in Munich includes neo-Impressionists, Secessionist artists, Cézanne, Gauguin and van Gogh. Corinth invites Jawlensky to exhibit with the Berlin Secession. Macke attends the Art Academy and Industrial Art Academy in Düsseldorf until 1906. Nolde in Italy, but unimpressed. Beckmann in Italy; studies Signorelli and Piero della Francesca.
Heinrich Mann's **Professor Unrat** published. Max Reinhardt becomes chief producer at the Deutsche Theater, Berlin. Strauss's **Salome** staged in Dresden. Hesse's **The Prodigy** published.	Death of Adolf von Menzel. Kirchner gains architectural diploma in Dresden; meets Schmidt-Rottluff studying architecture; with Bleyl and Heckel they form Die Brücke. Heckel rents studio in Dresden's Berlinerstrasse, shared by co-founder members and models. Jawlensky working in Brittany and Provence, influenced by Cézanne, van Gogh and Matisse. Kubin meets Redon in Paris, visits Italy. Rohlfs working in Soest, meets Nolde who has just sold first painting to the Folkwang Museum, Hagen. Klee visits Paris. Macke visits Italy. Dix apprenticed to a decorative painter until 1909. Beckmann settles in Berlin.
Turpitz demands greater naval expansion. Munch completes third version of **The Frieze of Life** for Reinhardt's Kammerspietheater, and set designs for Ibsen's **Ghosts.** Hauptmann writes **Und Pippa tanzt** (And Pippa Dances). De Chirico visits Munich, influenced by Böcklin. Birth of Carl Zuckmayer.	Munch exhibition staged by the Artists' Union of Saxony. Nolde invited to join Die Brücke following exhibition of his work at Arnold Art Salon in Dresden. Pechstein meets Heckel and joins Die Brücke following alterations to his design for the Dresden Industrial Arts Exhibition ceiling. Schmidt-Rottluff spends summer at Nolde's home on the island of Alsen. Modersohn-Becker in Paris influenced by Cézanne and Gauguin. Marc travels to Greece, visits Mount Athos. Barlach visits Russia, impressed by peasant life and religion. Meidner in Paris meets Modigliani. Kandinsky living at Sêvres in France exhibits at Salon d'Automne – and also in 1907. Klee exhibits with Munich Secession. Feininger in Weimar and Paris. Beckmann wins Villa Romana Prize from German Artists' League, Weimar; joins Berlin Secession; meets Munch and Nolde. Die Brücke produces first of the yearly portfolios. First Die Brücke exhibition staged in Seifert's lighting factory.
Formation of Deutsche Werkbund in an attempt to fuse industrial process and the arts and crafts movement.	Death of Paula Modersohn-Becker. Liebermann retrospective in Berlin to celebrate his 60th birthday. Die Brücke exhibition at the Richter Gallery, Dresden; Nolde leaves the group and joins Berlin Secession; Pechstein visits Italy then Paris, impressed by van Dongen's work. Jawlensky working in Matisse's studio, Paris. Kandinsky has one-man exhibition in Frankfurt; exhibits with **Les Indépendents.** Feininger in Paris abandons illustration and cartoons, devotes himself to painting.
Munch returns to Norway; suffers mental breakdown. Von Tschudi dismissed as Director of National Gallery, Berlin by the Kaiser. Kollwitz's poster **Die Heimarbeiter** banned by the Empress Auguste Victoria. Schönberg and Berg experimenting with atonal music. Lenin and Rosa Luxemburg meet in Berlin. Worringer's **Abstraction and Empathy** published.	Death of Leistikow. Kirchner living in Fehmarn in the summer; Pechstein settles in Berlin; van Dongen joins Die Brücke. Mueller moves to Berlin. Macke visits Paris and Italy. Hofer in Paris. Kandinsky returns to Munich; living during summer at Murnau with Münter, Jawlensky and Werefkin. Barlach settles in Güstrow (remains until his death in 1938). Feininger returns to Berlin. Kandinsky meets Worringer.
Von Tschudi made Director of Bavarian State Galleries. Kubin's novel **Die andere Seite** (The Other Side) published in Munich. Strauss's **Elektra** staged in Dresden. Matisse's **Notes d'un Peintre** (published 1908) translated into German; first one-man exhibition in Germany, Berlin.	Die Brücke portfolio by Schmidt-Rottluff with cover by Kirchner; Bleyl leaves group. Pechstein exhibits with Berlin Secession, gains acclaim; moves to Nidden on the Baltic coast. Heckel and Kirchner working at the Moritzburger Lakes. New Artists Union formed In Munich; founder members Kandinsky, Jawlensky, Münter, Werefkin, Erbsloh, Kanoldt, Kubin, Schnabel, Witten; exhibit at the Thannhauser Gallery, Munich. Nolde at Rüttebull. Grosz studying at Dresden Academy.

1910 Death of Edward VII; succeeded by George V. Death of Tolstoy. First Cubist Exhibition in Paris. **Manifesto of Futurist Painting** and **Technical Manifesto of Futurist Painting** published in Italy, signed by Balla, Severini, Carra and Boccioni. Diaghilev Ballet stage Stravinsky's **The Fire Bird** in Paris. Hodler receives honorary doctorate from Basle University.

1911 Second Cubist exhibition in Paris. Kokoschka's play **The Burning Thornbush** staged in Vienna.

1912 Fourth **Futurist Manifesto** issued using typography and advertising methods later adopted by the Dadaists. **Du Cubisme** by Gleizes and Metzinger published in Paris. Kokoschka, Kraus and Loos publish a defence of Schönberg in Vienna. Diaghilev Ballet première Debussy's **L'Après-Midi d'un Faune** in Paris.

RELATED SOCIAL AND CULTURAL EVENTS IN GERMANY	GERMAN IMPRESSIONIST AND EXPRESSIONIST ARTISTS
Hewarth Walden starts **Der Sturm** in Berlin. Founding of the Berlin Branch of the International Psychoanalytical Association. Hesse's **Gertrud** published. Matisse in Munich for an Islamic exhibition.	Liebermann awarded honorary doctorate by Berlin Academy. Work by twenty-seven young artists, including Die Brücke, rejected by Berlin Secession. New Secession formed with Pechstein as President: includes Die Brücke. Die Brücke issue portfolio by Kirchner with cover by Heckel; exhibit at Arnold Gallery, Dresden. Mueller joins Die Brücke, having met Schmidt-Rottluff and Feininger in Berlin. Pechstein meets Marc and Macke and visits the Saxon Lakes with Kirchner and Heckel. Rohlfs in Berlin. Nolde in Hamburg and Berlin; denounces Liebermann and the Secession in an open letter. Jawlensky meets Marc in Munich; Marc living in Sindelsdorf meets Macke, Kandinsky, Werefkin and Klee. Second New Artists Union exhibition held at the Thannhauser Gallery, Berlin; includes Picasso, Braque, Derain, Rouault, van Dongen, Vlaminck. Dix studying at Dresden Kunstgewerkschule until 1914. Kokoschka provides a portrait drawing for every edition of **Der Sturm**; exhibits at Cassirer Gallery, Berlin and Folkwang Museum, Essen. Kubin illustrates **The Gold Bug** by Poe.
Agadir crisis; withdrawal from Morocco; claims compensation; reduction of demand to avoid confrontation with Britain. Worringer first uses the term Expressionism to describe plastic arts in **Der Sturm** (August). Strauss's **Der Rosenkavalier** staged in Dresden. Mann's **Buddenbrooks, Tonio Kröger** and **Death in Venice** published. Wedekind's **Franziska, ein modernes Mysterium** produced.	Death of von Uhde; von Stuck. Kandinsky, Münter and Marc leave New Artists Union; formulate plans for Der Blaue Reiter; exhibit at the Thannhauser Gallery (First Exhibition of the Editorial Board of the Blaue Reiter). Kandinsky, Marc, Klee and Macke contribute to the symposium **The Struggle for Art** published in Munich to answer the nationalistic **Protest Deutscher Künstler** by Vinner. Die Brücke issue portfolio by Heckel with cover by Pechstein; work illustrated in **Der Sturm**. Pechstein visits Florence. Schmidt-Rottluff visits Norway and settles in Berlin, as do Heckel and Kirchner. Nolde meets Ensor in Holland. Kirchner and Pechstein form the Moderner Unterricht in Malerei Institut. Macke and Feininger meet Delaunay in Paris. Macke living in Bonn; meets Marc and Campendonk in Sindelsdorf; all three visit Kandinsky in Murnau. Grosz studying at Dresden Academy. Beckmann leaves the Berlin Secession. Kandinsky produces non-representational **Improvisations.**
Der Sturm opens its gallery in Berlin; in April shows Futurist work; in May contemporary French graphics. Sonderbund Exhibition held in Cologne. Hauptmann receives Nobel Prize for Literature. Strauss's **Ariadne auf Naxos** staged in Stuttgart. Death of Georg Heym.	Die Brücke issue portfolio by Pechstein with cover by Mueller; exhibit at the Gurlitt Gallery, Berlin; Pechstein leaves, rejoining Secession. Kirchner and Heckel decorate the chapel at the Cologne Sonderbund. Heckel develops friendship with Marc, Macke and Feininger. Kirchner and Mueller spend summer painting near Prague; Schmidt-Rottluff at Dangast; Heckel at Lake Hidden on the island of Rügen, visits Kirchner on Fehmarn. Brücke travelling exhibition in Switzerland and Prague; involved in second Blaue Reiter exhibition. Rohlfs returns to Hagen. Meidner paints series of apocalyptic images; forms a group called The Pathetic Ones. Blaue Reiter work reproduced in **Der Sturm**. Kandinsky writes **Concerning the Spiritual in Art.** Kubin illustrates **The Double** by Dostoievsky. Marc attacks German Impressionists in **Pan**. Beckmann replies in defence. Barlach writes **Der tote Tag.** Blaue Reiter exhibition moves to the Gerlonsklub, Cologne and Der Sturm Gallery, Berlin; Kandinsky and Marc edit **Der Blaue Reiter Almanac;** at Sturm Gallery pictures by Klee, Kubin, Jawlensky and Werefkin added; exhibition travels on to Folkwang Museum, Hagen and Goldschmidt Gallery in Frankfurt. Marc and Macke travel to Paris; visit Delaunay. Klee visits Picasso and Delaunay in Paris. Klee and Macke visit Tunisia. Grosz receives scholarship for the Arts and Crafts School, Berlin.

1913	Birth of Camus. Apollinaire writes **Les Peintres Cubistes.** Roger Fry establishes Omega Workshops in London. Diaghilev Ballet première Stravinsky's **Le Sacre du Printemps** in Paris.
1914	Franz Ferdinand of Austria assassinated by Serbian nationalist whilst on a state visit to Bosnia; Austria invades Serbia. Outbreak of First World War. Tsar appointed Commander-in-Chief of Russian Forces. Fifth **Futurist Manifesto** issued in Italy.
1915	Italy enters the war. Rasputin in virtual control of Russia. Future Dadaists Tzara, Arp, Janco, Ball and Huelsenbeck meet in Zurich. Malevich exhibits Suprematist works at 0.10 Exhibition in Moscow.
1916	Rasputin murdered. Death of Redon. Hugo Ball opens Cabaret Voltaire in Zurich; formation of Dada. Mondrian, van der Leck and van Doesburg formulate the principles of **de Stijl.** Hodler awarded an honorary Professorship at Ecole des Beaux-Arts, Geneva.
1917	U.S.A. enters war. Russian Revolution; June: Lenin in Finland unable to unseat provisional government; Kerensky forms liberal/socialist coalition; Trotsky strengthens army; November: Kerensky dismissed; Bolsheviks seize government buildings in Petrograd; Soviet government formed; Lenin Chairman. Death of Degas; Rodin. **Dada I** and **Dada II** published in Zurich.
1918	Armistice: Treaty of Versailles. White Russian army fighting in Siberia; Britain, France, America, Finland send forces to assist; Russia cancels foreign debts; pledges support for international revolution; Tsar Nicholas and family assassinated. Kandinsky working with the People's Commissariat of Public Education and teaching at the Moscow Academy. Death of Apollinaire; Klimt; Schiele. **Dada III** published in Zurich.

RELATED SOCIAL AND CULTURAL EVENTS IN GERMANY	GERMAN IMPRESSIONIST AND EXPRESSIONIST ARTISTS
General Staff decide war with the Triple Alliance (Britain, France and Russia) is inevitable; preparations made for war. Hitler moves to Munich. Magazine **Revolution** appears in Berlin. Schiele writing and illustrating for **Aktion** in Berlin. Carl Sternheim writes **1913**. Marinetti in Berlin.	Following Kirchner's writing **Chronik der Brücke** the group is officially dissolved. Pechstein visits Rome. Grosz visits Paris. Hewarth Walden arranges first German **Salon D'Automne** in Berlin which includes abstract work; 360 works in all including Der Blaue Reiter, Kokoschka, Kubin, Rohlfs, Nolde, Feininger, Baumeister, the Futurists, Delaunay, Gleizes, Metzinger, Picabia, Chagall, Archipenko, Brancusi, Epstein, Larionov, Mondrian, Arp, Ernst, 20 works by Rousseau and Oriental and folk art. Nolde takes part in the Külz-Leber anthropological expedition to Palau and the South Sea Islands; travels through Russia, Siberia, China, Japan and New Guinea. All ex-Brücke artists exhibit with Berlin Secession; one-man shows at the Gurlitt Gallery, Berlin.
Kubin publishes **Blätter mit dem Tod,** a newspaper which continues until 1916. Heinrich Mann's **Untertan** published; Kaiser's **Burghers of Calais** staged. Richter working for **Die Aktion.** Frank's **Die Räuberbande** published. Hasenclever writes **Der Sohn.** Death of Christian Morgenstern; Georg Trakl on the Galician front.	Chagall visits Berlin; exhibits at Der Sturm Gallery. Corinth delivers lecture to the Berlin Free Student Association attacking primitivism in contemporary painting. Kandinsky and Jawlensky, as aliens, return to Russia. Jawlensky then settles in Geneva with Werefkin. Hofer shows at Cassirer Gallery, Berlin; interned in France as an alien until 1917. Grosz enters the army; Kirchner volunteers as an artillery driver. Pechstein visits Palau; Nolde returns via Burma, Java and the Suez Canal; Pechstein arrested by occupying Japanese forces on Palau; returns to Germany via America. Marc enlists. Macke in North Africa with Klee in April; Macke in the trenches in August, September killed in action. Beckmann enlists as a medical orderly.
Death of August Stramm on the Russian Front.	Corinth President of the Berlin Secession. Slevogt made a member of the Academy of Fine Arts, Dresden. Schmidt-Rottluff called up for military service until 1918. Heckel, medical orderly in Ostend, meets Ensor, Beckmann and Permeke. Pechstein enlists until 1917. Mueller called up for military service until 1918. Beckmann invalided to Frankfurt, remains there until 1933. Münter moves to Scandinavia and stays until 1920.
Heartfield, W. Herzfelde and Grosz found Malik-Verlag publishing house and launch **Neue Jugend** magazine. Mass demonstration against the war in Berlin led by Liebknecht. Bahr writes **Expressionismus.**	Richter one-man exhibition Galerie Hans Goltz, Munich. Hofmann teaching at Dresden Academy until 1928. Marc killed in action at Verdun. Meidner drafted into army; produces two volumes of poetry **Neck of the Stormy Sea** and **September Cry.** Kirchner has breakdown and returns to Berlin. Klee drafted. Grosz invalided out of army, returns to Berlin. Beckmann appointed at Frankfurt Academy.
In order to reduce pressure on the Eastern Front, Lenin transported across German-held territory to aid the Russian Revolution. Massive industrial strikes.	Huelsenbeck and Hausmann with Grosz and Heartfield form Berlin Dada group. Kirchner in sanatorium near Davos, Switzerland; on recovery settles nearby. Slevogt teaching at Berlin Academy after visit to Egypt. Kokoschka settles in Dresden; remains until 1924. Grosz recalled for military service; put in an asylum; discharged, returns to Berlin.
Germany and Russia sign Treaty of Brest; Russia cedes Poland and Baltic Lands to Germany and Austria; Ukraine and Finland declared independent. Treaty of Versailles: Germany loses Alsace-Lorraine, Poland, Danzig; alliance forbidden with Austria; losses 13% of land area, 12% of population, 48% of steel production, 18% of agricultural production, 10% of industrial plant, all colonies. November, sailors mutiny in Kiel; revolution; Kaiser Wilhelm II abdicates. Communist Republic declared in Bavaria. December, Sparticist Revolt led by Rosa Luxemburg and Karl Liebknecht. Death of Wedekind. Thomas Mann's **Reflections of a Nonpolitical Man** published. Walden's **Expressionismus: Die Kunstwende** published.	Hofer in Berlin. Meidner exhibition at Cassirer Gallery, Berlin. Pechstein produces stained glass windows for Gurlitt Gallery, Berlin; leader of Novembergruppe.

1919	Communist uprising in Hungary fails. In Italy D'Annunzio calls for Nationalism. Mussolini forms Fascist Party. Kandinsky appointed Director of the Museum of Pictorial Culture in Moscow. Suprematist and Non-Objective exhibition in Moscow organised by State. Dada moves to Paris from Zurich. Death of Renoir.
1920	Kandinsky made a Professor of Moscow University and organises the Academy of Artistic Science; sets up 22 museums throughout Russia to promote popular education.
1921	Commercial treaty between Sweden, Britain and Germany. In Italy Fascists win parliamentary representation. Dada festival in Prague.
1922	Lenin gives up office due to ill-health; Stalin made Secretary General of Russian Communist Party. Fascists seize power in Italy. Munch exhibition in Basle. International Dada Exhibition, Paris.
1923	In Italy elections secure Fascist majority.
1924	Fascists gain 65% majority in Italy; introduce censorship and violent suppression of opposition. Breton publishes **First Manifesto of Surrealism.**
1925	Trotsky dismissed from office in Russia. Breton publishes first instalment of **Surréalisme et la Peinture;** Surrealist exhibition at the Gallery Pierre, Paris.
1926	General Strike in Britain. Death of Monet. Surrealist exhibition at the Galerie Surréaliste, Paris.

RELATED SOCIAL AND CULTURAL EVENTS IN GERMANY	GERMAN IMPRESSIONIST AND EXPRESSIONIST ARTISTS
Eisner head of Communist Republic of Bavaria defeated in elections and assassinated; army restores order and links with the right-wing parties; increase in anti-semitism and anti-left factions. Weimar government set up. Sparticist Revolt crushed by army; Luxemburg and Liebknecht murdered. Military regain political importance. **Job** and **The Burning Thornbush** by Kokoschka staged in Berlin by Max Reinhardt. Kubin suggested to design sets for the film **The Cabinet of Dr. Caligari** but not used. Worringer's **Critical Thoughts on New Art** published in **Genius II**.	Bauhaus formed in Weimar by Gropius, encouraged by the Grand Duke of Saxe-Weimar. Pechstein returns to Berlin until 1933. Hofer made a Professor of Applied Arts at the Berlin Academy. Schmidt-Rottluff returns to Berlin and elected President of the Secession. Schames, dealer for the former members of Die Brücke, increases their prices tenfold. Mueller exhibition at the Cassirer Gallery, Berlin. Schwitters, founder of the Hanover Dada Group, invents **Merz**, exhibits at Der Sturm Gallery, Berlin; poems and prose published in **Der Sturm**. Barlach illustrates **Der Kopf** by Walter von Rheinold (published by Cassirer). Grosz and Einster publish **Die Pleite**; confiscated after the third issue. Beckmann publishes **Hell** portfolio. Death of Lehmbruck.
National Socialist party created. Kapp-Putsch – nationalist counter revolution – defeated by Berlin workers. Nationalist seizure of Bavaria. Frank publishes **Die Mensch ist gut**; Werfel publishes novel **Nicht der Mörder, der Ermordete ist schuldig** (Not the Murderer, the Victim is Guilty). Kaiser writes **Gas**. Death of Richard Dehmel.	Death of Klinger. Rohlfs made a member of the Berlin Academy. Kokoschka made a Professor at Dresden Academy although forbidden to teach in Austria. Mueller a Professor at Breslau Academy until his death; trips to Ragusa, Split, Hungary and Roumania. Klee joins Bauhaus staff; Albers enters as a student and continues as a member of staff. Liebermann President of Berlin Academy of Fine Arts. Marc's **Aufzeichnungen und Aphorisms** Vol. I published in Berlin. Barlach writes **Die echten Sedemunds**. Huelsenbeck publishes **En Avant Dada**. International Dada Exhibition in Cologne closed by police.
War Reparations Committee fix sum to be paid by Germany at £6,600m, to be paid £100m annually. Lang's film **Der müde Tod** released.	Jawlensky moves to Wiesbaden. Kandinsky returns to Germany due to official opposition to abstract art in Russia. Schwitters ostracised by Berlin Dadaists for being a 'bourgeois reactionary'. Kubin illustrates Barbey d'Aureyvilly's **Devil's Children**. Richter produces abstract film **Rythm 21**. Grosz fined for slandering the Reichswehr.
Foreign Minister Rathenau assassinated. Increasing inflation. Exchange rate 760 marks to £1. Lang's **Dr. Mabuse der Spieler** and Murnau's **Nosferatu** released. Brecht writes **Trommeln in der Nacht.**	Kandinsky and El Lissitsky join Bauhaus staff. Moholy-Nagy exhibits at Der Sturm Gallery, Berlin. Pechstein becomes a member of the Prussian Academy of the Arts, Berlin. Heckel paints frescoes for Erfurt Museum. Dix teaching in Düsseldorf until 1925. Grosz in Russia and Denmark.
Hitler in Landsberg Prison following failure of Hitler-Ludendorff Putsch. French occupy the Ruhr. Heller's Putsch in Bavaria fails. Resignation of government; new Chancellor, Stresemann. Deepening economic crisis: January 7200 marks to £1, November 16,000,000,000 marks to £1. Pabst's **Der Schatz** released; Grune's **Die Strasse**, sets by Meidner.	Corinth in Switzerland. Schmidt-Rottluff visits Italy with Kolbe. Moholy-Nagy joins Bauhaus staff. Grosz produces **Ecce Homo** portfolio which is confiscated by police; Grosz tried and fined and 30 plates destroyed. First Neue Sachlichkeit (New Objectivity) exhibition staged in Mannheim, including Grosz, Dix, Beckmann and Hofer. Grosz works for **Der Knüppel** the communist weekly paper.
Dawes Plan provides two year pause in payment of war reparations. French withdraw from Ruhr. 800 million gold marks loan from U.S.A. 2·5 million unemployed. Hitler released from Landsberg. Death of Kafka. Thomas Mann's **The Magic Mountain** published, sells 50,000 copies in one year.	Death of Thoma. Kandinsky, Klee, Feininger and Jawlensky form Die Blaue Vier and exhibit together for a decade; exhibition in San Francisco; considerable success in U.S.A. Rohlfs made a member of the Prussian Academy, Berlin, Hofer exhibits in Mannheim. Schmidt-Rottluff in Paris. Kokoschka leaves Dresden and Germany. Novembergruppe breaks up. Hostility to Bauhaus increases. Kirchner illustrates Heym's **Umbrae Vitae**; exhibits at Basle Kunsthalle. Klee delivers lecture **Concerning Modern Art** at Jena Museum; published 1925.
Locarno treaty signed with Italy, Britain, Belgium and France. Feuchtwanger's **Jud Süss** published. Berg's **Wozzeck** staged using Schönberg's 12 tone system and based on a play by Büchner. Krenek's **Johnny Spielt auf** (Jazz Opera) staged. Kafka's **The Trial** published.	Death of Corinth in Zaandvoort, Holland. Schmidt-Rottluff visits Dalmatia. Pressure forces Bauhaus to move to Dessau. Corinth, Rohlfs, Hofmannsthal, Hauptmann, Einstein, Kokoschka, Reinhardt, Schönberg sign appeal in its defence. Klee's **Pedagogical Sketchbook** published. Grosz in France.
Germany joins League of Nations. Hitler Youth formed for boys of 14-18. Lang's film **Metropolis** and Murnau's **Faust** released. Death of Rilke. Kafka's **The Castle** published.	Blaue Vier travelling exhibition in U.S.A. Bauhaus publishes Kandinsky's **Point, Line, Plane**. Kubin's **Damonen und Nacht-gesichte** published in Dresden.

1927	Trotsky expelled from Communist Party.
1928	Complete edition of **Surréalisme et la Peinture** by Breton published.
1929	Trotsky exiled from Russia. Breton's **Second Manifesto of Surrealism** published. Dali and Bunuel's film **Le Chien Andalou** première in Paris.
1930	Breton edits **Le Surréalisme au Service de la Revolution**, Paris.
1931	Dali and Bunuel's film **L'Age d'Or** shown in Paris; forbidden by police.
1932	Famine in Russia.
1933	U.S.A. recognises U.S.S.R. Surrealists produce **Minotaure** magazine in Paris.

RELATED SOCIAL AND CULTURAL EVENTS IN GERMANY	GERMAN IMPRESSIONIST AND EXPRESSIONIST ARTISTS
Zweig's pacifist novel **Der Streit um der Sergeanten Grischa** published. **Berlin-Symphonie einer Grosstadt** released. Kafka's **America** published. Hesse's **Steppenwolf** published.	Böcklin exhibition, National Gallery, Berlin. Dix made a Professor at Dresden Academy. Kollwitz visits Russia. Exhibition Ways and Directions of Abstract Painting in Europe held in Mannheim; included work by Klee, Archipenko, Braque, Delaunay, Gleizes, Feininger, Kandinsky, Leger, El Lissitsky, Moholy-Nagy, Mondrian, Picasso, Schwitters.
Formation of Hitler Youth for boys 10-14, girls 14-18. Walden leaves Germany for Russia; **Der Sturm** no longer appears. **The Threepenny Opera** by Brecht and Weill staged. Lang's film **Spione** and Pabst's **Joyless Street** and **Pandora's Box** (based on second half of Wedekind's **Lulu**) released.	Hofer retrospective at Berlin Secession to celebrate his fiftieth birthday. Gropius resigns as director of Bauhaus, succeeded by Bayer. Grosz convicted for blasphemy as result of publishing **Hintergrund.**
War reparations cut to £2,000m. British and Belgian troops leave. Further economic deterioration following death of Stresemann. Lang's **Die Frau im Mond** released. Thomas Mann wins Nobel Prize for Literature for **The Magic Mountain.** Death of Arno Holz.	Ernst exhibition at the Flechtheim Gallery, Berlin. Richter publishes **Filmfeinde von Heute, Filmfreunde von Morgen.** Grosz acquitted on charge of blasphemy.
National Socialists win 107 seats in Reichstag with Hindenberg as puppet-leader; rules by decree. De Chirico designs sets for Krenek's **Orestes** in Berlin. World première of von Sternberg's **The Blue Angel** starring Emil Jannings and Marlene Dietrich in Berlin. Feuchtwanger publishes **Erfolg.** Pabst's New Objectivity film **Westfront 1918** released.	Death of Mueller. Schmidt-Rottluff at German Academy in Rome. Klee leaves Bauhaus and takes a post on the staff of Düsseldorf Academy.
Hesse resigns from Prussian Academy of Literature due to its failure to counter growing conservatism. Lang's **M,** Sagan's **Mädchen in Uniform,** Pabst's **Kameradschaft** and **Threepenny Opera** released. Kafka's **Great Wall of China** published.	Kubin's **Mein Werk** published. Schmidt-Rottluff made a member of the Prussian Academy, Berlin, as are Dix and Kirchner. Feininger Retrospective at the National Gallery, Berlin. Münter returns to Murnau. Kokoschka exhibition in Paris; returns to Vienna, remains until 1934; 1935 goes to London. Grosz's work exhibited in New York.
Third of the male population unemployed. National Socialists win 230 seats in the Reichstag; 196 in second election. Communist film **Kühle Wampe** released.	Death of Slevogt. Bauhaus transfers to Berlin; dissolved shortly afterwards.
Death of Stefan George. Hitler made Chancellor. Goebbels made Minister of Propaganda and Public Enlightenment; sets up State Chambers of Culture, with single State Trade Union, the Deutsche Arbeitsfront. Reichstag fire; Communists accused; increasing pressure on the left and Jews. Germany walks out of disarmament conference and withdraws from League of Nations. Public burning of books of an un-German spirit. Jewish actors and producers from the cinema and theatre leave. Mann, Zweig, Feuchtwanger leave. Lists published of artists and writers to lose citizenship because of un-German activities. Lang's **Das Testament des Dr. Mabuse,** Weifel's **Die vierzig Tage des Musa Dagh** and Leni Riefenstahl's **Der Sieg des Glaubens** (Victory of Faith) released.	Kandinsky moves to Paris. Feininger returns to America in 1936, having been proscribed by the National Socialists. Kirchner deprived of membership of Prussian Academy; 1937 639 of his works removed from museums by National Socialists; suicide at Davos 1938. Schmidt-Rottluff deprived of membership of Prussian Academy and classified as a 'degenerate artist' and 608 works removed from public museums; forbidden to paint 1941. Pechstein deprived of membership of Prussian Academy and work proscribed. Heckel, 729 works removed from German museums and confiscated as 'degenerate art' in 1937. Nolde, work proscribed and forbidden to paint by National Socialists. Liebermann's work proscribed as being of non-Aryan origins; dies abandoned by friends 1935. Kollwitz loses membership of the Prussian Academy, dies 1945. Beckmann moves to Berlin after being dismissed from professional post at the Städelschule, Frankfurt; emigrates to Paris 1937. Dix dismissed from professional post at Dresden Academy; 1934 forbidden to exhibit by National Socialists and in 1937 eight paintings included in the Exhibition of Degenerate Art and 260 works removed from German museums. Grosz emigrates to New York; 1938 becomes American citizen. Heartfield emigrates. Klee dismissed from post at Düsseldorf Academy, returns to Berne, 17 pictures included in Exhibition of Degenerate Art. Rohlfs classified as a 'degenerate artist', works removed from public museums and many destroyed. Meidner classified as a 'degenerate' in 1935; remains in Berlin until 1939 when he flees to London. Hofer dismissed from his post at the Prussian Academy in 1934 and banned from teaching.

**Catalogue of the 19th and 20th century German Paintings,
Drawings, Prints and Sculpture in the permanent collection
of Leicestershire Museums and Art Gallery.**

All measurements in the catalogue and for the illustrations
accompanying the preceding text are in centimetres, height before width.

Ernst Barlach

1870-1938

Barlach was born at Wedel. At the age of eighteen he went to Hamburg to train as an art teacher and then studied at the Dresden Academy. His early work displayed many of the curvilinear qualities of Jugendstil. In 1895 his visit to Paris reinforced his earlier interest in Millet and Meunier and the depiction of lives led close to the soil. A more decisive stimulus to the development of his work came in 1906, with a visit to Russia which heightened his vision of the simplicity, profundity and primitive religious belief of those who toil on the land. For inspiration and direction he turned to the wood carvers of mediaeval Germany who projected a feeling of mystical intensity. His later work grew increasingly symbolic, the figures losing their individuality and becoming psychological types, as in his plays. Between 1899-1910 he was in Hamburg and Berlin. In 1909 he made his last trip abroad, to Italy. In 1910 he settled in Güstrow where he remained, in almost monastic isolation, until his death. In 1916 he was conscripted into the army but was discharged through the intervention of Liebermann and Slevogt. In 1933 he was proscribed by the National Socialists and in 1935 confined to his studio. His importance lies not only in the field of sculpture but also in his work as a printmaker, illustrator and playwright.

1   **Der Kuss II**

The Kiss

1921

Bronze 16·5 × 19·5 × 12

Purchased from the Bruton Gallery, Bruton, Somerset with a national grant-in-aid administered by the Victoria and Albert Museum 1976.

Coll: Dr. Arnold Haskell, CBE.

Lit: Carl Dietrich Carls: *Barlach,* 1969, p.89, illus. 73.

Originally a wood carving, the bronze casts were made by Flechtheim, Barlach's dealer. The cast illustrated in Carls' book is from the Kunsthistorisches Museum, Vienna, and also illustrated is a charcoal drawing of the subject produced in 1921 from the Barlach Estate, Güstrow.

176'1976

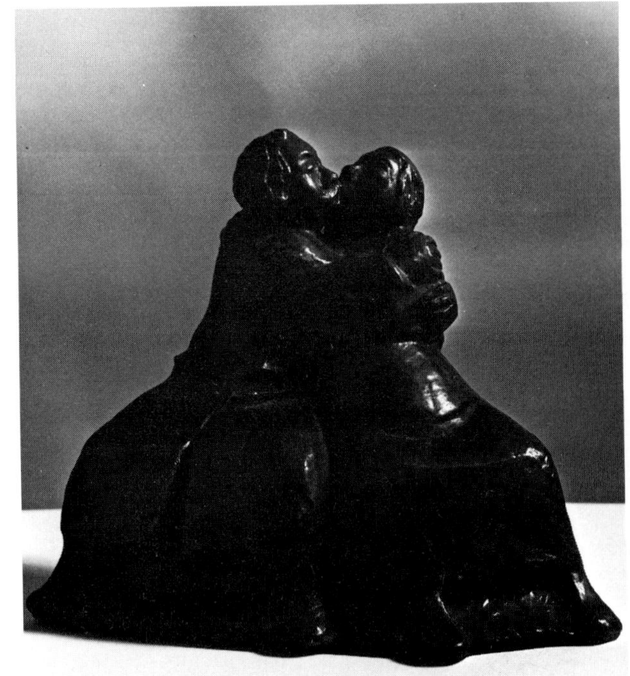

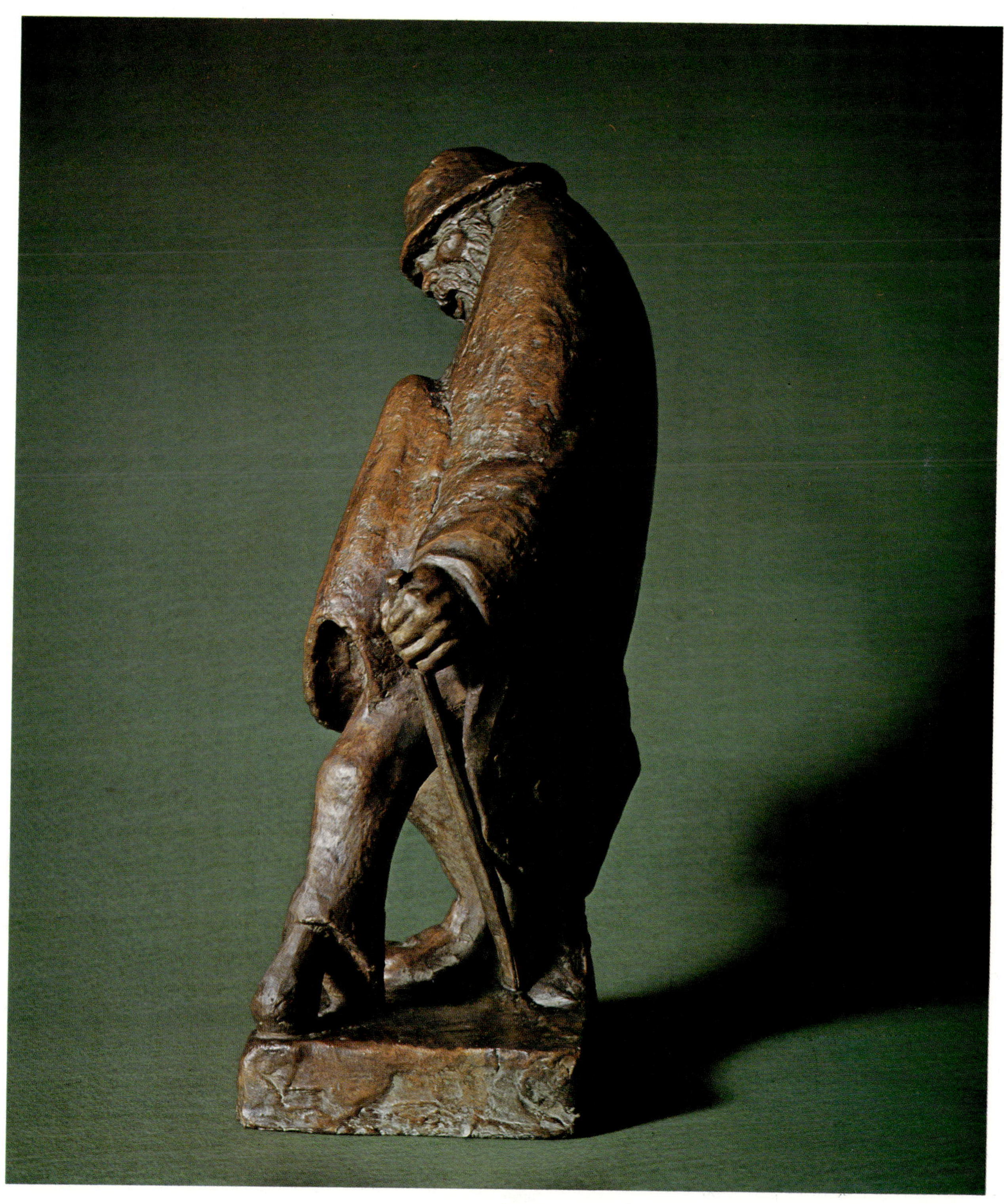

2 **BARLACH**
Das fröhliche Einbein 1934

2 **Das fröhliche Einbein**
Jolly Peg-Leg

1934

Bronze, height 53·5

Purchased from Galerie Alex Vomel, Düsseldorf with a
national grant-in-aid administered by the Victoria and
Albert Museum 1961.

Schult 451

Lit: Carl Dietrich Carls: *Ernst Barlach,* 1969, pp.200,
212, pl. no. 87.

This piece is closely related to a lithograph, **Jolly
Peg-Leg II** (Schult II 226) produced in 1922,
illustrated by Carls in his book (pl. no. 86). Schult
mentions four bronze casts in public and private
collections but does not specify this as being the
original number produced.

10 A 1961

Max Beckmann
1884-1950

Beckmann was born in Leipzig. He entered the Weimar Academy in 1900 and
studied there until 1903. In subsequent years he travelled extensively in
Europe, particularly Florence and Paris. He admired the work of Rembrandt,
Piero della Francesca and Signorelli. In 1905 he settled in Berlin and became
involved with the Secessionist movement and the Impressionist influence of
Liebermann, Corinth and Slevogt. In 1905 and 1906 he exhibited with the
Berlin Secession. He met Munch in 1906 but his real interest rested in artists
such as Delacroix and El Greco rather than his contemporaries. In 1910 he
became an executive member of the Berlin Secession but resigned in the
following year. In 1914 he enlisted as a medical orderly but was invalided out
in 1915 to Frankfurt, where he remained until 1933. After the war he
developed a simpler compositional style using constricted and distorted
perspectives reflecting his growing preoccupation with Germany's mediaeval
heritage, with its direct symbolism and harsh realism. In his work aesthetics
gave way to direct representation of the emotional content of the subject
often involving sex, violence and horror. In the 1920's he was involved with
the New Objectivity movement reflecting the social turmoil within Germany.
With the increasing power of National Socialism he was forced to leave
Frankfurt in 1933 and moved to Berlin but was forced to flee Germany to
Amsterdam. In 1947 he moved to New York, where he died.

3   **Bildnis Heinrich Simon**
Portrait of Heinrich Simon

1922

Lithograph 58·5 × 40

Signed: *Beckmann* in pencil

Purchased from Mrs. Margaret Fisher, London 1972.

Glaser and Meier Graefe 198

Heinrich Simon was chief editor of the *Frankfurter Zeitung,* a democratic and liberal newspaper which remained free of party influence. The paper championed modern developments in the arts, particularly poetry and drama. In 1931 he said:

> 'It is good to remember that time in which the advocates of freedom, the advocates of a humane Germany, experienced hostility and persecution. It is good to remember that these persecutions did not cause them to surrender a single iota of their convictions. Where did this courage come from? From the belief in the other Germany which, through the centuries, again and again interrupted sabre-rattling self-laceration, even when force sought to condemn it to silence. This newspaper has lived, to this day, on the belief in this other Germany of freedom and humanity.'

Excerpts from a speech delivered on 29 October 1931 quoted in 'Ein Jahrhundert Frankfurter Zeitung, begrundet von Leopold Sonnemann', special number of *'Die Gegenwart'* XI, 29 October 1956, p.39.

In 1930 Simon published a work on Beckmann, *Max Beckmann,* (Berlin/Leipzig 1930).

13 A 1972

4   **Garderobe**
Dressing Room

1922

Drypoint 20·5 × 15·5

Signed: *Beckmann.* Numbered 88/125 (not by artist)

Purchased from Mrs. Margaret Fisher, London, with a national grant-in-aid administered by the Victoria and Albert Museum, 1975.

Gallwitz 164; Glaser and Meier Graefe 167

From a series entitled **Jahrmarkt,** published in 1922 by the Marées Gesellschaft.

818'1975

Illustrated on page 25

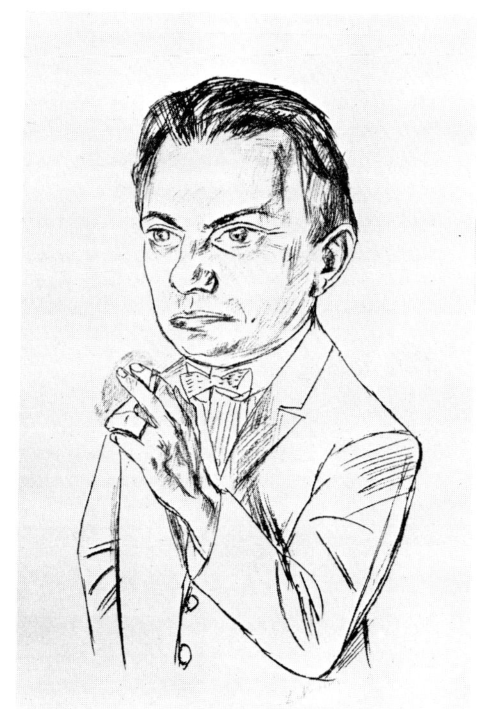

Adam Brenner
1800-91

Brenner was born in Vienna where he later studied at the Academy under Kupelwieser and Waldmuller. He was an adherent of the academic attitudes prevalent in German 19th century painting and like many of his contemporaries looked to the Italian Masters, in particular Raphael. He painted genre, religious and historical subjects and also worked as an illustrator for *Die Himmelrose.* He died in Vienna.

5 **Jesus ruft Seine Ersten Jünger, Simon, Andreas, Jakob und Johannes**

Christ calling His First Disciples, Simon, Andrew, James and John

1839

Oil on canvas 62·5×79

Signed and dated: *Adam Brenner pinx. 1839*

Presented by Mrs. L. Jarratt, Leicester 1964.

Brenner's treatment of the subject is very close to that of the Nazarenes, a group of German artists who lived and worked in Rome and who hoped to create a synthesis of style between the traditions of Dürer and Raphael.

146 A 1964

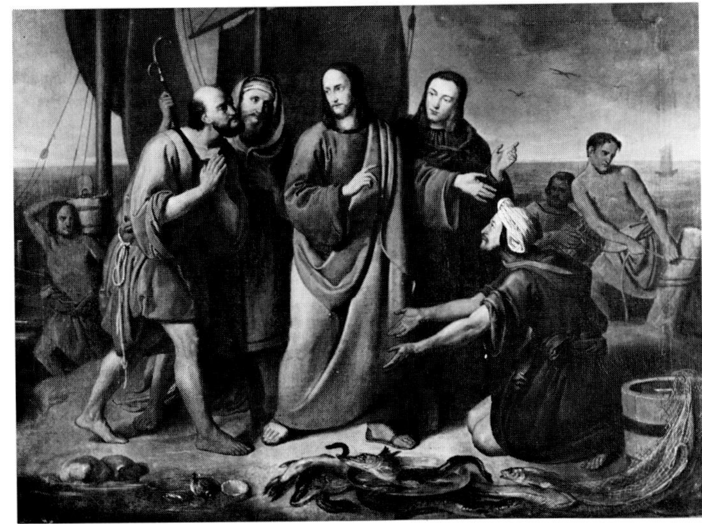

Lovis Corinth
1858-1925

Corinth was born in Tatiau, the son of an East Prussian craftsman, and studied in Königsberg 1876-80, Munich 1880-81, Antwerp, summer of 1884 and at the Académie Julian in Paris 1884-87. In 1891 he settled in Munich where he met Liebl and Trubner and was influenced by the Jugendstil movement. In 1900 he moved to Berlin where, on the advice of Liebermann, who helped to advance him, he joined the Berlin Secession. In 1902 he was elected to the Committee of the Secession and was its director in 1911-12 and 1915. His productive artistic life in Berlin was ended by a serious illness in 1911-12 which left him debilitated for life. The late paintings that he was able to produce combine the sensuous nature of his early work with a newly found spiritual quality, which brought his work closer to that of his younger contemporaries in the Expressionist school. He died at Zaandvoort in Holland.

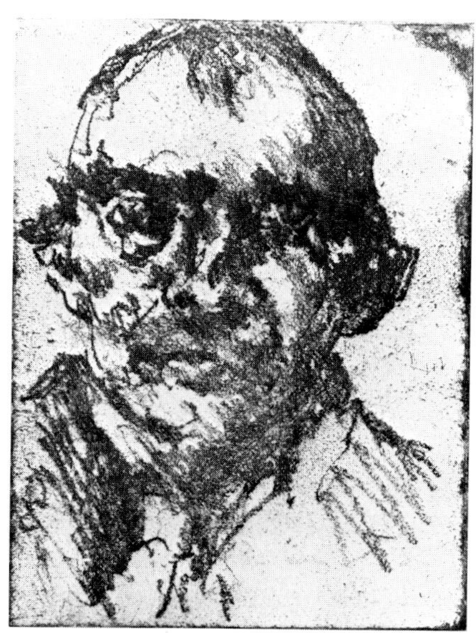

7 **CORINTH**
Selbstbildnis 1921

6 **Bildnis Carl Ludwig Elias 7¼**
Portrait of Carl Ludwig Élias aged 7¼

1899

Oil on canvas 68·5 × 54·5

Signed and dated: *Lovis Corinth 1899* and inscribed: *Carl Ludwig Elias 7¼*

Purchased from Mrs. B. Levy, London, with the assistance of a national grant-in-aid administered by the Victoria and Albert Museum 1968.

48 A 1968
Illustrated on page 6

7 **Selbstbildnis**
Self Portrait

1921

Vernis mou 11·75 × 9·1

Signed: *Lovis Corinth* in pencil

Purchased from Mrs. Margaret Fisher, London 1976.

In his later years Corinth produced a large number of self-portrait prints and drawings in which he used increasingly expressionistic means to explore his own psychology and emotions.

974'1975

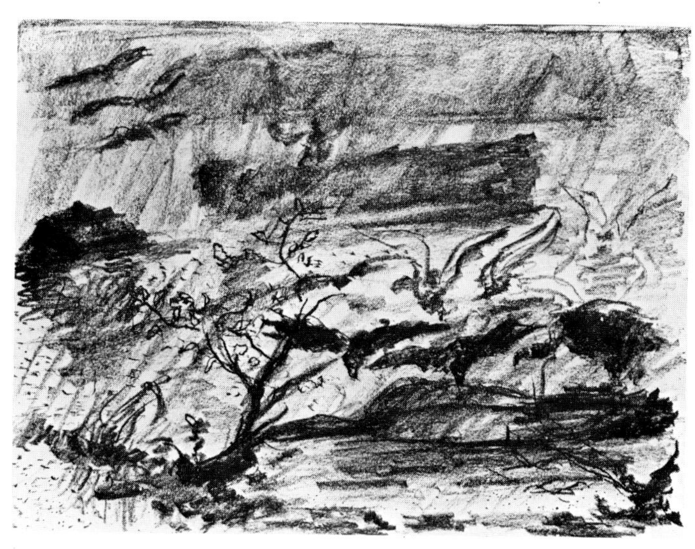

8 **Die Wasser steigen**
The Waters Rise

1923-1925

Lithograph 56 × 76

Signed: *Lovis Corinth* in pencil

Purchased from Mrs. Margaret Fisher, London 1974.

Müller 819

Plate 5 from the folio **Die Sündflut** (The Deluge) published by Euphorion Verlag.

441'1974

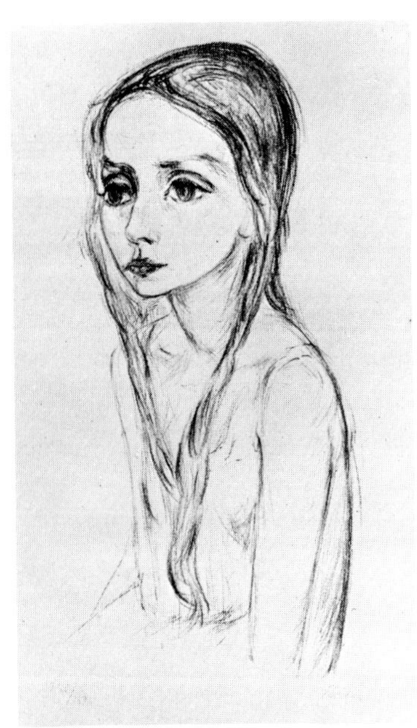

Georg Ehrlich

b. 1897

Ehrlich was born in Vienna. Between 1912-15 he studied at the Vienna Kunstgewerbeschule. From 1915-18 he served with the Austrian army. In 1919 he exhibited in Vienna including illustrations of Verlaine and Dostoievsky and moved to Munich. In 1920 he exhibited in Munich with Barlach, Beckmann, Corinth, Kokoschka and Klee at the Graphische Sammlung. In 1921 he moved to Berlin, exhibiting at Paul Cassirer's gallery. In 1924 he returned to Vienna and exhibited with the Hagenbund. In 1926 he turned to sculpture which was to become his prime interest. During the thirties and forties he exhibited extensively in Vienna, London, Europe and America. In 1937 he settled in London, leaving in 1948-49 to teach at the Art School in Columbus, Ohio, USA.

9 **Ein junges Mädchen**

A Young Girl

1922

Lithograph 64 × 43

Signed and dated: *Ehrlich 22*

Purchased from Mrs. Margaret Fisher, London 1973.

303'1973

Max Ernst

1891-1976

Ernst was born in Brühl near Cologne, the son of a schoolmaster and amateur artist. In 1909 he entered Bonn University and planned to specialise in psychiatry. In 1910-11 he studied the art of mental patients in order to investigate 'those vague and dangerous territories on whose border madness lies'. In 1911 he met Macke and through him other young German artists. The remaining pre-war years were vital to his evolution as an artist with the 1912 Cologne Sonderbund, his meeting with Delaunay and Apollinaire in 1913 and, the following year, the beginning of his lifelong friendship with Hans Arp 1887-1966. During the war he served as an artillery engineer and later wrote:

> 'On 1 August 1914 Max Ernst died. He was resurrected on 11 November 1918 as a young man who aspired to find the myths of his time.'

Following the war he became a prominent figure in Cologne Dada. In 1919 he began experimenting with collage but not as a formal device as used by the Cubists but as a record of 'a faithful and fixed image of hallucination'. In 1920 he had his first one-man show in Paris at the invitation of André Breton, b.1896. In 1922 he moved to Paris and painted works such as *Hommes n'en Sauront rien* (Tate Gallery) which contained all the elements inherent in Surrealism, although it preceded Breton's 'First Surrealist Manifesto' by a year. The irrational juxtaposition of images and use of association linked with a use of diagrams, fantastic landscapes and eroticism developed in the 1920's, remained central to his work throughout his life. In 1925 he developed 'frottage', the technique of obtaining rubbings from different materials and combining them with fantastic images. He later adopted this technique for oil painting as in *La Ville Entière* 1935 (Tate Gallery).

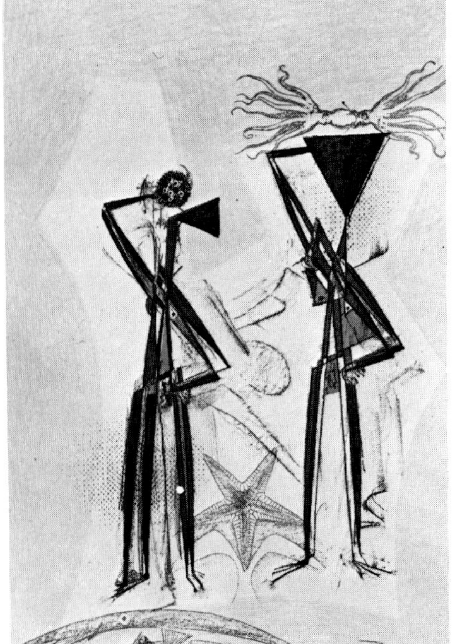

10 **ERNST**
Etoile de Mer 1950

In 1925 his first 'frottage' drawings were published as the book **Histoire Naturelle** and in 1929 his first book of collages **La Femme Cent Têtes** appeared. In 1934 he published his most famous book of collages, **Une Semaine de Bonté.** In 1938 he left the Surrealist group after quarrelling with Breton. In 1941 he settled in New York and married Peggy Guggenheim but later moved to Sedona, Arizona and remarried, this time Dorothea Tanning. In Arizona he discovered close affinities with the local landscape and with the life and sacred art of the Hopi Indians. In 1954 he won first prize at the Venice Biennale and only at that time a regular sale for his work. Since then he has had major retrospective exhibitions in Berne (1956), Paris (1959), and New York (1961). He died in Paris.

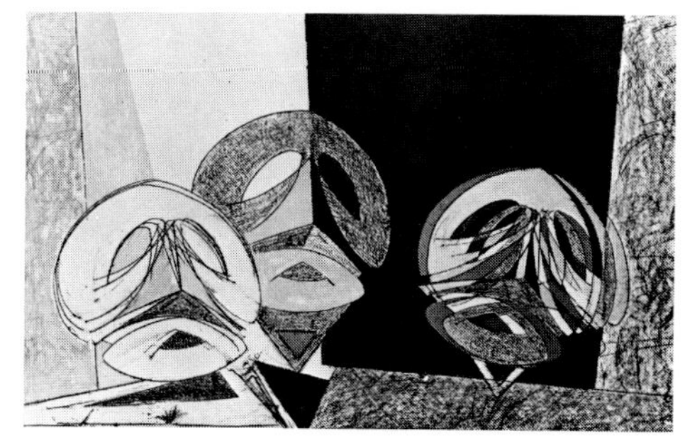

10 **Etoile de Mer**

Starfish

1950

Lithograph 42·5 × 26·5

Signed: *Max Ernst*

Purchased from the Anglo-French Art Centre, London 1951.

Brusberg 63P

12 A 1951

11 **Masques**

Masks

1950

Lithograph 38 × 56

Signed: *Max Ernst*

Purchased from the International Guild of Engravers, London 1952.

Brusberg 59P

26 A 1952

Lyonel Feininger
1871-1956

Feininger was born in New York, the son of German emigré musicians. In 1887 he went to Hamburg to study music but decided to become a painter instead and enrolled at the Industrial School of Art. In 1888 he went to the Berlin Academy where he studied under Hancke, Schlabitz and Friedrich who helped to develop his draughtsmanship. Between 1890 and 1906 Feininger produced illustrations and cartoons for *Ulk* and *Lustige Blätter* in Berlin. In 1890 he attended the Jesuit College in Liège and in 1892-93 the Atélier Colarossi in Paris, before returning to Berlin. In 1906 he visited Weimar, returned to Paris and met the German painters in Matisse's circle at the Café du Dôme. He also met Delaunay, Pascin and Götz (and through the latter discovered the colour theories of Seurat). In 1920 Feininger exhibited at the Berlin Secession, in 1911 at the Salon des Indépendants and in 1913 at the First German Autumn Salon. He held his first one-man show at the Sturm Gallery in Berlin, 1917, and was invited by Walter Gropius to join the staff of the Bauhaus at Weimar in 1919, where he worked until 1924 as artistic director of the printing shop and 'master of form'. In 1924 he joined the **Blaue Vier** (Blue Four), lived in Dessau from 1925-33 and in Halle from 1929-31. He returned to America in 1936 when his work was proscribed by the Nazis, and died in New York.

12 Traumstadt
Dream City

1911

Etching on zinc 13·8 × 21·3

Signed on plate u.r.: *Leinoel Einfinger.* Signed and dated l.r. below image: *Lyonel Feininger 1911.* Inscribed l.r. below image: *Traumstadt.*

Presented by Herold Goddard Esq., Leicester 1964.

Prasse E 38, illus.

The print was also titled *Vergessene Stadt* (Forgotten City). Besides this impression, three others are known, dated 1911: another on cream paper, one on yellow paper and one inscribed *I. Druck.* It is possible that an edition of about twenty-five were printed from the existing plate in the early 1950's for the artist by L'Imprimerie Lacounière, Paris. A posthumous edition was printed in 1965 at Editions M. Lacounière (formerly the above), Paris.

Another example is in the public collection, Saarbrucken.

139 A 1964

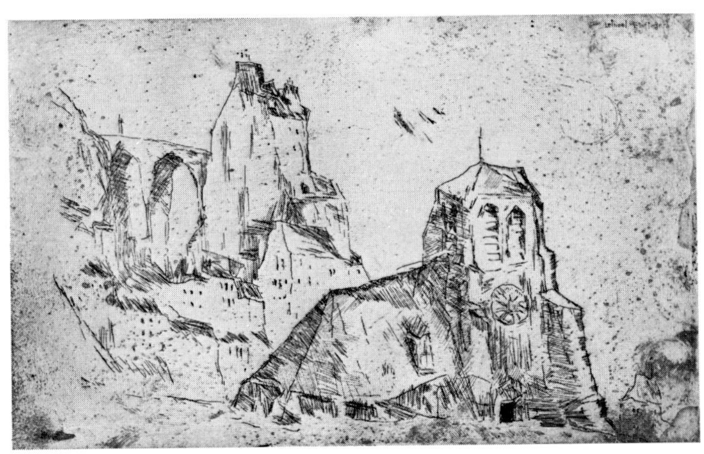

13 Hinter der Stadtkirche
Behind the Church

1916

Alternative Title: The Square

Oil on canvas 73·5 × 90

Signed and dated: *Feininger 1916.* On back of stretcher in pencil: *March 1916.*

Purchased from Mrs. T. Hess, Leicester 1944.

Coll: Georg Kaiser, Weimar, Germany; Alfred Hess, Erfurt, Germany.

Exh: Berlin, *Kunstausstellung 'Der Sturm',* 1917 (32) as *Platz an der Kirche;* Royal Academy, London: *Primitives to Picasso,* 1962 (282); Munich and Zurich: *Lyonel Feininger 1871-1956,* 1973 (89), repr.

Lit: Leicester Museums and Art Gallery: *Collection of Paintings,* 1958, p.21 (61), repr. 13F; Hans Hess: *Lyonel Feininger,* London 1961. Oeuvre Catalogue No. 155 as compiled by Mrs. Julia Feininger, repr. p.262; Barry Herbert: *German Expressionists at Leicester,* Arts Review 19th June 1971, Vol. XXIII No. 12, p.377 repr.

9 A 1944

Illustrated on page 27

Marcel Frishman

1900-52

Frishman was born in Lodz and studied at the Berlin Academy in the early 1920's. In 1926 he joined the staff of the political and satirical weekly *Simplicissimus* as a cartoonist. When the magazine was taken over by the Nazis in 1933, he was compelled to leave Germany, working in Copenhagen and then, in 1937, Australia where he remained for thirteen years, working in factories. In 1950 he returned to Europe with deteriorating health to continue his work.

14 Strassenszene

Street Scene

Etching and drypoint 20×13·5

Signed: *Marcel Frishman*

Purchased from Mrs. Margaret Fisher, London 1975.

359'1975

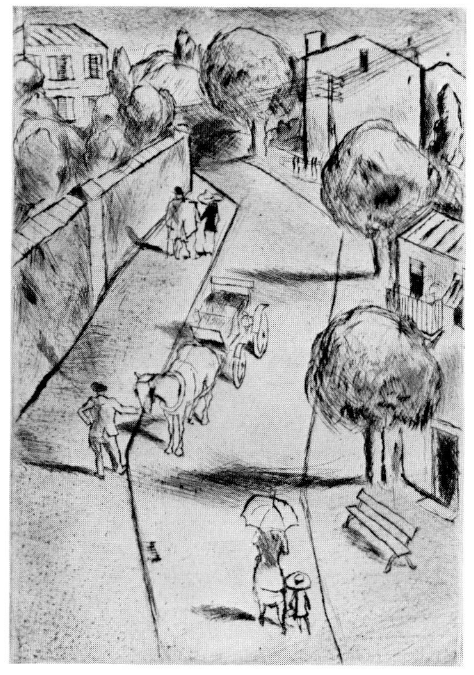

George Grosz

1893-1959

Grosz was born in Berlin but his family moved to Stolp in 1898. However, upon the death of his father in 1900 the family returned to Berlin. In 1908 he was expelled from grammar school and the following year entered the Dresden Academy where he remained until 1911. In 1912 he returned to Berlin and attended the Art School attached to the Museum of Arts and Crafts until 1917. In 1913 he visited Paris, studying at the Atélier Colarossi. The following year, with the outbreak of war, he enlisted in the army but was released from service in 1915. On his return to Berlin he met Wieland Herzfelde and had a drawing and poem published in *Der Sturm.* In 1916 he worked on Herzfelde's magazine *Die Neue Jugend* but the following year was recalled for military service; almost immediately he suffered a mental breakdown and was invalided out. On his recovery he again worked for Herzfelde and the following year with John Heartfield on an animated film *Pierre in St. Nazaire.* In 1919 he joined the Berlin Club Dada whilst working for Herzfelde's publishing house Malik-Verlag and producing collages in conjunction with Heartfield. In 1920 he illustrated publications for both *Malik* and *Sektion Dada* and ran a political cabaret with Heartfield called *Schall und Rauch* in the basement of Reinhardt's theatre, for whom he also produced theatre designs. In 1921, whilst continuing all these activities, he was tried and fined 300 marks for slandering the Reichswehr. In 1922 he visited Petrograd, Moscow and Denmark. **Ecce Homo**, a portfolio of drawings published in 1923, was confiscated by the Public Prosecutor for obscenity and the following year Grosz was tried and fined 6,000 marks. From this time until 1927 he worked for the Communist weekly paper *Der Knüppel.* In 1925 he again visited France and on his return his work was represented at the New Objectivity exhibition in Mannheim. In 1928 the publication of his portfolio

Hintergrund caused his trial on a charge of blasphemy, for which he was convicted but the subsequent year acquitted. In 1931 his work was shown in New York and two years later he was offered teaching posts at the Arts Students League and the Sterne-Grosz School in New York where he moved the same year. He remained in the USA until 1959 when he returned to Germany but died in Berlin within two months of his return.

15 **Zur Erinnerung an Rosa Luxemburg und Karl Liebknecht**

Remember: In Memory of Rosa Luxemburg and Karl Liebknecht

c.1919

Pen, brush and ink heightened with white 56×40·5

Inscribed: _Meinem liebern Freunde Erich & s.l. Frau z. müssten an in erinnern die grosse Zeit der_ (word illegible) _& Roter Kampfe in Freundschaft. George Grosz. Bayside 1935 Nov._ (My dear friend Erich and your dear wife in order that the great time of the —— and Red conflict be remembered in friendship. George Grosz. Bayside 1935 Nov.) Dated: _January 1919_ (probably not in Grosz's hand).

Purchased from Fischer Fine Art Ltd., London with the assistance of a national grant-in-aid administered by the Victoria and Albert Museum 1976.

Coll: Erich Cohn; Barnett Shine, London

Lit: Hans Hess: _George Grosz,_ London 1974, p.81, repr. pl. 76 on p.83.

The dedication was written in November 1935 from Grosz's American home at Bayside, 40-41 221st Street, Long Island. Erich Cohn and his wife were avid patrons of his work.

394'1976

Illustrated on page 22

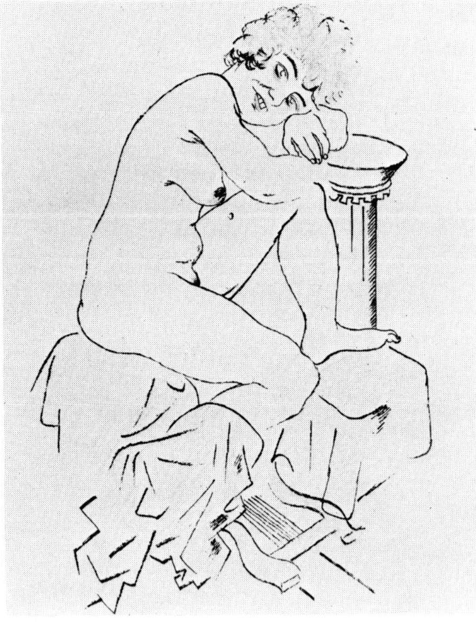

16a **GROSZ**
Lady Hamilton . . .
Facing title page

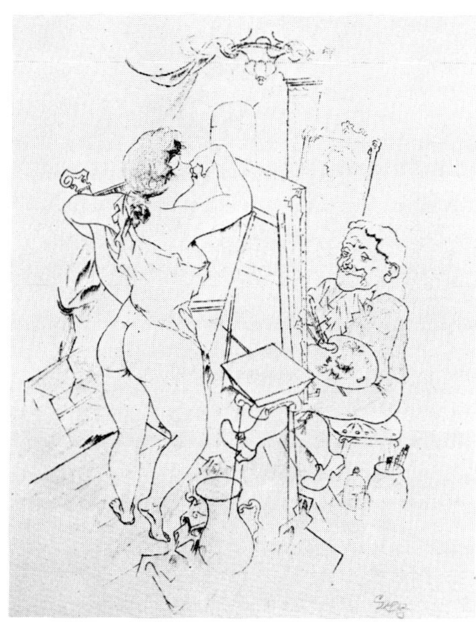

6b Facing p. 16

16 **Lady Hamilton oder die Posen – Emma oder vom Dienstmädchen zum Beefsteak à la Nelson. Eine ebenso romanhafte wie auch novellenschankelnde durchwachsene Travestie von Alfred Richard Meyer. Fleissigt und fleischigst bebildert von George Grosz.**

Lady Hamilton or The posturing of Emma or From housemaid to Nelson's bit of crackling. A fantastic and romantic travesty by Alfred Richard Meyer. Most industriously fleshed out by George Grosz.

1923

Book with eight illustrations hand-coloured with coloured pencil 30·25×25·5

Signed on each plate l.r.: *Grosz.*

Purchased from Mrs. Monika Kinley, London, with the assistance of a national grant-in-aid administered by the Victoria and Albert Museum 1976.

Lit: Hans Hess: *George Grosz,* 1974, p.159

Published by the Fritz Gurlitt Verlag, Berlin. An edition of 250 was printed, of which the first 50 copies were hand-coloured and signed. The final page of text is signed *Richard Meyer* and the copy numbered XXXI.

In 1921 Grosz illustrated Meyer's book *Munke Punke Dyonisus groteske Liebesgedichte.*

7'1976

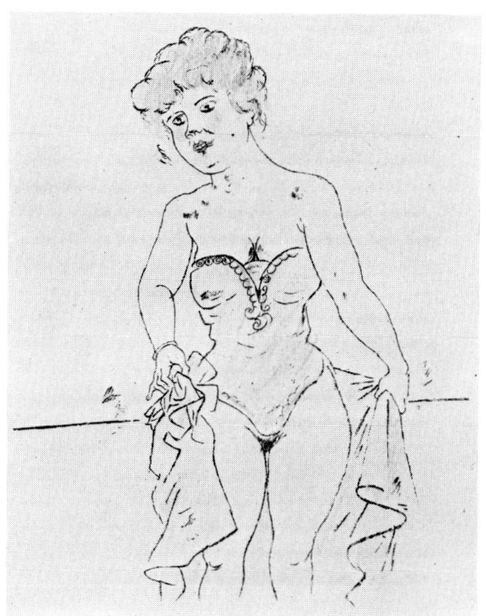

6c Facing p. 20

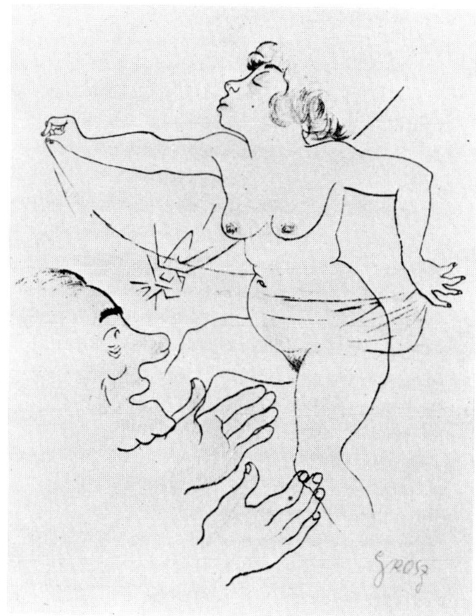

16d Facing p. 24

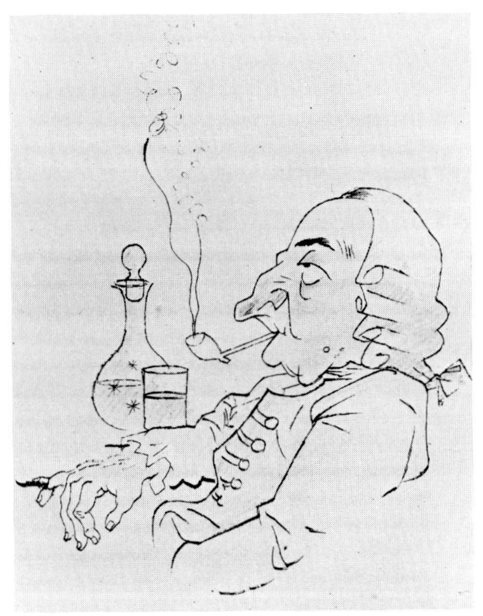

16e   Facing p. 32

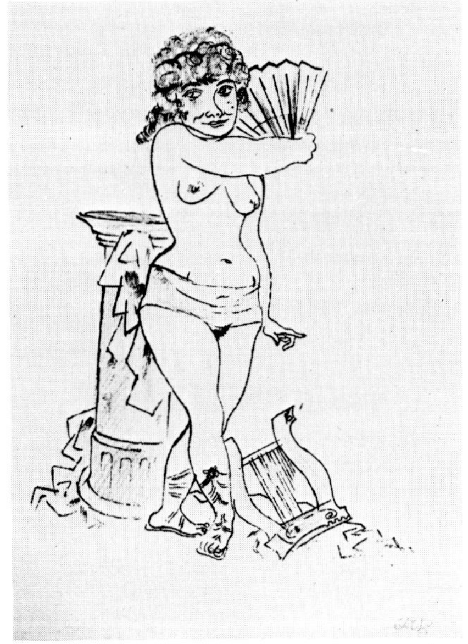

16f   Facing p. 40

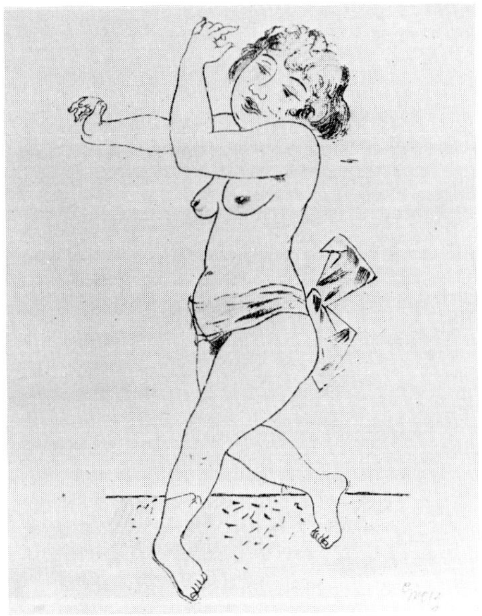

16g   Facing p. 44

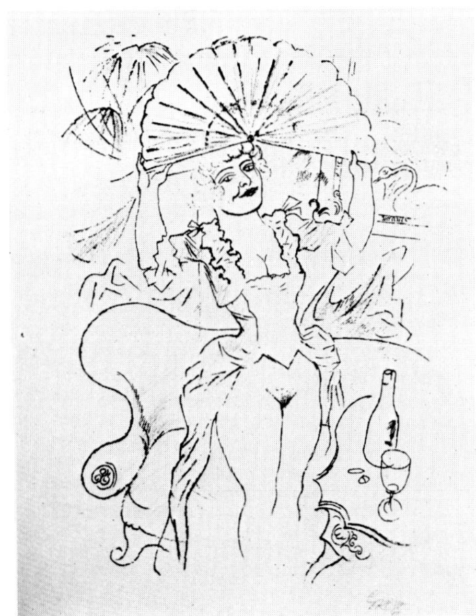

16h   Facing p. 48

17   Hinterbliebene
The Bereaved

c.1930

Pencil 59 × 44·5

Signed l.r.: *Grosz.* Inscribed: *No. 70 Hinterbliebene*

Purchased from Mrs. Margaret Fisher, London, with the assistance of a national grant-in-aid administered by the Victoria and Albert Museum 1974.

This is probably one of the series of drawings and watercolours on which Grosz was working circa 1930 for a portfolio called **Natural History of the German Middle-Classes** and for which he wrote a text. Grosz had not completed the work before he left Germany in 1933 to escape Nazi persecution.

440'1974

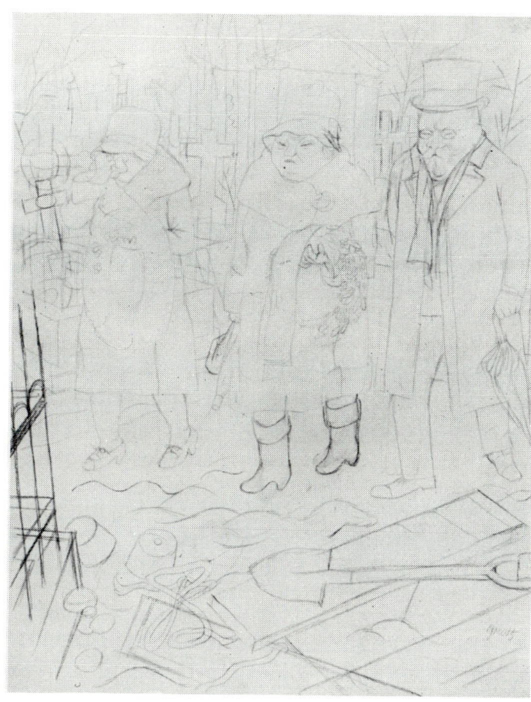

17 **GROSZ**
Hinterbliebene c.1930.

18 **Das Innere eines Zimmers in Berlin**
Interior of a Room in Berlin

1954

Set Design for the film version of the play *I am a Camera* based on the novel *Goodbye to Berlin* by Christopher Isherwood published in 1939.

Watercolour 32×42

Signed: *Grosz* and numbered *36* l.r.

Purchased from Mrs. Margaret Fisher, London, with the assistance of a national grant-in-aid administered by the Victoria and Albert Museum 1975.

Grosz came to London from Berlin in September 1954 to design the decor for the Remus film *I am a Camera,* staying until 6th November at White's Hotel, Hyde Park.

The room represented is probably that of Sally Bowles.

817'1975

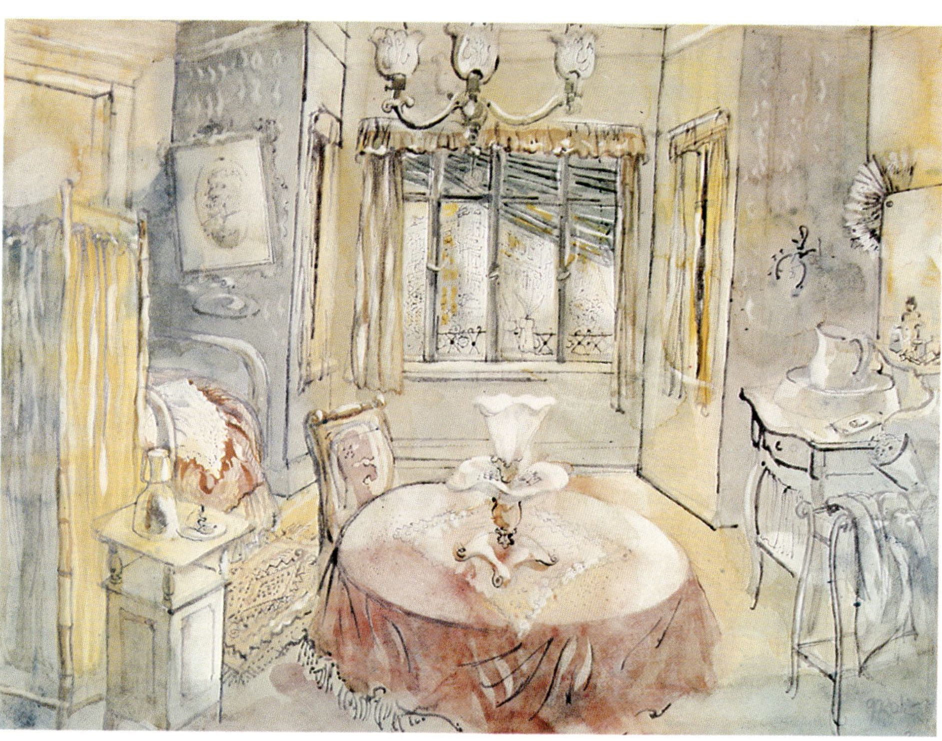

Erich Heckel
1883-1970

Heckel was born at Dobeln in Saxony. At school in Chemnitz he became
friendly with a fellow pupil, Karl Schmidt (later Rottluff), with whom he
attended the twice weekly meetings at the local Kunstverein. In 1904 he
moved to Dresden to study architecture at the Technical College and was
introduced by his elder brother to Kirchner. The following year **Die Brücke**
was formed and Heckel rented the group's first communal studio in the city's
working class district of Friedrichstadt. He worked in the drawing office of the
architect Wilhelm Kreis and established useful contacts that enabled the
unknown group to launch its first public exhibition in the showroom of a local
lamp factory in October 1906. In 1907 Heckel produced the first expressionist
book illustrations when he executed twelve woodcut plates to Oscar Wilde's
Ballad of Reading Gaol. In 1909 he painted at Moritzburg for the first time
with Kirchner. Throughout the group's stormy eight-year life-span it was
Heckel who dedicated himself most selflessly to preserving its unification
which was constantly being threatened by differences of opinion between
Kirchner and Schmidt-Rottluff. In 1911 Heckel moved to Steglitz in Berlin
and exhibited with the **Brücke** at the international exhibition of the Cologne
Sonderbund in 1912, for which he and Kirchner also painted the interior of a
large chapel. The following year the group was dissolved. From 1915-18
Heckel was a medical orderly in Belgium where he met James Ensor. He
returned to Berlin at the end of the war where he found a success that had
been denied the **Brücke** during its formative years. In 1937 his work was
discredited by the National Socialists and 729 of his works were confiscated
from German collections. In 1944 his Berlin studio was destroyed in an air
raid and many works were destroyed including the only copy of the illustrated
book *Odi Profanum Vulgus,* a joint **Brücke** collaboration. Heckel moved to
Hemmenhofen on the Bodensee and taught at the Karlsruhe Academy from
1949-55.

19   **Mann in der Ebene**

Man on a Plain

1917

Woodcut 38×27

Signed and dated: *Erich Heckel 17*

Dube H 305

Purchased from Mrs. Margaret Fisher, London, with
the assistance of a national grant-in-aid administered
by the Victoria and Albert Museum 1977.

This self-portrait exemplifies the austere stylisation
and attenuation of form which distinguished
Heckel's technique during the strain of the war years
when despair and pessimism replaced his earlier
delight in visual energy of shape and colour.

346'1977

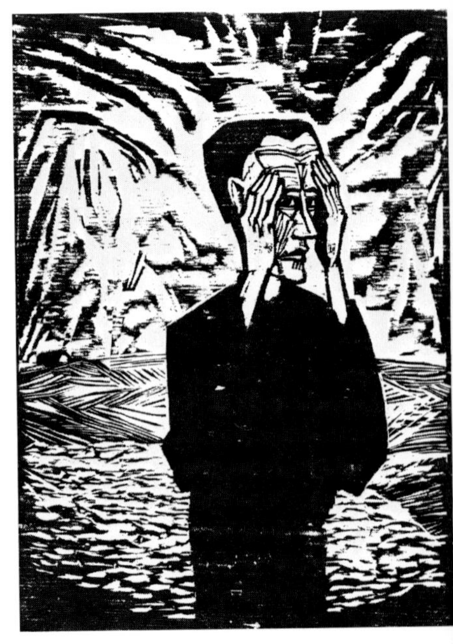

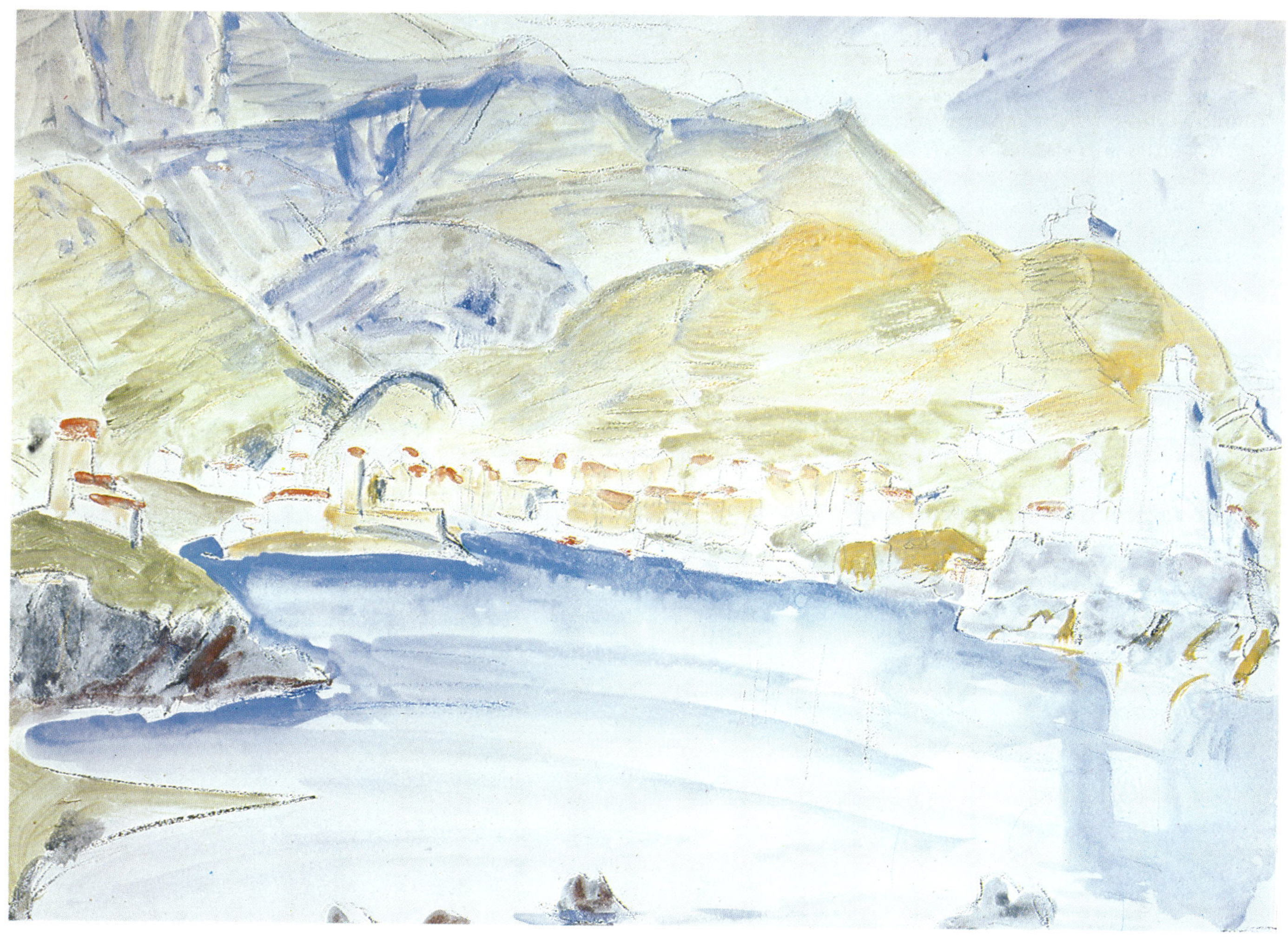

20 Marseilles

1926

Watercolour 54·5 × 71

Signed and dated: *Erich Heckel 26*

Presented by Herold Goddard Esq., 1956.

Lit: Leicester Museums and Art Gallery: *Watercolours and Drawings* 1963 (152)

Heckel had always been attracted to landscape painting and by the 1920's it eventually came to dominate his work. Compared to the anguished distortion of the early **Brücke** compositions, his style by this time had become much more restrained and abstract, probably due in part to the fact that basically he was more intellectual than emotional.

44 A 1956

Karl Hofer

1878-1955

Hofer was born in Karlsruhe and studied at the Academy there from 1896-1900 under Thoma. In 1901 he returned to his native city to study, having spent a year in Paris. From 1902-03 he studied at the Stuttgart Academy. At this time he made friends with Dr. Theodor Rheinhardt under whose sponsorship he spent five years, from 1903-08, studying in Italy where he came under the influence of the idealistic and monumental work of Marées. From 1908-13 he worked in Paris but made two trips to India, 1909 and 1911, again with the help of Rheinhardt. At the outbreak of war he was in France and was interned as an alien until 1917. Throughout his time in Paris and following his return to Berlin in 1918 his work was strongly influenced by Cézanne. In 1919 he became Professor of Applied Arts at the Berlin Academy. In the post-war period his work showed increased affinity with Expressionist painting, particularly with the artists of **Die Brücke**. In 1936 the National Socialists removed him from his post at the Academy and in 1937 his work was included in the 'degenerate art' exhibition held in Munich. In 1943 his studio was totally destroyed in an air raid and Hofer attempted to repaint all the works that had been lost. After the war he became a Professor at the Academy again, Director of the Hochschule for Plastic Arts, a member of the Kulturbund for the Democratic Revival of Germany and in 1947 editor of *Die Bildende Kunst*. He died in Berlin.

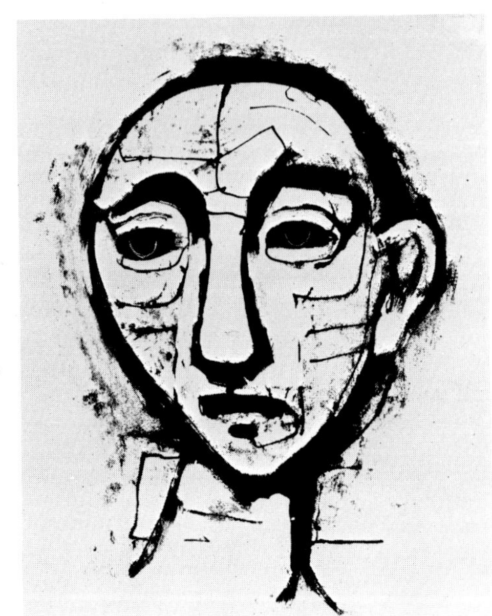

21   **Kopf eines Mannes**
Head of a Man

Lithograph 35×24·75

Signed: *K. Hofer*

Purchased from Mrs. Margaret Fisher, London 1976.

178'1976

Ludwig von Hofmann

1861-1941

Hofmann was born in Darmstadt. In 1883 he entered the Dresden Academy and then in 1888 he studied under Keller in Karlsruhe. In 1890 he went to Paris and studied at the Académie Julian. In Paris he was influenced by the work of Puvis de Chavannes who with Böcklin, Marées and later Munch shaped the development of his work. From 1891 to 1894 Hofmann lived in Berlin where he became friendly with Leistikow and Liebermann and in 1892 when the exhibition of paintings by Munch was closed at the Verein Berliner Künstler he and Liebermann formed **Gruppe XI** which was the core of the Berlin Secession established in 1898. The influence of Symbolism on his work was reinforced in 1894 when he moved to Rome, where he came into contact with Marées. He remained in Rome until 1900. Hofmann was one of the major German Jugendstil painters and in the Berlin Secession exhibition of 1905 his work was shown with that of Klimt, Klinger and Hodler. In 1903 he was invited to teach at Weimar Art School and from 1916-28 he taught at the Dresden Academy. He died in Pillnitz near Dresden.

22a-l   **Taenze**
Dances

1905

Folio of twelve lithographs 41×51

Signed: *L v H* on stone

Published by the Insel-Verlag, Leipzig.

Purchased from Mrs. Margaret Fisher, London 1975.

Lit: Edwin Redslob: 'Ludwig von Hofmanns Lithographien und Holzschnitte' *Die Kunst* Vol. 32, 1917, p.354, repr. pp.356, 357.

Dance was a theme which Hofmann dealt with in numerous works, which suited his symbolic and decorative style. The folio was originally produced with a text by Hugo von Hofmannsthal.

363'1975/1-12

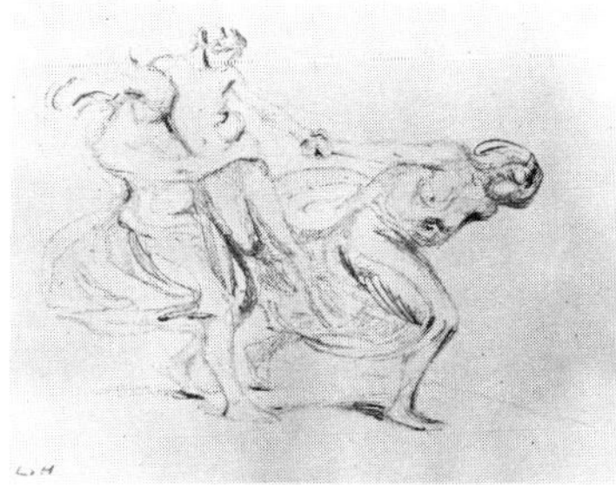
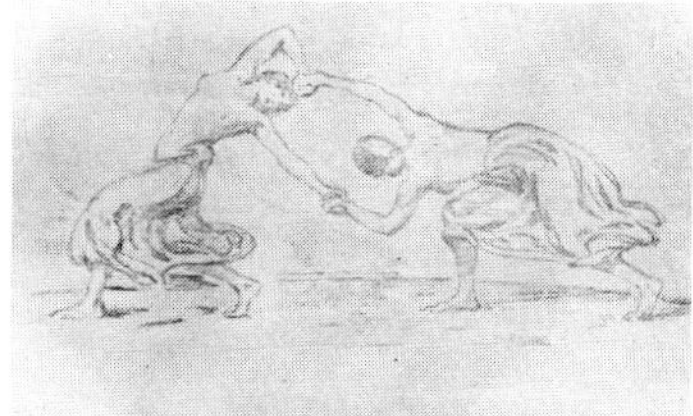
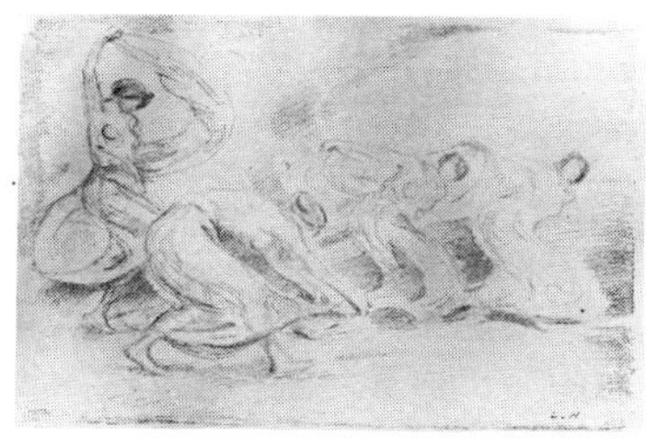
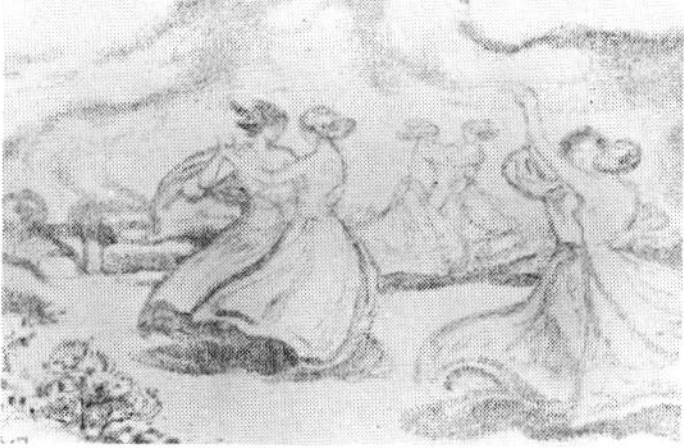
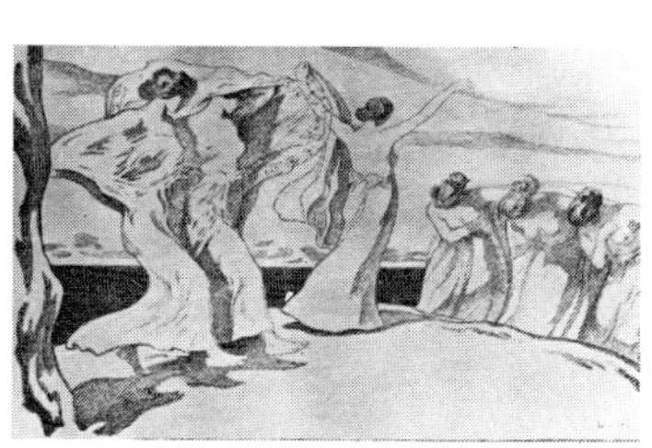
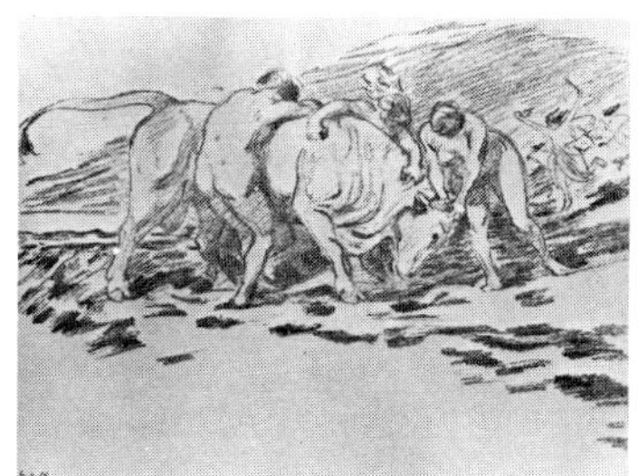
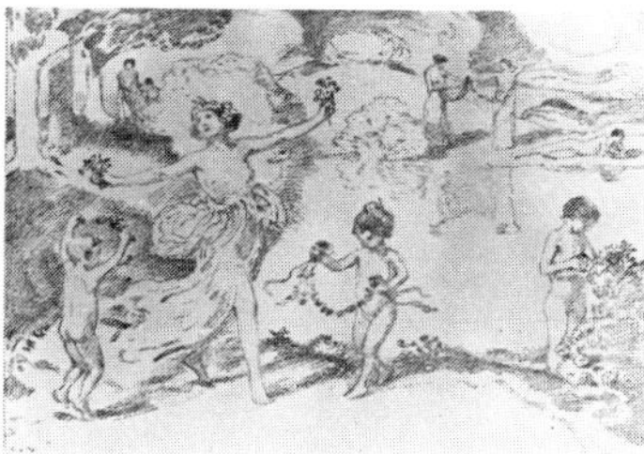
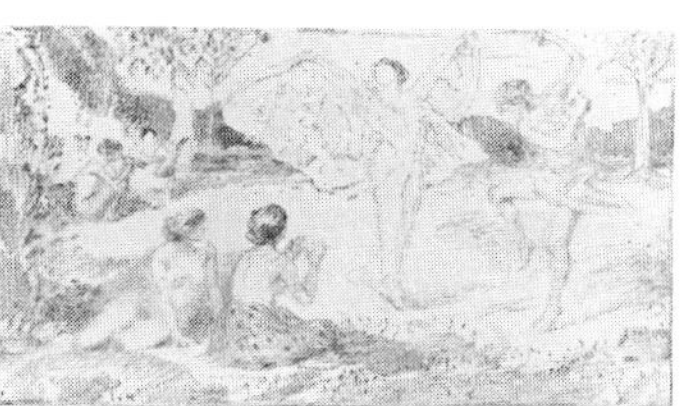
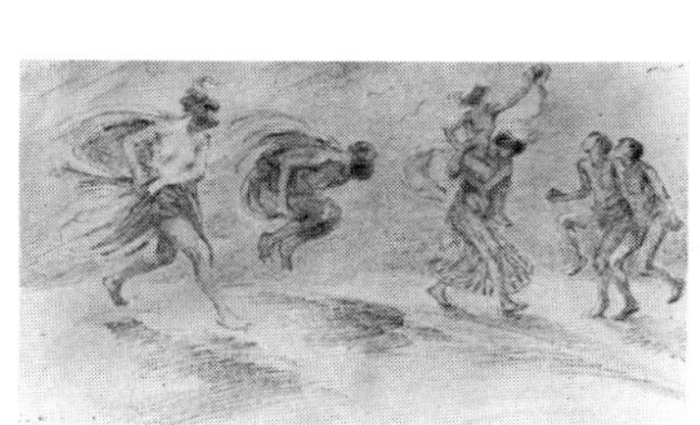
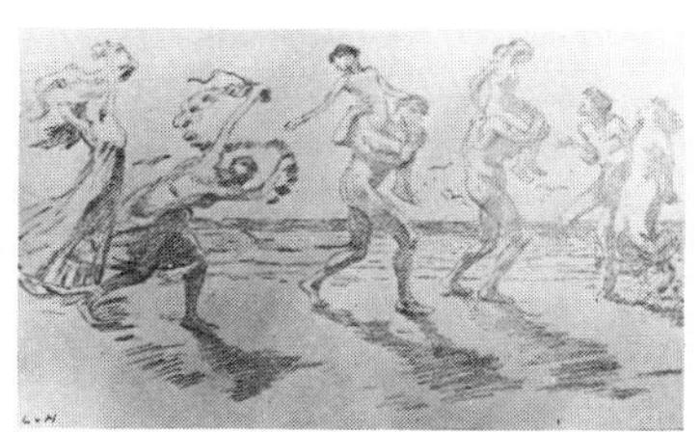
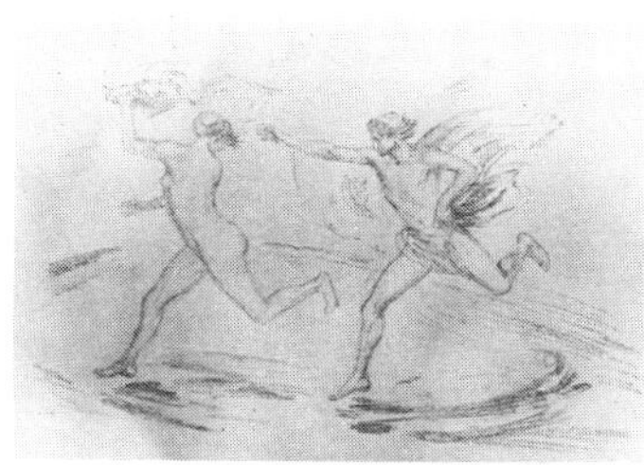
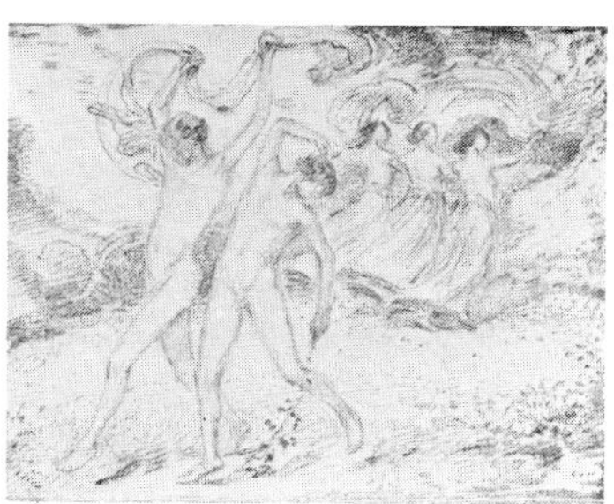

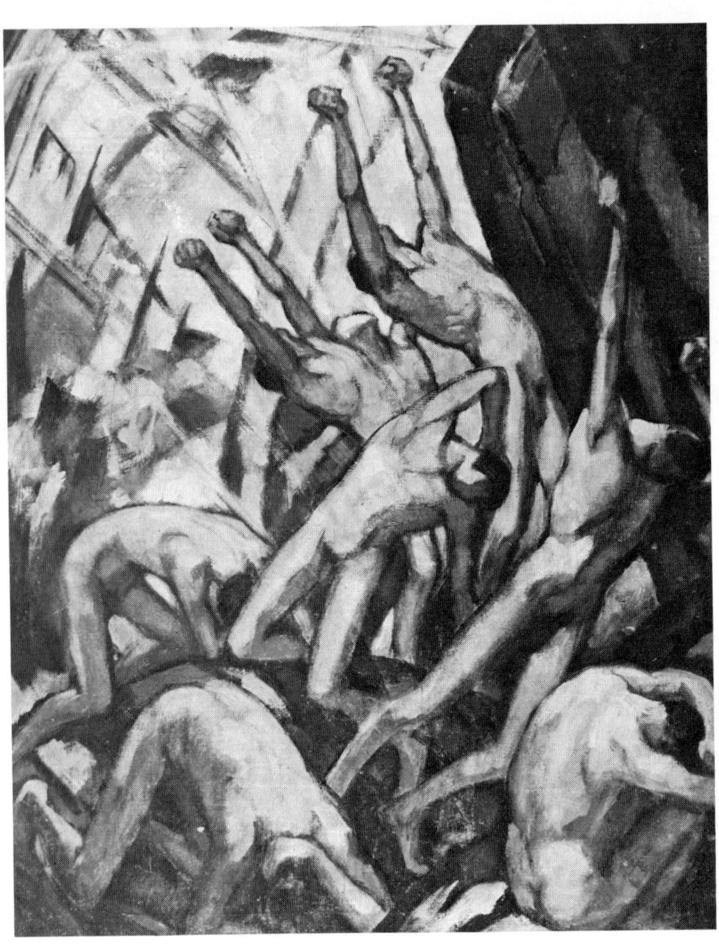

23 Das Zusammenbringen
The Levelling

c.1914

Oil on canvas 88·9 × 69·8

Initialled: *L v H*

Purchased from the Piccadilly Gallery, London, with the assitance of a national grant-in-aid administered by the Victoria and Albert Museum 1971.

Exh: Durham, Sheffield, Leicester: *Germany in Ferment* 1970 (45)

One of the apocalyptic themes prevalent in German painting before the First World War.

24 A 1971

Alexej von Jawlensky
1864-1941

Jawlensky was born in Torschok, Russia. In 1889, whilst serving with the Alexander-Nevsky Regiment in St. Petersburg, he became interested in painting and attended evening classes at the Academy. In 1891 he met Marianne von Werefkin, an Academy student disillusioned by the conservative nature of the staff, and together they emigrated to Munich in 1896. He studied in the studio of Azbé where he met Kandinsky in 1897. In 1903 he exhibited with the Munich Secession and with the Berlin Secession the following year. In 1905 he visited Brittany and Provence where his work was influenced by van Gogh, Cézanne and particularly Matisse, in whose studio he worked in 1907. In 1909 he was instrumental in the formation of the **Neue Kunstlervereinigung München** (New Artists Union). In 1910 he met Marc. With the outbreak of war in 1914 he was forced, as an alien, to leave Germany and returned to Russia. However, within the year he had settled in St. Prex, Switzerland. In 1924, with Kandinsky, Klee and Feininger, he founded **Die Blaue Vier** which exhibited successfully for the following decade, particularly in America. Unfortunately, in the late 1920's he was stricken with severe arthritis, although he continued to paint using colour and line in an increasingly symbolic manner. He died in Wiesbaden, Germany.

24 Kopf in Schwarz und Grün
Head in Black and Green

Colour lithograph 53·5 × 49·5

Signed: *A. Jawlensky* with stamp

Purchased from the Redfern Gallery, London 1957.

An oil painting on card of the same subject and identical dimensions was produced in 1913.

15 A 1957

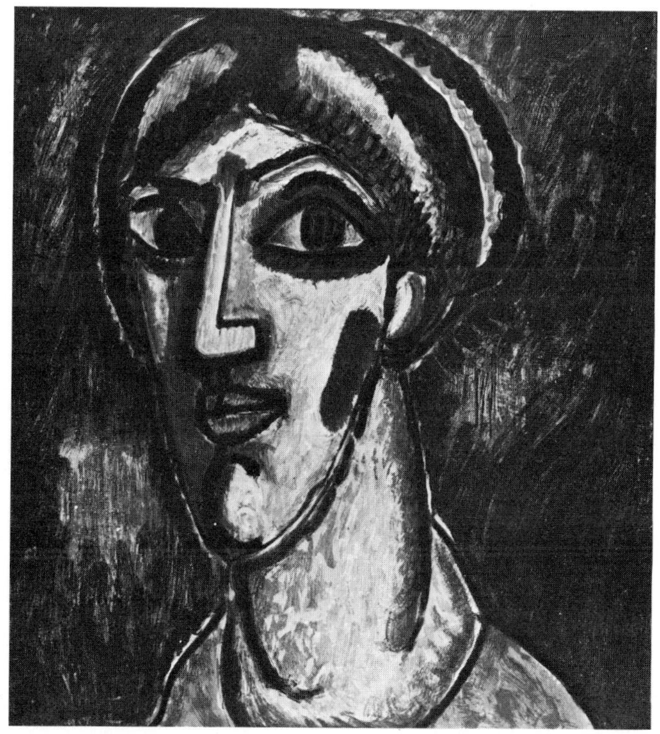

Wassily Kandinsky
1866-1944

Kandinsky was born in Moscow. He studied law at Moscow University and began to paint at thirty. In 1896 he emigrated to Munich where he studied painting under Azbé and Stuck. From 1900-03 he began to teach art and founded the association **Phalanx,** devoted primarily to exhibitions of its members' work and also of contemporary European artists. In 1902 he met the German painter Gabriele Münter with whom he lived until the First World War. Between 1903-08 they visited Italy, Holland and Tunis, with an extensive stay in Paris in 1906-07, where he exhibited at the Salon d'Automne. Between 1908-14 Kandinsky and Münter were living in Munich during the winter months and the village of Murnau for the summer where they established a colony which, at various times, included Jawlensky, Werefkin, Marc and Macke. Kandinsky became first president of the **Neue Künstlervereinigung München** but, after differences, left in 1911 with Marc to organise two exhibitions of contemporary art and publish an almanac, all entitled Der Blaue Reiter. In 1914 he returned to Russia where, following the Revolution, he had a leading role in its cultural policy, re-organising the provincial museums and proposing a programme of art instruction for Inkhuk (Institute of Artistic Culture). In the face of growing hostility he accepted a post as Professor at the Bauhaus (1921), holding the post until 1933 when it closed. In 1924, with Jawlensky, Feininger and Klee, he formed **Die Blaue Vier;** in 1926 the Bauhaus published his *Point and Line to Plane.* In 1933 he moved to Paris, where he died.

25 Unbetitelte Radierung
Untitled Drypoint

1924

Drypoint 21·8 × 20·8

Monogrammed and dated in the plate lower left.
Signed in pencil: *Kandinsky* and numbered 17/30.

Roethel 183, illus.

Presented by Herold Goddard Esq., Leicester 1964.

Further examples in Bauhaus-Archiv, Darmstadt (G 12984) and Pasadena Art Museum, USA.

Kandinsky was a pioneer of abstract painting. In addition to his oil paintings and watercolours, he produced a remarkable body of graphic work including **Klange** (1913) and **Kleine Welten** (1922). He was also a philosopher and poet. After an early period of experimentation, he pursued very precise aims and his work, despite its increasingly abstract appearance, retained a specific, though well concealed, thematic content, often of an apocalyptic or eschatological nature.

138 A 1964

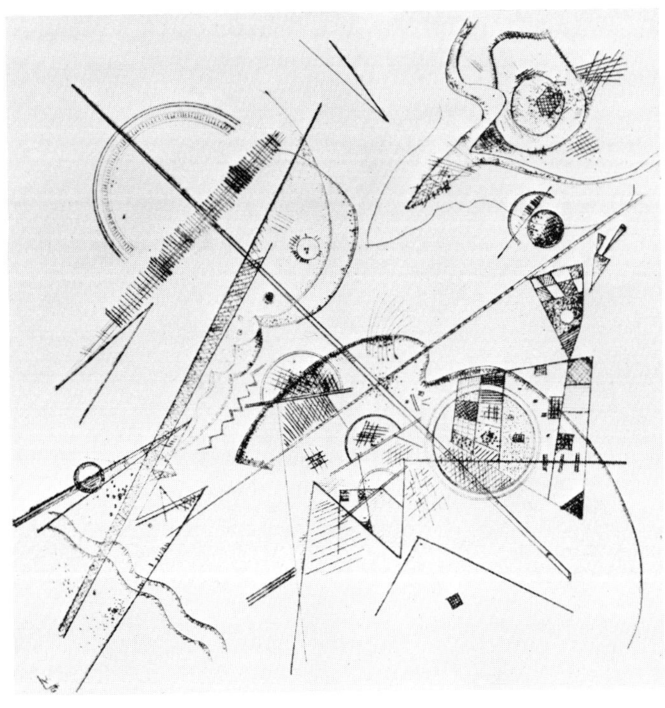

Wilhelm von Kaulbach
1805-74

Kaulbach was born in Arolsen, the son of a goldsmith. His father taught him to draw and in 1822 he entered Düsseldorf Academy where he studied under the Nazarene painter, Peter von Cornelius 1783-1867, whom he followed to Munich in 1825. In 1826 he was commissioned to paint the fresco *Apollo among the Muses* for the Odeon, Munich. He continued to receive major commissions from the German nobility and official bodies throughout his career. In 1835 he visited Venice and in 1838-39 he visited Rome. In 1847 he became Director of the Munich Academy. Kaulbach, although he inherited much from Cornelius and the Nazarenes, did not invest his monumental depictions of history with the same idealism, so that his work often appears merely academic and grandiose. Following his death, his reputation waned so that by the end of the century he was largely remembered for his illustrations for Goethe and Schiller, particularly *Das Narrenhaus* 1835 and *Reineke Fuchs* 1840-46.

26 Series of nine drawings to illustrate an unidentified subject.

Pencil on sheets 52·5 × 75·5, each numbered below image.

Presented by J. E. Sarson, Leicester 1926.

15 A 1926/1-9

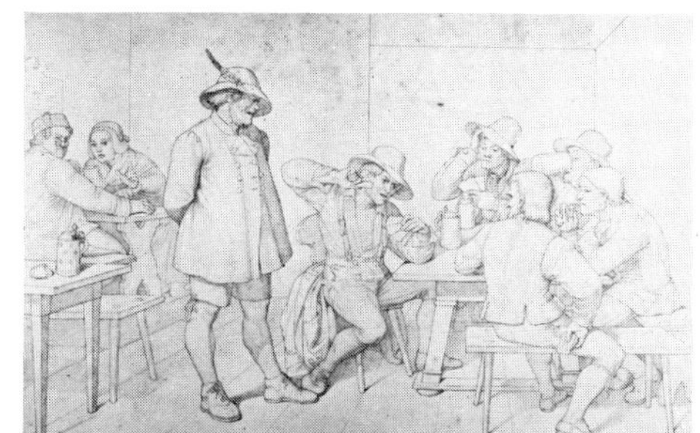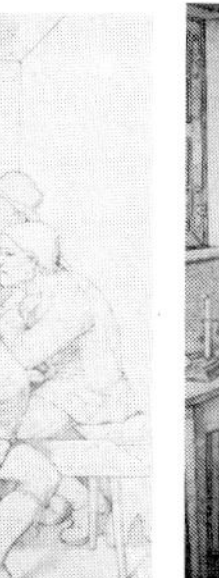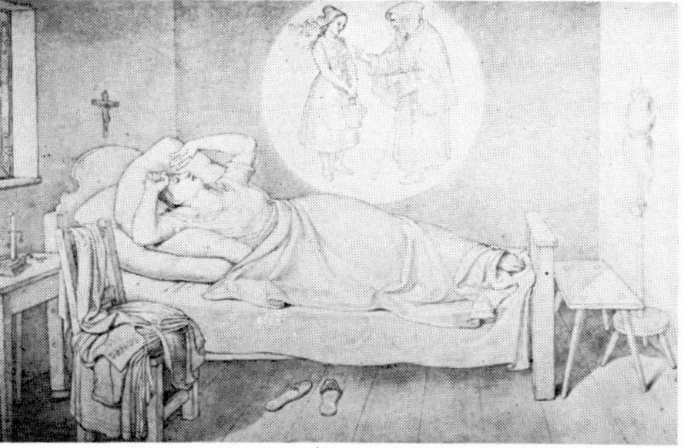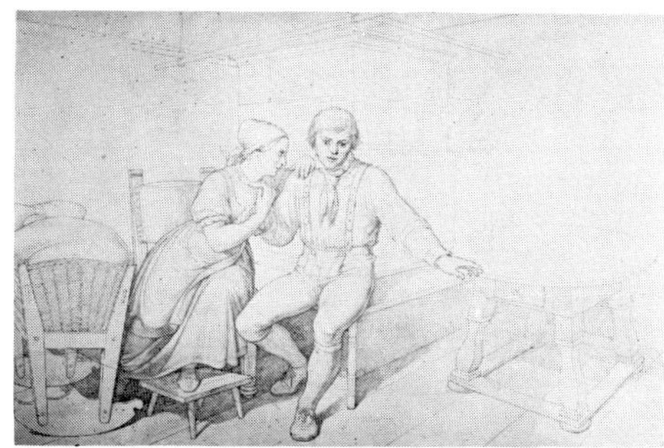

KAULBACH

One

Two

Three

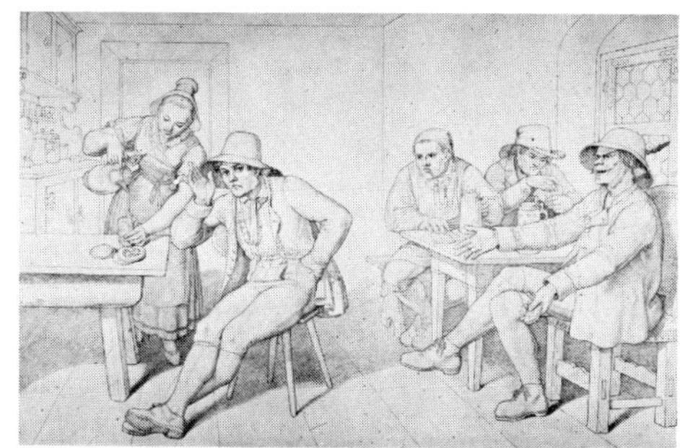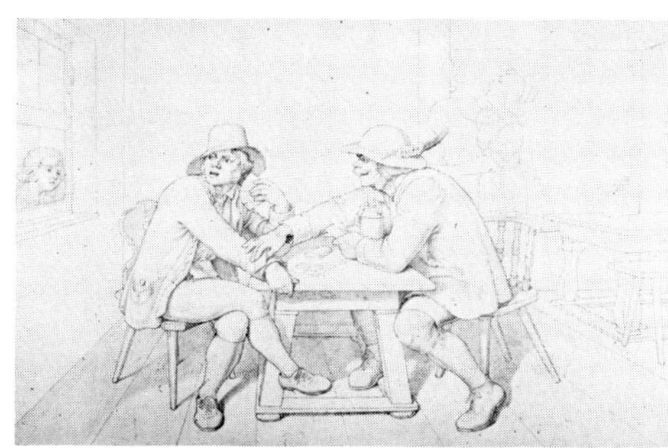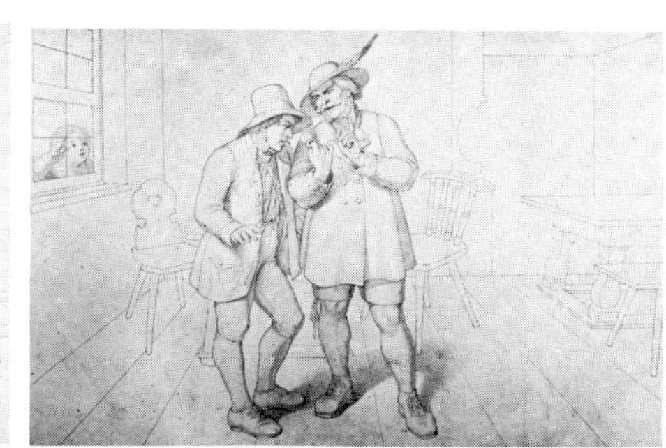

Four

Five

Six

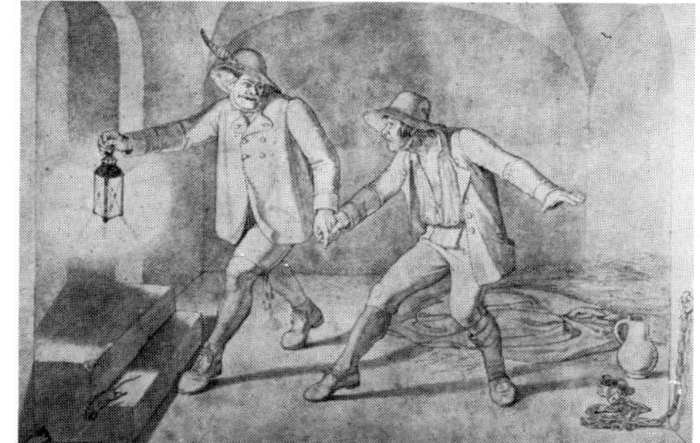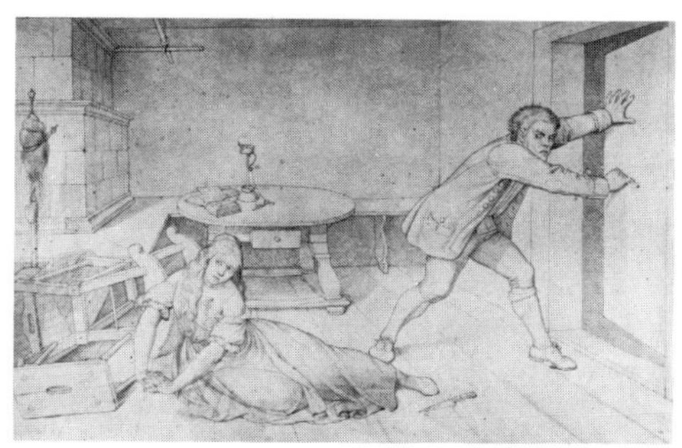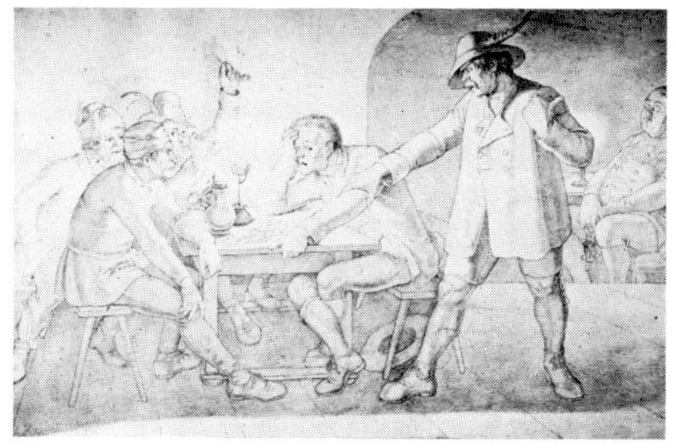

Seven

Eight

Nine

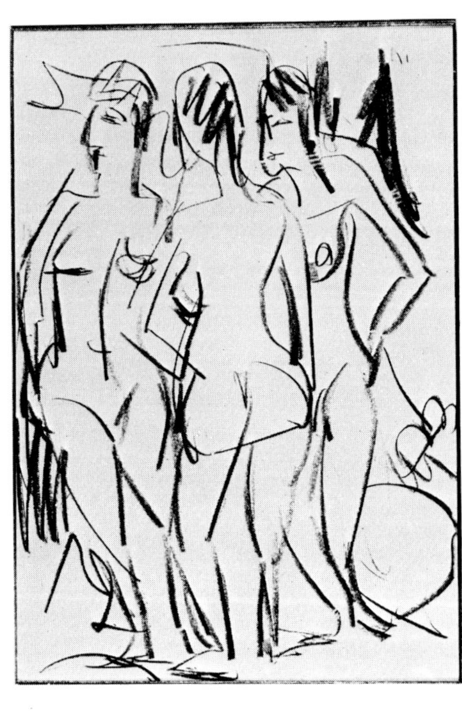

Ernst Ludwig Kirchner
1880-1938

Kirchner was born at Aschaffenburg. His father was a chemical engineer
who, after the family had moved to Chemnitz, sent his son to study
architecture at the Technische Hochschule in Dresden. Kirchner, however, had
every intention of becoming an artist and in 1903 absented himself from the
course to study art in Munich. On his return to Dresden he met Heckel and
Schmidt-Rottluff and in 1905 the **Brücke** was formed. During the next six
years they established themselves as one of Germany's foremost avant-garde
groups pioneering a flat, two-dimensional, brilliantly coloured and
aggressively agitated picture surface. Kirchner was the group's most ambitious
and radical member whose intelligent and rapid understanding of such
modern progressives as Matisse combined with his innate yearning after the
unspoilt cultural traditions of the German Mediaevalists and primitive African
and Melanesian art forms produced a completely new German art form. Whilst
experimenting with new methods of technical expressiveness he remained
faithful to the Bohemian fin-de-siècle interest in the world of the demi-
monde: nudes, circuses, cabarets and big city street scenes were his basic
subjects and his landscape paintings are always most successful when they
involve a human element. After the group moved to Berlin in 1911 individual
ambitions displaced their earlier dedication to the **Brücke** as a coherent
group activity and it was dissolved by mutual consent in 1913. Kirchner
suffered a complete mental and physical breakdown as a result of his wartime
service as an 'involuntary volunteer' in the artillery and he subsequently went
into self-imposed exile in Switzerland, living near Davos. His highly-strung
temperament, which lent such intense neurotic power to his most successful
work and created considerable personality conflicts with his **Brücke**
colleagues, was finally stricken by the condemnation and confiscation of his
work by the National Socialists in 1937. He shot himself in the following year.

27 **Drei Akt**
Three Nudes

1920

Black crayon 45·5 × 31

Stamped with the Nachlass mark on the reverse: *E. L. Kirchner KDon/Bf 14* and *20453* in pencil.

Purchased from Mrs. Margaret Fisher, London 1977.

Coll: Studio of the artist; Roman Norbert Ketterer, Lugano, Switzerland; American Masters Gallery, Los Angeles 1969; Sotheby's July 1, 1976 (618), illustrated.

The gratuitous ugliness of Kirchner's treatment of the naked female form was one of the most blasphemous extremes to which the **Brücke** went in their rejection of conventional prejudices and taboos. Kirchner's calligraphic draughtsmanship was largely inspired by the drawings of Rembrandt which had exerted a powerful influence over his imagination as a youth when he first saw them at the Alte Pinakothek during his stay in Munich in 1903.

344'1977

Oskar Kokoschka
b. 1886

Kokoschka was born in Pocklarn, Austria. In 1905 he received a scholarship to attend the Vienna School of Arts and Crafts where he was influenced by the work of the Vienna Secessionists and the art nouveau linearism of Gustav Klimt 1862-1916, to whom he dedicated an illustrated book of poetry, *Die Traumenden Knaben* (The Dreaming Boys), published in 1908. At this time he also produced decorative work for the Wiener Werkstätte under the leading Jugendstil architect, Joseph Hoffmann 1870-1956. However, these decorative influences soon gave way to an interest in more aggressive and emotional means of expression, particularly in a series of portraits produced between 1907 and 1912 where he abandoned any lyrical qualities for an analytical study of the sitter's neurosis and illness. In 1908 he entered his work for the Vienna Kunstschau and was vociferously denounced by the press and conservative academic circles. He was immediately dismissed from the School of Arts and Crafts but became the focus for the progressive artists and writers of Vienna. In 1909 his entries to the Vienna Kunstschau were again badly received, as were his two plays *Murderer, Hope of Women* and

Sphinx and the Straw Man. The reaction to his work and these plays, which dealt with sex and violence, was so great that his friends thought it safer for him to leave Austria. He settled in Switzerland but in 1910 visited Munich and then settled in Berlin, where he found himself surrounded by young artists and writers of a similar spiritual and emotional persuasion. In the German capital, Paul Cassirer became his dealer and Walden employed him on *Der Sturm.* Between 1912 and 1915 he produced his most Expressionist work, dealing particularly with the conflict between man and woman stemming from his traumatic love affair with Alma Mahler. In 1915 he enlisted and was seriously wounded in 1916 on the Russian Front. Invalided out of the Forces, he went to Sweden but returned to Germany, settling in Dresden where he remained until 1924. In 1920 he was appointed to a professorship at the Dresden Academy, whilst still forbidden to teach in Austria. His stay in Dresden and contact with Expressionism heightened the tone of his palette and stimulated a use of violent colour. When he left Dresden he travelled extensively in Europe, North Africa and Israel, returning to Vienna in 1931 where he became increasingly involved with politics. However, with the rise of National Socialism, he moved to Prague in 1934, remaining until 1938 when he fled to England, settling in London. In 1947 he moved to Switzerland.

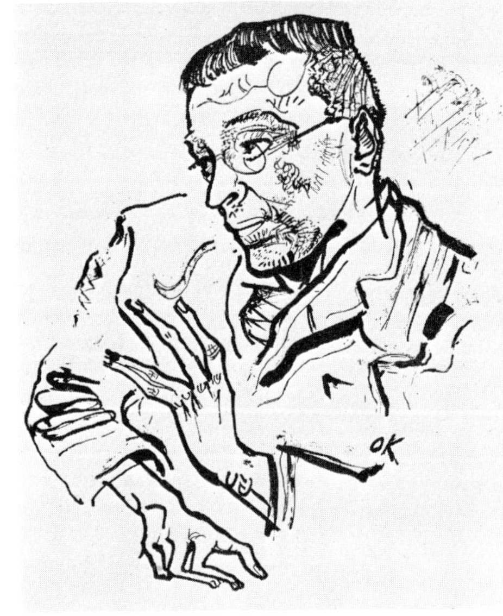

28　Bildnis Karl Kraus
Portrait of Karl Kraus

1910

Lithograph 35·5 × 28·5

Signed: *OK* on stone

Purchased from Mrs. Margaret Fisher, London 1971.

Exh: London, Margaret Fisher: *Kokoschka* 1974

Lit: Edith Hoffmann: *Kokoschka, Life and Work,* 1947, p.76, Fig. 5; Oskar Kokoschka: *My Life,* 1974, p.58, pl.9; Peter Vergo: *Art in Vienna 1898-1918,* 1975, illus. 164 of original drawing (1909).

Karl Kraus 1874-1936, whom Kokoschka called 'the scourge of the Viennese conscience' in his autobiography, was one of the leading literary figures of pre-war Vienna. A satirist, poet and critic, he founded the magazine *Die Fackel* (The Torch) in 1899 and from 1911 wrote it entirely himself allowing no advertisements so as to safeguard its total independence. He attacked corruption and the general moral decline, employing the misuse and disintegration of grammar and language as its symbol. He enjoyed the idea of being a martyr and consequently indulged in protracted feuds with other Viennese and Berlin critics. Those artists, such as Kokoschka, whom he supported he helped to his utmost but those he disliked, such as Klimt, he attacked incessantly. Prophetic in his vision of the coming war, he was at his zenith during the war years, expressing pacifist ideals and debunking militaristic ethics. In 1922 he published *The Last Days of Mankind* which was a satirical panorama of the war.

Kraus helped Hewarth Walden financially in the creation of *Der Sturm* magazine and this portrait of him was the first drawing by Kokoschka to appear in the magazine. Whilst working for the magazine (he was the first regular illustrator), Kokoschka produced a series of portraits of men and women who were in the centre of contemporary intellectual and artistic life. In 1914 Kokoschka illustrated Kraus's *Chinese Wall.*

14 A 1971

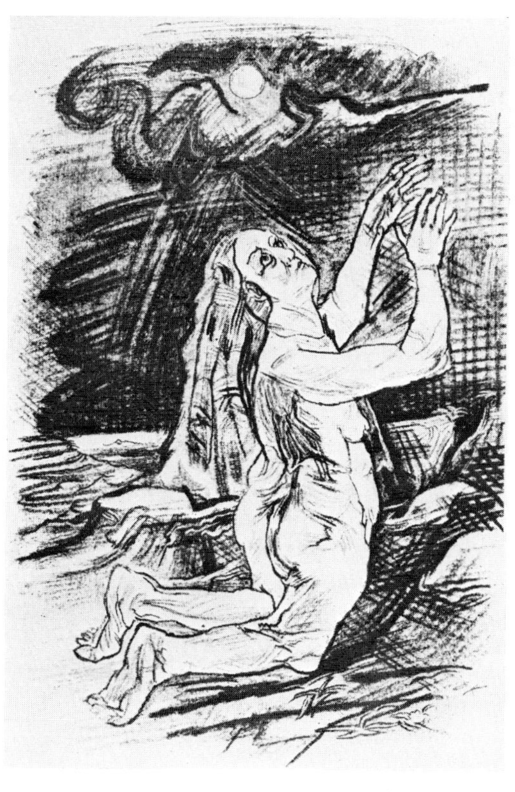

29 Herr, ich warte auf Dein Heil
Lord, I Await Your Salvation

1914

Lithograph 42×29

Signed: *OK* on stone

Purchased from Mrs. Margaret Fisher, London 1976.

Lit: Edith Hoffmann: *Kokoschka, Life and Work,* 1947, p.124; Lothar Lang: *Expressionist Book Illustration in Germany 1907-27,* 1976, repr. p.106.

From the series *O Ewigkeit – Du Donnerwort. Worte der Kantate nach Johann Sebastian Bach* (O Eternity – Thou Fearful Word. Words from the cantata by Johann Sebastian Bach), of eleven lithographs published as a folio by Fritz Gurlitz in an edition of 125 in 1914. In 1918 Gurlitz published the series as a book, in an edition of 125, in the collectors series *Die Neuen Bilderbücher.*

The Staatliche Galerie Moritzburg has in its collection the pen and ink sketches and manuscript text (illus. Lang pp.100-104) which give the text for the image in this collection as being:
Die Hoffnung:

*Herr, ich warte auf dein Heil,
Ich warte auf dein Heil, ich warte auf dein Heil
dein Heil! Herr, ich warte auf dein Heil*

*Ich weiss vor grosser Waurigkeit nicht,
wo ich mich für wende; mein ganz erschrocknes
Herze bebt, dass mir die Zung am Gaumen klebt.*

The words of the cantata by Knorr von Rosenroth appear to have been more important to Kokoschka than the music of Bach. The musicologist Paul Bekker in the *Kunstblatt* in 1917 wrote that Kokoschka's images 'had little more than the title in common with Bach's cantata'. Rather than illustrate the themes of the cantata Kokoschka used the words as a vehicle for the representation of those ideas which preoccupied him. Following his turbulent love affair with Alma Mahler he saw man as an impassive victim of fate whilst woman could be both his greatest hope and his most intense symbol of fear. The male and female figures in the series bear a strong resemblance both to Kokoschka and Alma Mahler.

175'1976

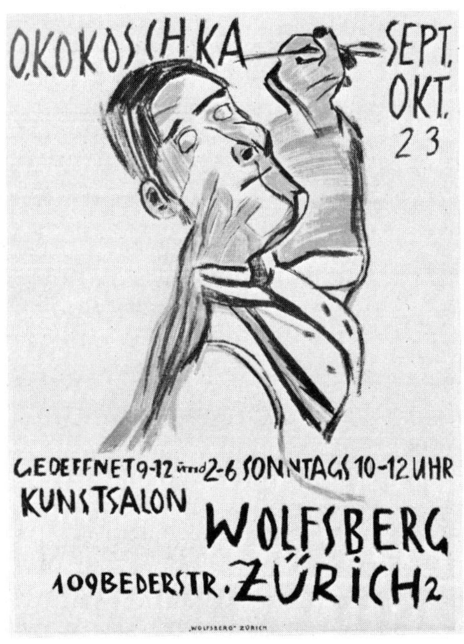

30   Selbstbildnis von zwei Seiten als Maler
Self-Portrait as a Painter from Two Sides

1923

Poster. Lithograph in four colours 127 × 90·1

Printed: *O. Kokoschka Sept. Okt. 23; Geöffnet 9-12 und 2-6 Sonntags 10-12 Uhr; Kunstsalon Wolfsberg 109 Beder Str. Zürich 2.*

Printed by J. E. Wolfensberger, Zurich. Publisher: Kunstsalon Wolfsberg, Zurich.

Wingler/Welz 164, illustrated

Purchased from C. R. Mendez, London 1966.

Exh: Durham, Sheffield, Leicester: *Germany in Ferment,* 1970 (49)

Lit: Bevis Hillier: *Posters,* 1974, illus. p.206

53 A 1966

Käthe Kollwitz
1867-1945

Käthe Kollwitz was born at Königsberg. She was primarily a graphic artist. After recognition of her work in 1897 her subjects and presentation changed little despite the radical changes in the visual arts occurring in France and Germany. Though often linked with the Expressionists she had little time for 'studio art', believing art should be the tool of social conscience. She depicted those who were oppressed by poverty, injustice, politics and war. Her earliest success as an etcher was the series *The Weaver's Revolt* 1897, based on Hauptmann's play *The Weavers,* followed by the series *Bauernkrieg* (The Peasants' War) 1908. Due to her obvious social intentions throughout her life she found much of her work criticised by the authorities and even banned. Later she extended her technique to include lithography and woodcuts and also produced a number of sculptures. The 1914-18 War had a deep effect on her, more so because she lost a son. In the aftermath of the revolution and under the Weimar Republic, she gave full voice to the despair felt by herself and other Germans that so little had been gained for all the effort and for all the losses. Never active in politics she was, however, drawn to Communism and in 1927 visited Russia. In 1933 she was forced to resign from the Prussian Academy by the National Socialists. She remained in Germany throughout the war until her death in Moritzburg.

31 **Zertretene**
The Downtrodden

1900

Etching 23 × 19

Klipstein 48, illustrated

Purchased from Mrs. Margaret Fisher, London 1971.

Lit: Otto Nagel: *Käthe Kollwitz,* repr. pl. 40

Left-hand panel from a triptych measuring 23 × 83·6
13 A 1971

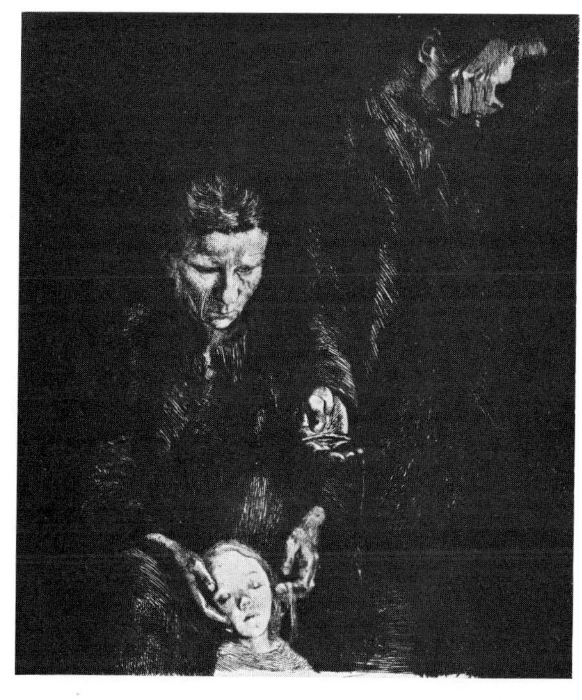

32 **Hamburger Kneipe**
Hamburg Drinking-Den

1901

Vernis mou 19·2 × 24·7

Signed l.r.: *Käthe Kollwitz*

Klipstein 58, illustrated

Purchased from Mrs. Margaret Fisher, London 1974.

Lit: Otto Nagel: *Käthe Kollwitz,* repr. pl. 44
439'1974

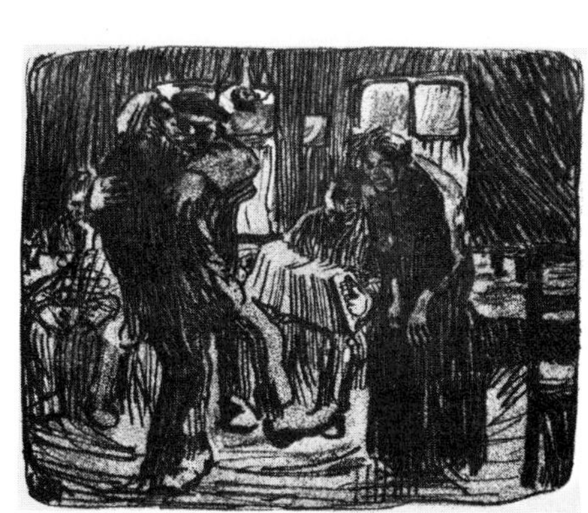

33 **Die Gefangenen**
The Prisoners

1908

Etching and softground with woven texture 32 × 43

Klipstein 98, illustrated

Purchased from Mrs. Margaret Fisher, London 1973.

Lit: Otto Nagel: *Käthe Kollwitz,* repr. pl. 54

Plate 7 from the series *Bauernkrieg* (Peasants' War)
1908
301'1973

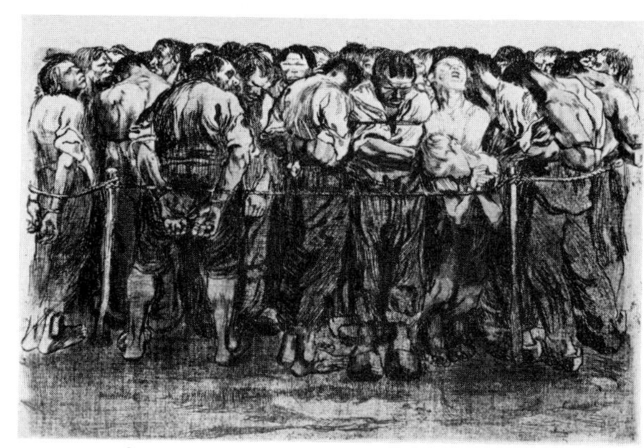

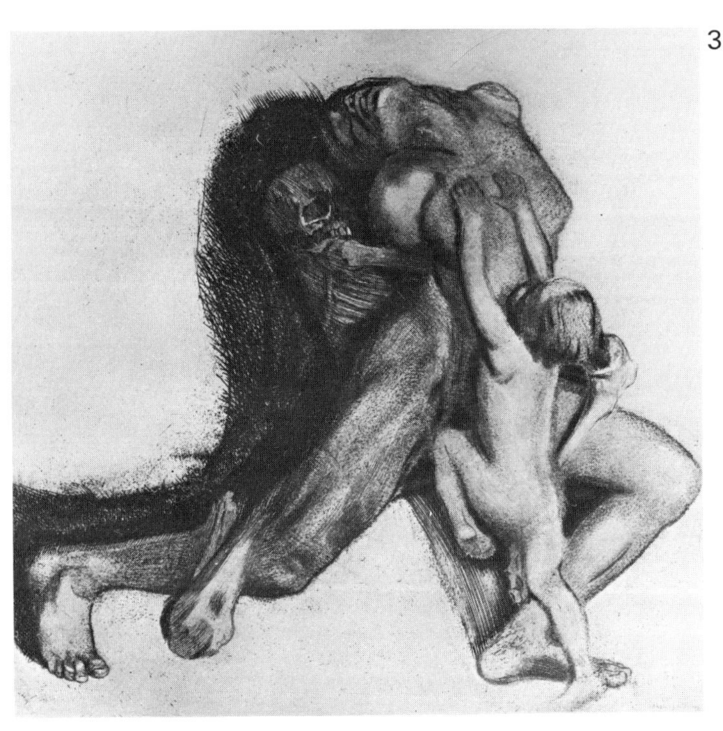

34 **Tod und Frau**
Death and Woman

1910

Etching and sandpaper softground 44·7 × 44·6

Signed with studio stamp

Klipstein 108, illustrated

Purchased from London Graphic Art Associates 1971.

Lit: Otto Nagel: *Käthe Kollwitz,* repr. pl. 77

11 A 1971

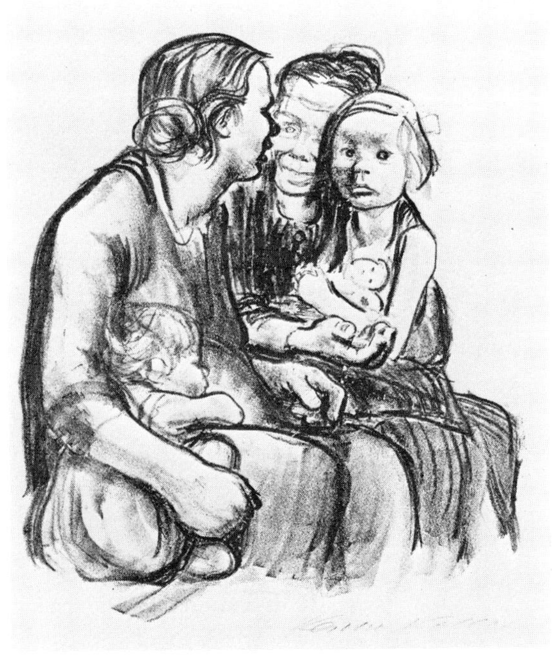

35 **Zwei schwatzende Frauen mit zwei Kindern**
Two gossiping Women with Two Children

1930

Lithograph 34 × 30

Signed: *Käthe Kollwitz*

Klipstein 240, illustrated

Purchased from Mrs. Margaret Fisher, London 1971.

12 A 1971

Alfred Kubin

1877-1959

Kubin was born in Leitmeritz, Bohemia. From 1891-92 he studied at the School of Industrial Art in Salzburg. When he left Salzburg he was apprenticed to a photographer in Klagenfurt until 1896. In 1887 his mother died, an event which haunted him throughout his life; in 1896 he attempted to commit suicide by her grave. In 1897 he entered the armed forces in an attempt to find a way of life which would provide him with some stability but he suffered a mental breakdown and was invalided out. From 1898 to 1901 he studied at a private art school and then moved to the Munich Academy. In 1902 his first exhibition was held at the Cassirer Gallery in Berlin and in 1903 a folio of his drawings was published. In the same year his fiancée died, which brought on a further psychological crisis. He married in 1904 which did bring him a new sense of security. In 1905 he visited Italy and the South of France and, the following year, Paris. He also bought the small castle at Zwickeldt in Austria, where he stayed for the rest of his life, apart from visits to Bosnia, Dalmatia, Paris, Switzerland and various other German cities. In 1908 he completed his novel *Die andere Zeit* (The Other Side) for which he gained considerable literary recognition, and subsequently illustrated over two hundred books, all close in subject to his own obsessions with fantasy and mythical dream worlds. In 1911 he joined the **New Artists' Union in Munich** and **Der Blaue Reiter** in 1912. In 1914 he suffered another nervous breakdown and turned to Buddhism to resolve his problems. In 1930 he was elected to the Prussian Academy and in 1937 obtained a post as professor. In 1947 he was given the freedom of the city of Linz and in 1949 was elected to the Bavarian Academy of Fine Arts. In 1952 he won the Ulisse Prize at the Venice Bienalle and in 1955 the international drawing prize at the São Paulo Bienal. He died in Zwickeldt.

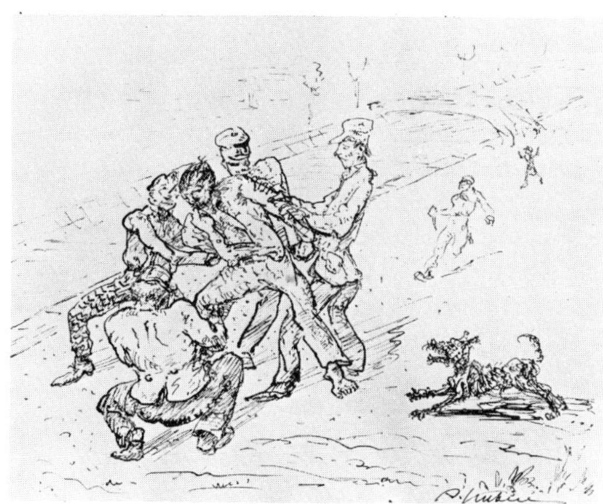

36   **Der Flüchtling**

The Fugitive

Lithograph 40×45

Signed: *Kubin*

Purchased from Mrs. Margaret Fisher, London 1975.

361'1975

Wilhelm Lehmbruck
1881-1919

Lehmbruck was born at Meiderich near Duisburg. He trained at the School of Arts and Crafts in Düsseldorf 1895-99 and worked as a sculptor's assistant until 1901. From 1901-08 he studied at the Academy of Art, Düsseldorf. During this period he visited Italy and Paris, where he was influenced by the work of Rodin and Maillol. In 1910 he moved to Paris to live, producing sculpture and line engravings. He returned to Berlin in 1914 when war broke out and committed suicide there in 1919.

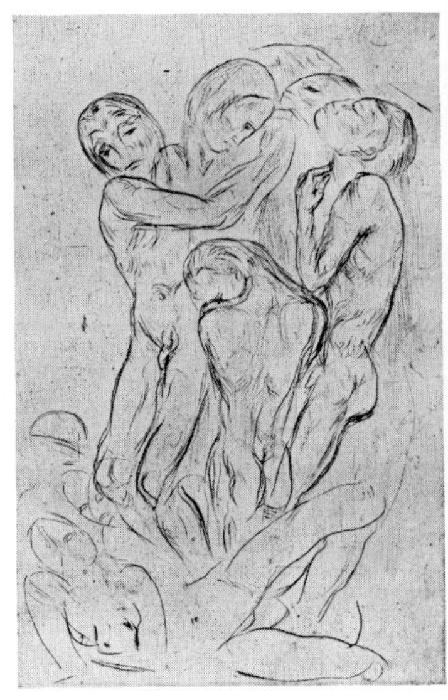

37   **Das Aufsteigen**

The Ascension

1913

Etching 29·8 × 19·7

Purchased from Mrs. Margaret Fisher, London 1972.

19 A 1972

Max Liebermann
1847-1935

Liebermann was born in Berlin of Jewish parents and studied under Karl Steffeck from 1866 to 1868 and at the Weimar Art School under Munkacsy from 1868 to 1872. During the 1870's he was living in France with occasional visits to Holland where he was influenced by the work of François Millet, Gustave Courbet, Josef Israels and Frans Hals and their paintings of peasant life. Twenty years later he was influenced by the atmospheric techniques of the French Impressionists and began to collect works by them as well as publishing articles on Manet and Degas. An important exhibition of his work was held in Berlin in 1897 and in 1899 he became President of the Berlin Secession. After 1914 he lived and worked almost exclusively at his country house at Wannsee, near Potsdam. He became President of the Academy in 1924 and Honorary president in 1933 but renounced all his honours after the Nazis came to power. His work was proscribed in 1933 on account of his non-Aryan origins. He died in Berlin.

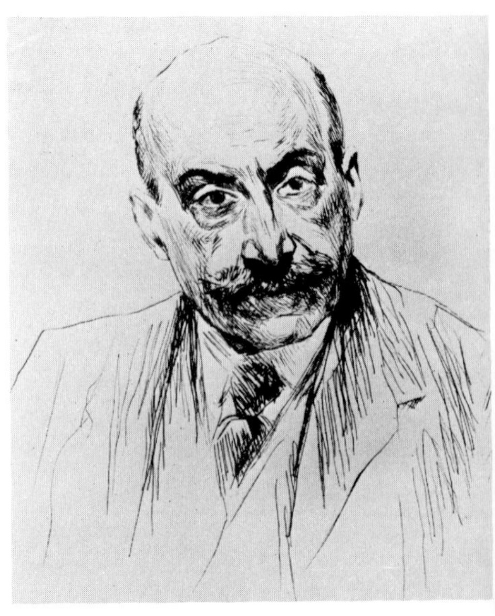

38   **Selbstbildnis**

Self Portrait

1913

Drypoint 23 × 17

Inscribed on plate: *Verlag Bruno Cassirer, Berlin*

Presented by Mrs. Margaret Fisher, London 1974.

Frontispiece of Erich Handck's monograph *Max Liebermann: sein Leben und seine Werke* published by Bruno Cassirer in Berlin, 1914.

23'1976

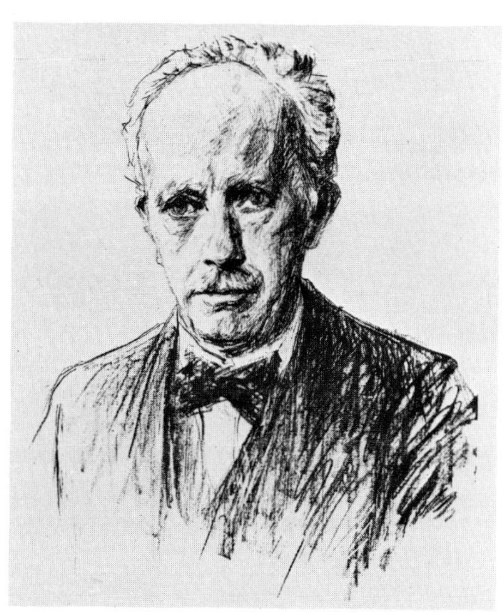

39 Bildnis Richard Strauss 1864-1949
Portrait of Richard Strauss

c.1918

Lithograph 54×48

Signed: *Max Liebermann* and inscribed in pencil
83/100

Purchased from Mrs. Margaret Fisher, London 1971.

Richard Strauss, prior to the First World War, was
Germany's most renowned contemporary composer.
Following the influence of Wagner, his early works,
due to their avant-garde elements, met with both
critical acclaim and conservative condemnation
amongst the Imperial circle. Under the Weimar
Republic, however, he became an accepted
establishment figure.

An oil portrait of Strauss by Liebermann, painted in
1918, was formerly in the National Gallery of Berlin.

16 A 1971

**40 Die Enkelin des Künstlers mit ihrem
Kindermädchen**
The Artist's Grand-Daughter with her Nurse

1919

Oil on canvas 53·5×43

Signed and dated: *Liebermann '19*

Purchased from Mrs. Margaret Fisher, London, with
the assistance of a national grant-in-aid administered
by the Victoria and Albert Museum and a private
donation, 1974.

Painted inside Liebermann's country house at
Wannsee, this painting is an interior companion
piece to the picture of the nurse and grand-child in
the garden of the house, painted in the same year
and formerly in the National Gallery of Berlin.

958'1974

Illustrated on page 8

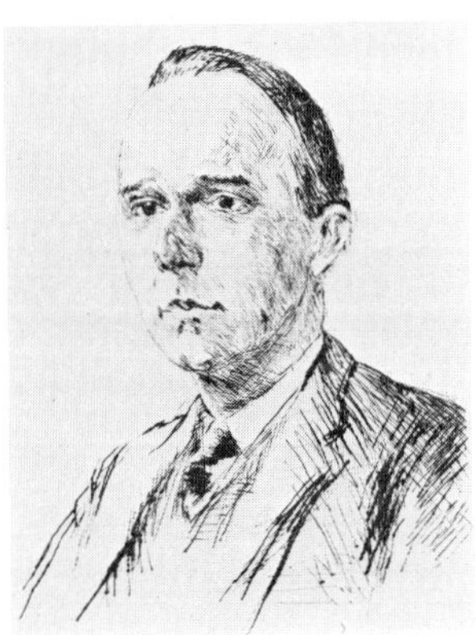

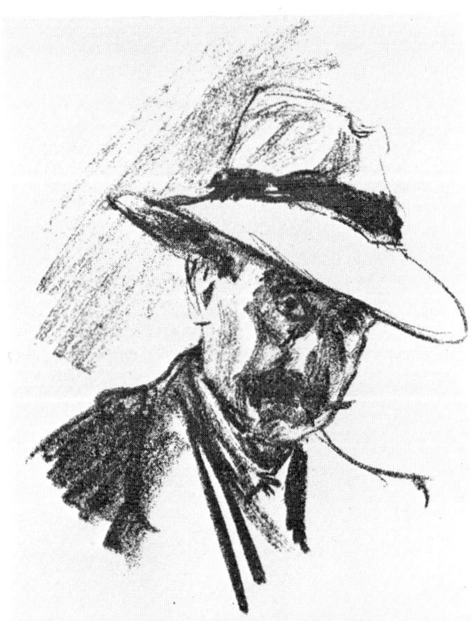

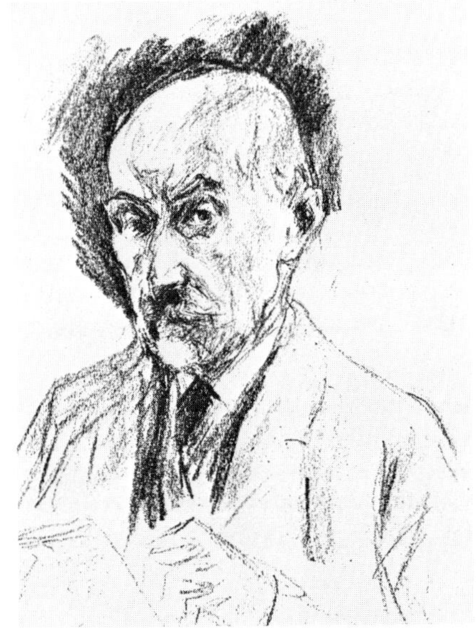

41 Bildnis Paul Cassirer 1871-1926
Portrait of Paul Cassirer

Etching and drypoint 30×23·5

Signed: *M. Liebermann*

Purchased from Mrs. Margaret Fisher, London 1976.

Paul Cassirer was an influential art-dealer and one of the progressive leading forces of the Berlin Secession in its early years.

179'1976

42 Selbstbildnis mit Hut
Self-Portrait with Hat

Lithograph 26×20·5

Signed: *Max Liebermann*

Purchased from Mrs. Margaret Fisher, London 1971.

17 A 1971

43 Selbstbildnis
Self-Portrait

1927

Lithograph 25·5×17

Presented by Mrs. Margaret Fisher, London 1974.

Printed as the frontispiece in the catalogue to the exhibition *Max Liebermann: Hundert Werke des Künstlers zu seinem 80 Geburtstage* held at the Prussian Academy of Arts in Berlin June-July 1927, on the occasion of Liebermann's 80th birthday. The catalogue was printed by Bruno Cassirer.

393'1976

Franz Marc
1880-1916

Born in Munich, Marc studied at the Munich Academy under Hackl and Diez. In 1903 and 1907 he visited Paris where he came into contact with French Impressionism and, during the second visit, began an exhaustive study of animals, their anatomy and movement. In 1908 he painted his famous series of horses in which constructive forms were allied with colour nuances. In 1910 he met Kandinsky and Macke, joined the **New Artists' Union in Munich** and with Kandinsky founded **Der Blaue Reiter,** which was composed of those who identified themselves with the progressive faction. Marc's use of colour became freer and more expressive which, combined with his earlier taste for Jugendstil, led him away from naturalistic painting towards abstraction. At this time he was also influenced by the Cubists and Delaunay's Orphism and their treatment of structural form and colour contrasts respectively. Alongside its basic simplicity, Marc's painting contains a deep vein of Romanticism which adds a deeper, almost religious, significance to his compositions. Towards the end of his abruptly shortened life – he was killed in action near Verdun – he was moving towards compositions built solely on colour. The overall designs of his later paintings are reminiscent of stained glass. The incorporation of natural and animal forms, whilst still present, are no longer the primary means of his artistic expression. Colour was increasingly taking over as the major vehicle for his ideas on composition.

44   Rote Frau

Red Woman

1912

Alternative Title: Mädchen mit Schwarzem Haar (Girl with Black Hair)

Oil on canvas 100·5 × 70

Signed and dated on back of canvas: *Fz Marc 12*

Purchased from S. Paulson Esq., Glasgow 1944.

Exh: Düsseldorf, Kunstpalast (208); Institute of Contemporary Arts, London: *Forty Years of Modern Art,* 1948 (51); Roland, Browse and Delbanco, London: *Fauve Paintings,* 1951 (38); Royal Academy, London: *Primitives to Picasso,* 1962 (281).

Lit: Klaus Lankheit: *Franz Marc,* 1950, repr. p.25 as Mädchen mit Grünen Haar; The Art Bulletin, Spring 1952; Leicester Museums and Art Gallery: *Collection of Paintings,* 1958, p.36 (101), repr. 13D; Klaus Lankheit: *Franz Marc – Katalog der Werke,* 1970, repr. p.61, Cat. No. 174 as Rote Frau; Barry Herbert: *German Expressionists at Leicester,* Arts Review, 19th June 1971, Vol. XXIII, No. 12, p.377 repr.

10 A 1944

Illustrated on page 16

Ludwig Meidner
1884-1966

Meidner was born in Bernstadt, Silesia. His early working life was spent as a plasterer's apprentice and fashion designer. After a dissatisfied period studying art in Breslau 1903-05 he spent a year in Berlin and then went to Paris where he studied at the Académie Julian and the Académie Cormon 1906-07, where he met Amedeo Modigliani before returning to Berlin. He was heavily influenced by Impressionism but the next five years were a period of privation and despair and in 1912 he helped to found a club called The Pathetic Ones, under which name its members held an exhibition in Berlin. With the outbreak of war Meidner became a 'hater of the Fatherland'. He was drafted into the army and whilst in uniform wrote *Neck of the Starry Sea* and *September Cry* 1916-18. In 1918 he joined the *Novembergruppe* in Berlin and continued to express his hatred for contemporary Germany. Under appalling conditions he continued to paint and write but moved to London from Berlin in 1939. He returned to Germany in 1953 and died at Darmstadt.

45 **Apocalyptische Vision**

Apocalyptic Vision

1912

Oil on canvas 72·5 × 88·5

Signed and dated: *LM 1912*

Purchased from Siegfried Oppenheimer Esq., London 1968.

Exh: Durham, Sheffield, Leicester: *Germany in Ferment* 1970 (42), repr. p.3.

49 A 1968

Illustrated on page 19

Adolf von Menzel
1815-1905

Menzel was born in Breslau. His early training was in his father's lithographic business and when his father died in 1832 he took over the business in order to support his family. For a short while he attended the Berlin Academy and then taught himself illustration. His early influences were those of Dahl and Constable and the early nineteenth century Berlin painters whose work was exhibited in Berlin in 1839. Menzel was initially concerned with historical subjects but the 1848 revolution drew his attention to the depiction of contemporary events. However, with the failure of the revolution he returned to subjects from national history but his interest in such subjects gradually waned. Menzel visited Paris in 1855, 1867 and 1868 and French painting had a profound effect on his work. His subjects became increasingly concerned with light and colour, although more as illumination than a phenomenon in its own right, as demonstrated by the Impressionists. Initially he was not concerned with 'plein air' painting and the harmonising effect of light but, with his 1867 visit to the French capital, his work displayed increasing interest in these developments. French painters and critics praised his work and in 1885 a large exhibition of his work was held in Paris. Degas thought highly of his work but Pissarro condemned it as being 'ponderous' and 'bourgeois', whilst Menzel considered Impressionism to be 'lazy art'. In 1856 he had been made a professor at the Berlin Academy and in 1898 he became a member of the hereditary aristocracy. In the 1870's and 1880's he travelled extensively in the Netherlands, Austria, Italy and Southern Germany. He died in Berlin.

46 Studien eines stehendern Mannes
Studies of a standing Man

1890

Pencil 20×12·5

Signed and dated: *A. Menzel 90*

Presented by P. R. W. Winter Esq., 1976.

975'1975

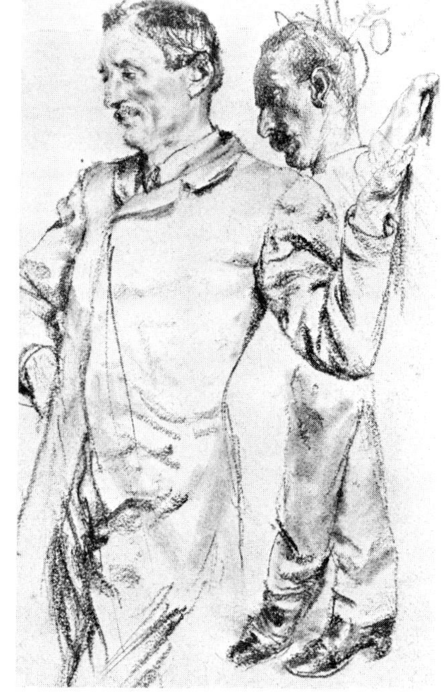

Wilhelm Morgner

1891-1917

Morgner was born in Soest, Westphalia, and studied at Worpswede under Georg Tappert in 1908. He joined the Berlin Secession in 1911, then made contact with **Der Blaue Reiter.** In 1912 he exhibited at the Cologne Sonderbund Exhibition. He died near Langemark.

47 Kopf eines Alten
Head of an Old Man

Woodcut 22·75×18

Signed: *Frau Morgner* and stamped *Nachlass Wilh. Morgner*

Presented by Mrs. Monika Kinley, London 1975.

926'1975

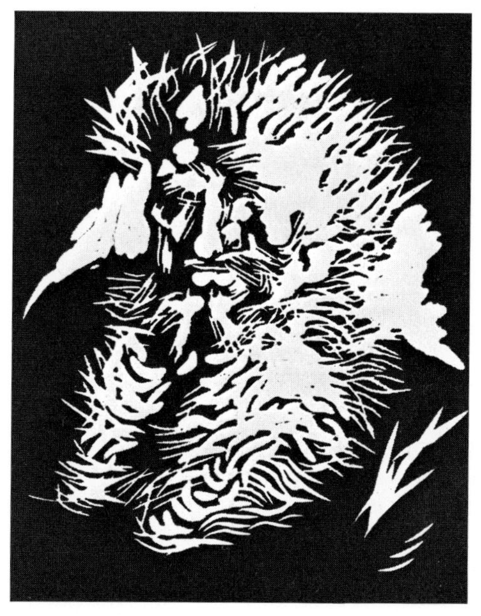

Otto Mueller
1874-1930

Mueller was born at Liebau in Silesia, allegedly a gipsy child who was
subsequently adopted by the aunt of Gerhart Hauptmann, the dramatist-poet,
who was an early influence. Between 1896 and 1898 Mueller studied at the
Dresden Academy but then withdrew to the lonely region of the
Riesengebirge mountains where he lived in self-imposed isolation with his
wife until 1908 when he moved to Berlin. He exhibited at the first **New
Secession** exhibition at the Maximilian Macht Gallery in 1910 where his
work was enthusiastically admired by the **Brücke** artists who immediately
invited Mueller to join their group, the last artist of significance to be
recruited. Mueller's characteristic subject matter of young naked girls in
arcadian landscape settings had an obvious appeal to the sensually inclined
Dresden artists but his temperament was otherwise more reserved and much
less intense than their flamboyant, nervous expressionism. In 1911 he visited
Bohemia with Kirchner and in 1912 he exhibited as part of the **Brücke** group
at the second **Blaue Reiter** exhibition in Munich and the Cologne
Sonderbund. In 1913 he supported Heckel and Schmidt-Rottluff's rejection
of Kirchner's highly personal account of **Brücke** history as set out in his
Chronicle, which led to the group's dissolution. From 1915 to 1918 Mueller
saw war service from which he emerged with his usual air of self-contained
impassivity. In 1920 he became a professor at Breslau Academy, where he
worked until his death.

48   **Drei Mädchen im Profil**
Three Young Girls in Profile

1921

Lithograph 29×39

Signed: *Otto Mueller*

Karsch 111

Purchased from Mrs. Margaret Fisher, London, with
the assistance of a national grant-in-aid administered
by the Victoria and Albert Museum 1977.

787'1977

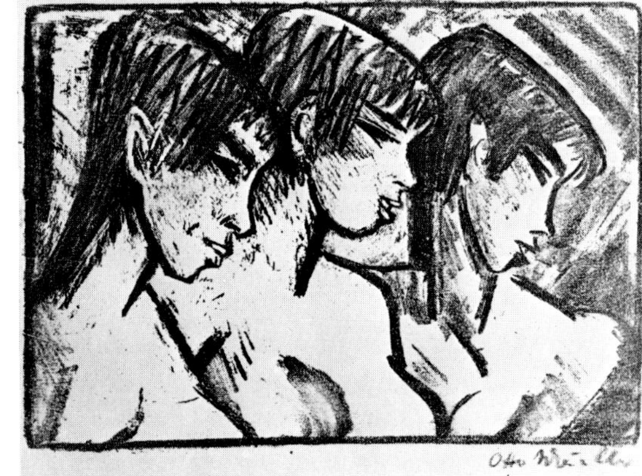

Heinrich Nauen
1880-1941

Nauen was born in Krefeld. He studied at Düsseldorf and Stuttgart. In 1902
he settled in Laetham-St. Martin where he remained until 1905. In 1911 he
moved to Dillborn in the Rhineland where he joined the circle of
Campendonk and Macke and contributed to the 1913 Rhenish Expressionists'
exhibition. His work, like many of his contemporaries, reflected the influence
of van Gogh and Matisse.

49   Bildnis Dr. Walter Kaesbach
Portrait of Dr. Walter Kaesbach

Lithograph 50·5×85·5

Presented by Hans Hess Esq., 1967.

Dr. Kaesbach was artistic adviser to Mr. Frank Stoop,
whose pictures are now in the Tate Gallery, including
all the early Braques and Picassos.

6 A 1967

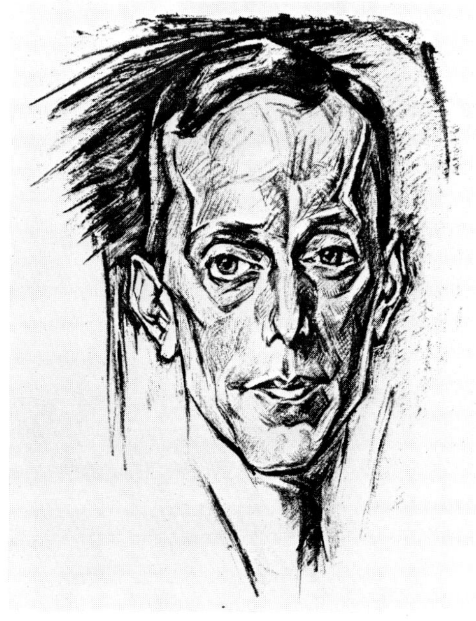

Emil Nolde
1867-1956

Emil Hansen was born in Nolde, which he adopted as his own name in 1902,
near Schleswig, the son of a farmer. Throughout his life he retained an
ardent passion for his native landscape, which provided him with one of his
major subjects. Although he expressed an early interest in becoming an artist,
he had no idea how to go about it. From 1885 until 1889 he was a student at
the Sauermann School of Woodcarving in Flensburg. From 1892-98 he
taught at the school of arts and crafts in St. Gallen, Switzerland. After selling a
popular series of grotesque watercolours, he was able to give up teaching in
order to paint, working independently after he was refused admission to the
Munich Academy. At this time he produced his first etchings. After studying
under Hölzel in Dachau 1899 he spent the following years travelling – to Paris
where he saw the Impressionists, Copenhagen and Berlin. From 1903 he lived
on the island of Alsen during the summer and in Berlin during the winter.
From 1906-07 he was a member of **Die Brücke.** In 1909 he started to paint
religious subjects. During 1913-14 he took part in the Kulz-Leber
anthropological expedition to the South Seas, via Moscow, Siberia, China,
New Guinea, Java and Burma where his discoveries about primitive art
influenced his work. When war broke out he returned to Germany. From 1916
he lived at Utenwarf, near Nolde, and from 1926 at Seebüll. Shortly after the
war he became a member of the National Socialist Party, naïvely confusing
his personal belief in racial purity with Nazi theories on racial superiority.
Despite repeated attempts at recognition, his work was officially classified as
'degenerate' in 1937 and 1,052 of his works were confiscated from public
collections and he was forbidden to paint. In 1940 he gave up his home in
Berlin to return to Seebüll, to work on the 'pictures I did not paint'.

50 **Der Maler Selbstbildnis**
Self-Portrait of the Painter

1905

Etching 17·8×12·9

Signed and dated: *Emil Nolde 05*

Schiefler Vol. I, No. 6 IV

Edition of 20, all numbered, No. 16

Purchased from Fischer Fine Art Ltd., London, with
the assistance of a national grand-in-aid
administered by the Victoria and Albert Museum
1976.

Exh: Marlborough Fine Art, London: *Edvard
Munch/Emil Nolde. The Relationship of their Art
1969* (138)

183'1976

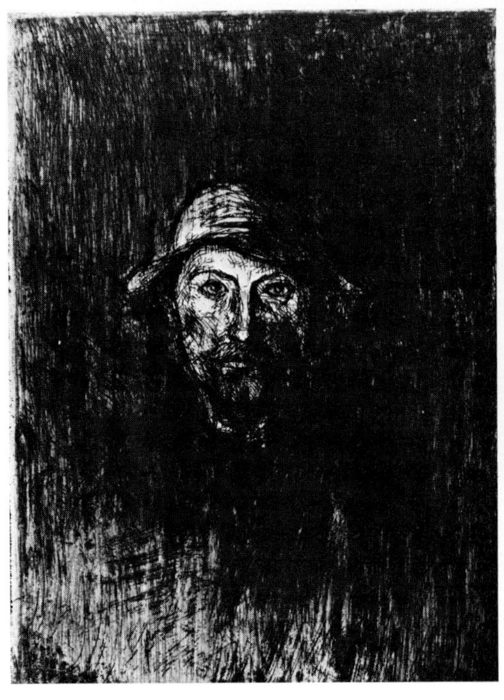

51 **Wie Vögel**
Like Birds

Lithograph 34·5×35·5

Schiefler Vol. 2, No. 14

Edition of 100

Purchased from Fischer Fine Art Ltd., London, with
the assistance of a national grant-in-aid
administered by the Victoria and Albert Museum
1976.

Exh: Marlborough Fine Art, London: *Edvard
Munch/Emil Nolde. The Relationship of their Art
1969* (149)

Nolde produced his first lithographs in 1907. The
two women shown in a moment of relaxed intimacy,
reflecting the influence of Toulouse-Lautrec, are Ada
Nolde, the artist's wife, and her sister Louise Vilstrup.

182'1976

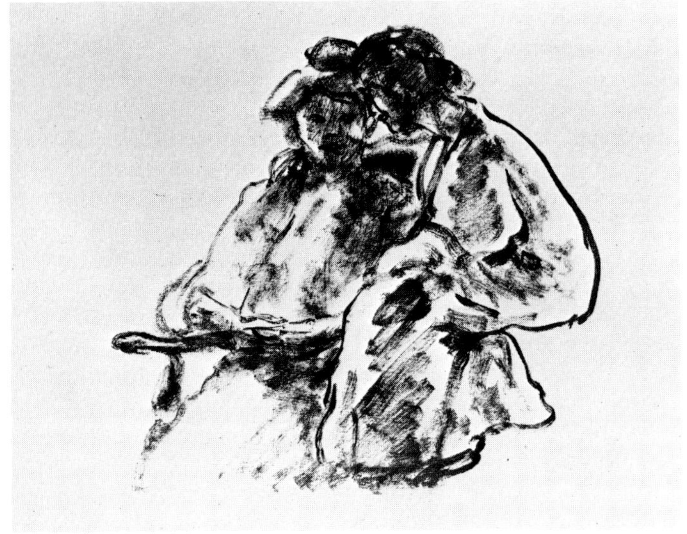

52 **Kopf mit rot-schwarzem Haar**
Head with red-black Hair

c.1910

Watercolour 40·25×32

Signed: *Nolde*

Purchased from Mrs. T. Hess, Leicester 1944.

Exh: Roland, Browse and Delbanco, London:
Expressionist Paintings 1952 (38)

Lit: Leicester Museum and Art Gallery: *Watercolours
and Drawings,* 1963 (235) as The Mask; Barry
Herbert: *German Expressionists* at Leicester, Arts
Review, 19th June 1971, Vol. XXIII, No. 12, p.377.

This watercolour probably belongs to the series of
heads produced in 1910.

8 A 1944

Illustrated as Frontispiece on page vii

Ernst Oppler
1867-1929

Oppler was born in Hanover. He studied at the Munich Academy, where his
work was greatly influenced by Max Liebermann and the French
Impressionists. He visited Holland and London where he became a member of
the International Society of Painters, Sculptors and Engravers of London. For
some time he lived in Sluis in Holland. In 1905 he settled in Berlin, where he
died.

53 **Isadora Duncan**

Etching 27×21

Signed: *Ernst Oppler*

Purchased from Mrs. Margaret Fisher, London 1972.

Isadora Duncan 1878-1927 was an American born
dancer who reacted against the grandiose balletic
style of the nineteenth century. She evolved a style
of dancing from the movement and costume
depicted on Greek vases, combined with classical
elements and movement derived from the
observation of natural phenomena. She taught for a
time in Russia where she influenced the future
impressario Diaghilev.

15 A 1972

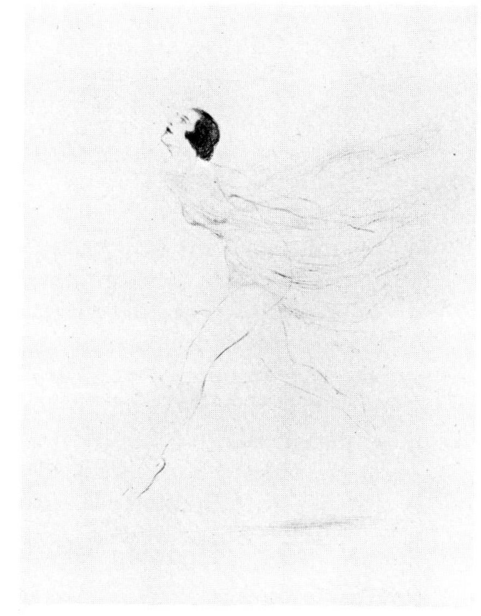

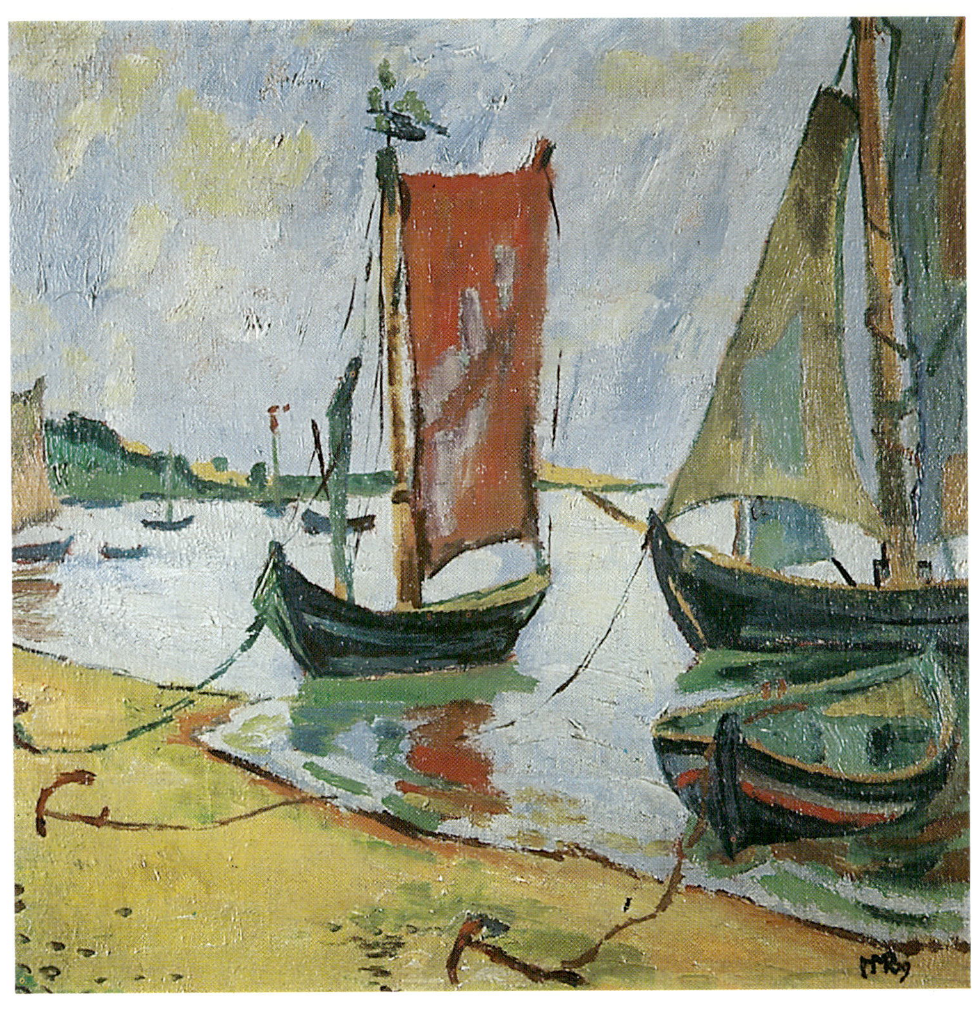

54 **PECHSTEIN**
Küstenszene mit Booten 1909

Max Herman Pechstein
1881-1955

Pechstein was born in Eckesbach, near Zwickau. He studied under Otto Gussman. In 1906 he became a member of **Die Brücke** in Dresden. In 1907 he visited Italy and Paris. He generally enjoyed greater public popularity than his Expressionist colleagues as his work tended to be less introverted and profound and therefore less challenging. He was greatly influenced by Matisse and there is often an imitative trend to be found in his work. In 1908 he settled in Berlin where he founded the **Neue Secession** in 1910. Like many of his contemporaries, Pechstein developed an interest in the primitive art of the South Seas. He visited Palau and the Caroline Islands in 1914 and produced a number of exotic, brightly coloured works in a flat primitive manner. His later work was less Expressionistic than that of the other **Brücke** artists. He died in Berlin.

54 Küstenszene mit Booten
Coast Scene with Boats

1909

Oil on canvas 50 × 50

Signed and dated: *HMP 09*

Purchased from the Leger Galleries, London 1952.

Exh: Roland, Browse and Delbanco, London:
Expressionist Painting 1952 (14)

Lit: Leicester Museums and Art Gallery: *Collection of
Paintings,* 1958, p.42 (119), repr. 13C

Painted at Nidden in East Prussia, where
Pechstein went with the money made from the sale
of his pictures at the Berlin Secession of 1909. Like
many works of this period it shows the influence of
van Gogh.

43 A 1952

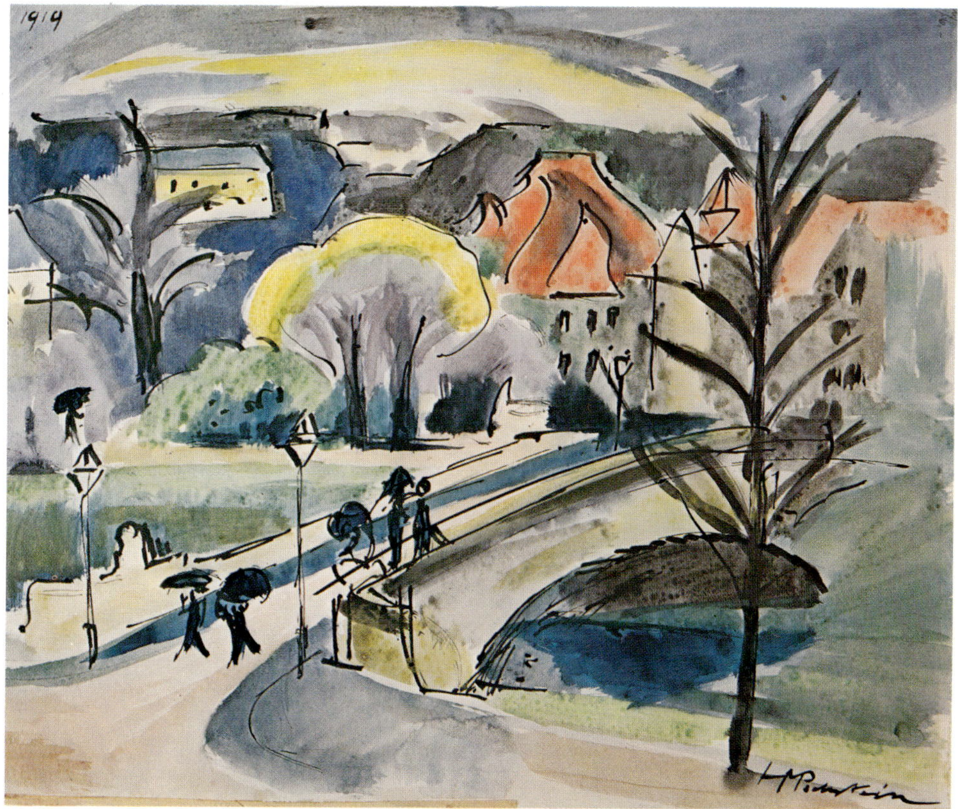

55 PECHSTEIN
Die Brücke in Erfurt 1919

55 Die Brücke in Erfurt
The Bridge at Erfurt

1919

Indian ink and watercolour 31·75×40·5

Signed and dated: *H. M. Pechstein, April 1919*

Presented by Mrs. T. Hess, Leicester 1944.

Exh: Durham, Sheffield, Leicester: *Germany in Ferment,* 1970 (28)

Lit: Leicester Museums and Art Gallery: *Watercolours and Drawings,* 1963, p.33 (238)

Painted between 6th April and 18th April 1919 during one of many visits Pechstein made to the home of the Hess family in Erfurt near Weimar. The visit is recorded in the Hess visitors' book.

11 A 1944

56 Dein Reich komme, Dein Wille geschehe, wie im Himmel also auch auf Erden
Thy Kingdom Come, Thy Will Be Done, on Earth as it is in Heaven

1921

Woodcut 40×29

Signed: *M. H. Pechstein*

Purchased from London Graphic Art Gallery 1969.

From the series of twelve woodcuts published in a portfolio in 1921 by Propyläen-Verlag, Berlin, entitled *Das Vaterunser* (The Lord's Prayer). An edition of 250 were printed of which the first fifty were hand-coloured.

13 A 1969

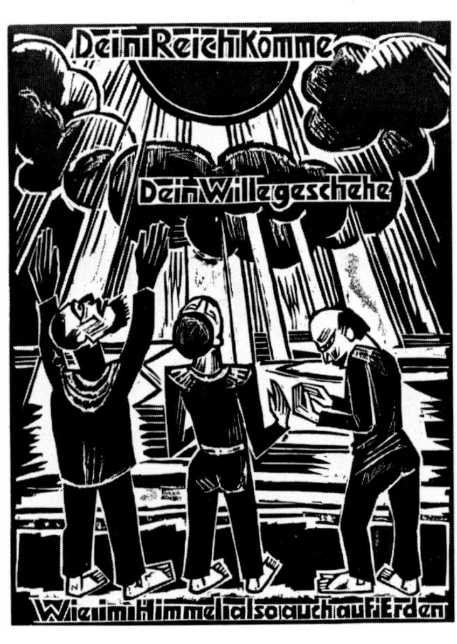

Alfred Rethel

1816-59

Rethel was born at Diepenabend, near Aachen, where he studied under J. Bastiné. From 1829-36 he attended the Düsseldorf Academy under Wilhelm von Schadow. From 1836-47 he attended the Stadel School in Frankfurt, where he lost all traces of his earlier Nazarene style. He visited Italy in 1844-45 and 1852-53. Rethel's work stands between the climax of Romanticism and the renewal of history painting. In his historical subjects he attempted to bring a contemporary feeling to the events. Throughout his work runs a haunting theme of spectres, skeletons and death. From 1853 Rethel suffered from a severe mental illness. He died in Düsseldorf.

57   Auch ein Todtentanz

Another Dance of Death

1849

Plates Three, Four, Five and Six from the set of six in the original folio. Wood engravings 15·5 × 32

Seventh edition. Published by the Leipzig Verlag von Bernard Schlicke. Folio cover: *Auch ein Todtentanz./ Erfunden und gezeichnet/von/Alfred Rethel./Mit erklärendem Text/von/Robert Reinick./Ausgeführt im akademischen Atelier für Holzschneidekunst zu Dresden unter Leitung von H. Bürkner./Du Bürger und du Bauersmann./Schaut reht Euch diese Blätter an!/Da seht Ihr nakt und ohne Kleid/Ein ernstes Bild aus ernster Zeit./Wohl kommt so mancher zu Euch her/Als ob's ein neuer Heiland wär,/Und spricht von Macht und Herrlichkeit/Die er für Alle hat bereit, Ihr glaubt es ihm, weil's Euch gefällt, -/Schaut her, wie es damit bestellt./Sechste Auflage./Preis ist Neugroschen./Leipzig, Verlag von Bernhard Schlicke.*

The first two plates, which are not in the folio, depict Death being given the attributes of Justice and then riding towards the town, where in inciting the people to insurrection he will obtain a great harvest.

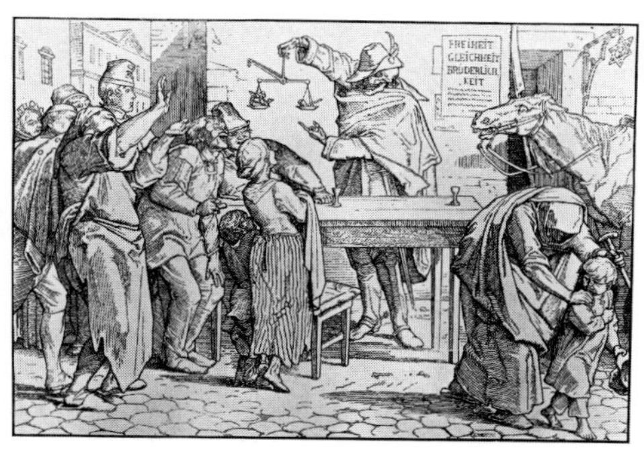

57a Plate Three

Er ist am Ziel. – Sieh, gleich am Thor/die Schenk' und mancher Gast davor;/beim Brandwein frecher Lieder Klang/und wüst' galächter Spiel und Zank! – . . .

He is near his goal. – Look, even at the entrance/to the tavern and with many of its customers;/ringing with insolent drinking songs/and wild laughter, play, and brawling! – . . .

57b   Plate Four

'Freiheit, Gleichheit und Brudersinn!'/Der Schrei wälzt durch die Stadt sich hin./Zum Rathaus' – Horch! Der Steinwurf saust . . .

'Freedom, Equality and Fraternity!'/The cry flew through the town./'To the town-hall!' – Hark! The whistling of stones being thrown . . .

57c   Plate Five

'Zur Barrikade!' 'Pflaster auf!!' – -/Da steht der Bau – und ober drauf/er, den zum Führer sie ernannt,/die blut'ge Zahn' in fester Hand! – . . .

'To the barricade!' 'Tear up the pavingstones!!' – -/It is erected – and upon it,/he, whom they have taken as their leader,/the bloody standard in his steadfast hand! – . . .

57d   Plate Six

Der sie geführt – es war der Tod!/Er hat gehalten, was er bot . . .

He that they followed – it was Death!/He has fulfilled, what he promised . . .

Illustrated on page 3

Lit: Bernard S. Myers: *Expressionism* 1963, p.15, repr. Ulrich Finke: *German Painting from Romanticism to Expressionism* 1974, pp.103, 104, repr. pl. 82.

This series, although a seemingly conservative reaction to the Peasants' Revolt of 1848, in its assumption that revolution and death are inexorably linked, was conceived prior to the event. It is, more importantly, Rethel's most overt statement of his preoccupation with death. Of Rethel's woodcuts and Reinick's poem, Baudelaire wrote it is 'a poem of reaction whose subject is the usurpation of all powers and the seduction of the people by the fatal goddess of death'. The whole series and particularly Plate Six look back to the work of Dürer and Holbein's *Dance of Death.* The woodcuts were produced in vast numbers, like handbills, as were Dürer's and Holbein's, and the images were assimilated into the German consciousness because of their massive circulation, although their creator was soon forgotten.

28 A 1944/1-4

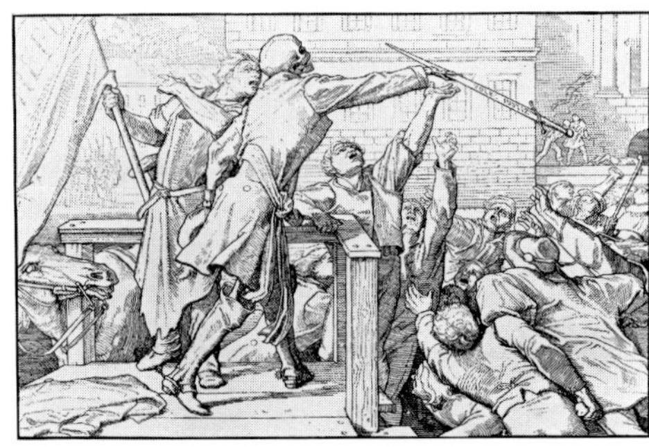

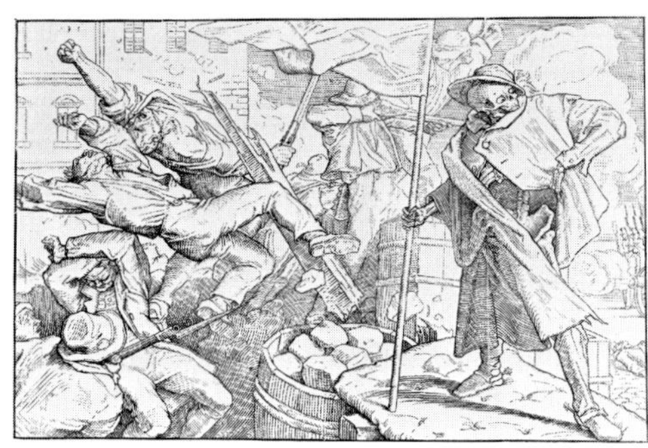

Christian Rohlfs
1849-1938

Rohlfs was born in Niendorf, the son of a peasant farmer. In 1870 he went to Berlin to study with Pietsch on the recommendation of the poet, Theodor Storm. However, in the same year Pietsch sent him to study at the Weimar Academy. In 1871 a severe illness forced him to leave but he returned in 1874, when he came into contact with Liebermann who was also studying at the Academy. Rohlfs remained in Weimar under the patronage of the Archduke. In the early 1890's he saw works by the major French Impressionists, which had a marked influence on his work. In 1901 he was invited to teach at Karl Ernst Osthaus' projected art school in Hagen and although the school never came into being Osthaus provided Rohlfs with a studio in the Folkswang Museum, Hagen. This museum had the first major collection of Post-Impressionist paintings in Germany including works by Cézanne, van Gogh and Gauguin. Rohlfs's contact with post-impressionism led to the development of an increasingly expressionist style although he was working in isolation from the main Expressionist groups. In 1905 and 1906 he spent the summer months in Soest where in 1906 he met Nolde. In 1922 he was awarded an honorary doctorate by the Technische Hochschule in Aachen and in 1925 by the University of Kiel. In 1924 he became a member of the Prussian Academy. From 1927 until his death he spent eight months of the year in Ascona, Switzerland. In 1936 the National Socialists closed his exhibition at the Barimer Ruhmershalle and he was expelled from the Prussian Academy. The following year his works were removed from private galleries and public collections. He died in Hagen, totally isolated from the art world.

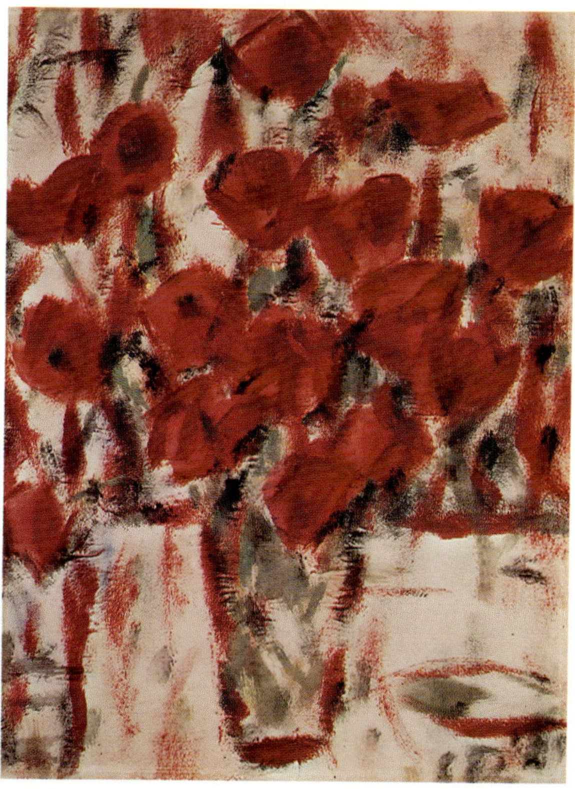

58 Roter Mohn in Vase

Red Poppies in a Vase

1929

Gouache 56 × 40·5

Signed and dated l.r.: *CR 29*

Presented by Sidney Pick Esq., Leicester 1965.

Exh: Durham, Sheffield, Leicester: *Germany in Ferment* 1970 (34), repr. p.20

45 A.1965

Karl Schmidt-Rottluff
1884-1976

Karl Schmidt was born in Rottluff, near Chemnitz, and added the name of his birth-place to his surname in 1905. At school in Chemnitz from 1897-1905 he met Erich Heckel and together they visited exhibitions of contemporary painting. They both studied architecture at Dresden and with Ernst Ludwig Kirchner and Fritz Bleyl formed **Die Brücke.** In the summer of 1906 Schmidt-Rottluff worked with Emil Nolde on the island of Alsen. From 1907-10 his summers were spent working at Dangast on the North Sea with Heckel. In 1911 he visited Norway and then settled in Berlin, where he became interested in primitive art forms. In 1912 he made bronze reliefs of the four apostles for the chapel at the Sonderbund exhibition in Cologne and met Lyonel Feininger. His rejection of all art theory appeared in the only public statement he made on his art in the March 1914 issue of *Kunst und Künstler.* After serving with the German Forces he produced many woodcuts and wood carvings with religious themes as their subject. In the period between the wars he had many exhibitions including Hanover 1921, Berlin 1927, 1929 and 1934, Dresden 1927 and Munich 1931. Under the National Socialists his work was proscribed and in 1941 he was forbidden to paint. 608 of his paintings were removed from public museums in Germany. After the war he was awarded a professorship at the Berlin Academy and has been recognised as one of the major exponents of Expressionism. The first exhibition of his work in Great Britain was held at Leicester Museum and Art Gallery in 1953. He died in Berlin.

59 **Hafen bei Ebbe**

Harbour at Low Tide

1907

Lithograph 27·5 × 34·8

Signed and dated: *Schmidt-Rottluff 1907* and titled: *Hafen bei Ebbe*

Schapire S 16

Bequeathed by Dr. Rosa Schapire 1955.

Schmidt-Rottluff signed only those prints with which he was entirely satisfied. Until 1913 he also inscribed the print's title and its year of production. From 1913 onwards he abbreviated this to a number only: the last 2 numerals of the year and the number of the print in chronological order, e.g. 245 means the 5th piece of work produced in 1924.

86 A 1955

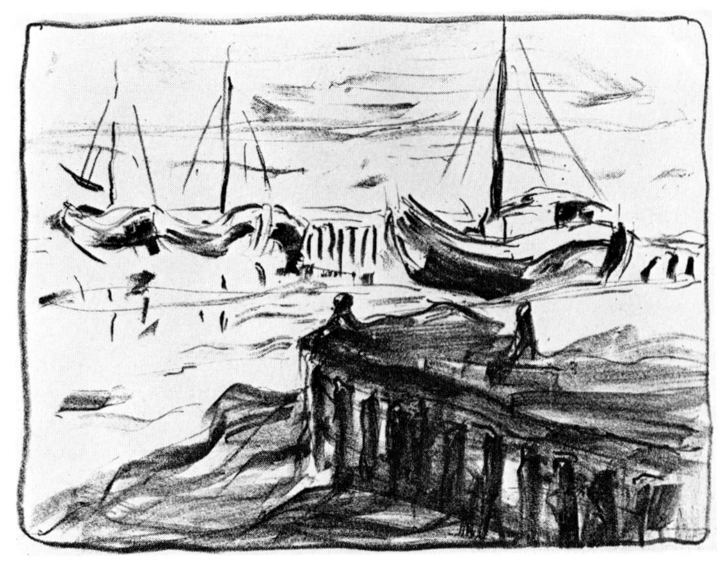

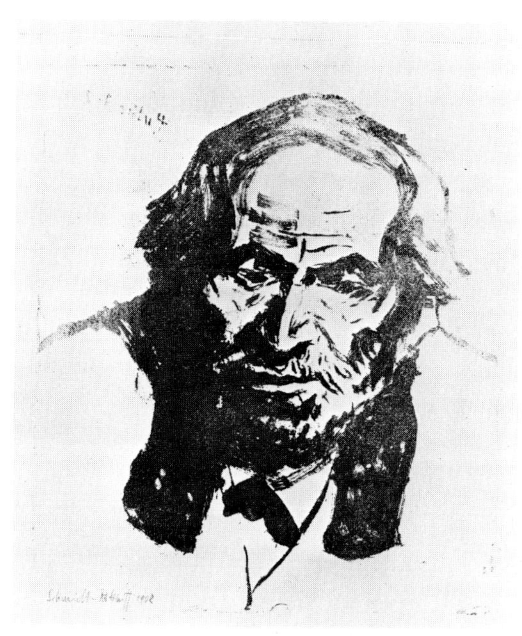

60 **Alter**
Old Man

1908

Lithograph 39·8 × 34

Signed and dated: *Schmidt-Rottluff 1908*

Schapire S 41

Bequeathed by Dr. Rosa Schapire 1955.

84 A 1955

61 **Liegender Akt**
Reclining Nude

1909

Lithograph 34 × 40

Signed: *S. Rottluff* (The paper has been trimmed for mounting and the title removed). It is also signed on the stone.

Schapire S 55

Bequeathed by Dr. Rosa Schapire 1955.

87 A 1955

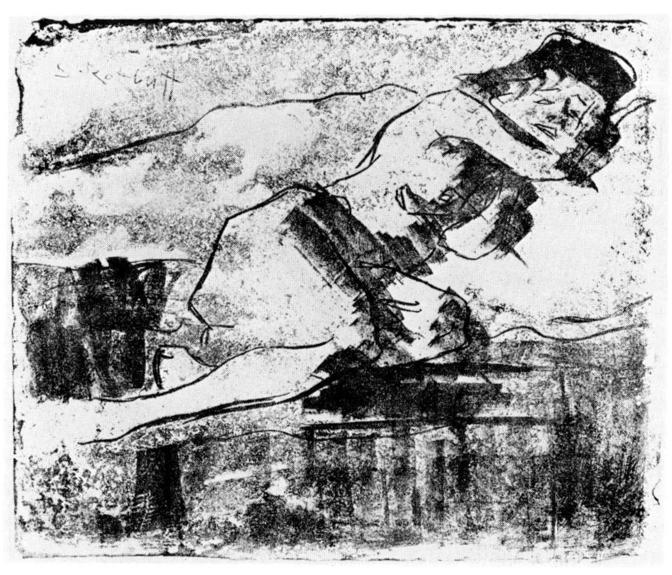

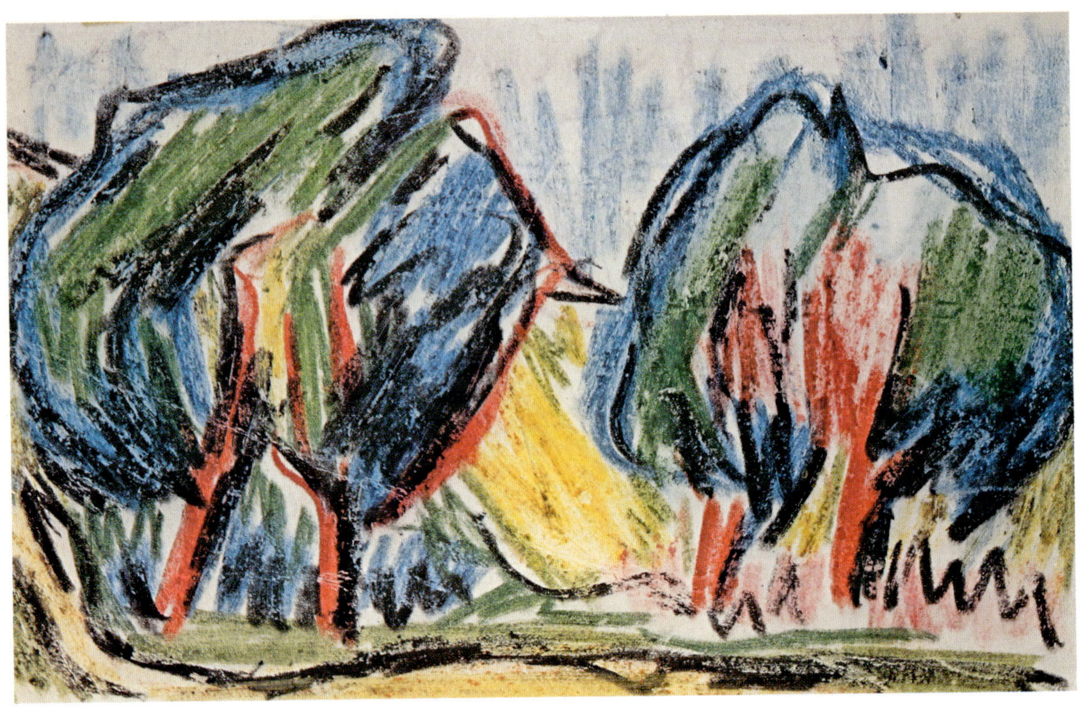

62 Landschaft mit Bäumen
Landscape with Trees

1909

Wax crayon 9×14

Sent as a postcard by the artist to: *Frl. Drphl Ro
Schapire, Hamburg horst. Osterbeck Str. 43 11.*
Postmarked: *Dangast 15.10.09.* Written on reverse:
*Frdl. Dank für die Rigaer Zeitung. Ist das dieselbe
Verfasserin? Bedeutend geschickter geschrieben, als
die Kritik im Börsen-Courier. Schade, dass nicht
umgekehrt. Herzl. Gruss.*
(Thank you for the Riga Newspaper. Is that the same
authoress? Written much better than the critic in the
Börsen-Courier. A pity, it is not the other way round.
Best wishes.)

Bequeathed by Dr. Rosa Schapire 1955.

Lit: Leicester Museum and Art Gallery: *Watercolours
and Drawings,* 1963 (286).

21 A 1955

63 **Häuser am Wasser**
Houses by the Water

1910

Woodcut 31·8 × 38·6

Signed and dated: *S. Rottluff 1910* and titled: *Häuser am Wasser*

Schapire H 33

Bequeathed by Dr. Rosa Schapire 1955.

90 A 1955

Illustrated on page 13

64 **Frau am Tisch**
Woman at a Table

1910

Woodcut 39 × 29·5

Signed and dated: *S. Rottluff 1910* and titled: *Frau am Tisch am Pappel* (on Poplar – probably an instruction written by the artist for the benefit of Dr. Schapire when she was compiling the catalogue raisonné of the artist's graphic work).

Schapire H 40

Bequeathed by Dr. Rosa Schapire 1955.

Exh: Durham, Sheffield, Leicester: *Germany in Ferment,* 1970 (18), repr. p.10.

92 A 1955

65 **Sonnenuntergang am Kai**
Quayside at Sunset

1910

Lithograph 40 × 33·7

Signed and dated: *S. Rottluff 1910*

The paper has been trimmed for mounting and the original artist's inscription of the title removed and rewritten in another hand.

Schapire S 70

Bequeathed by Dr. Rosa Schapire 1955.

85 A 1955

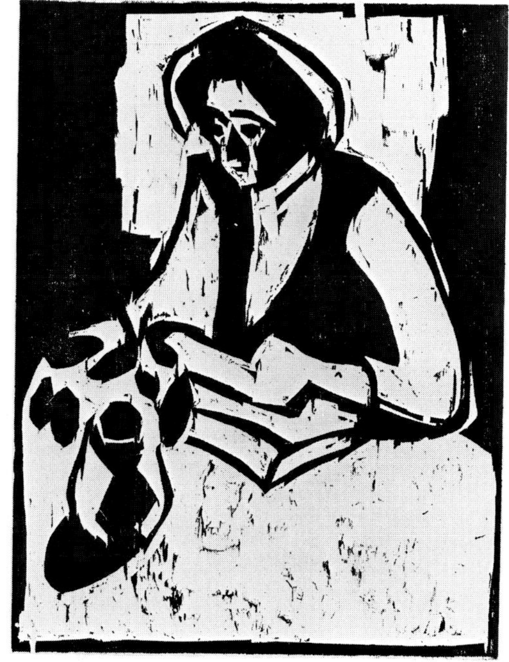

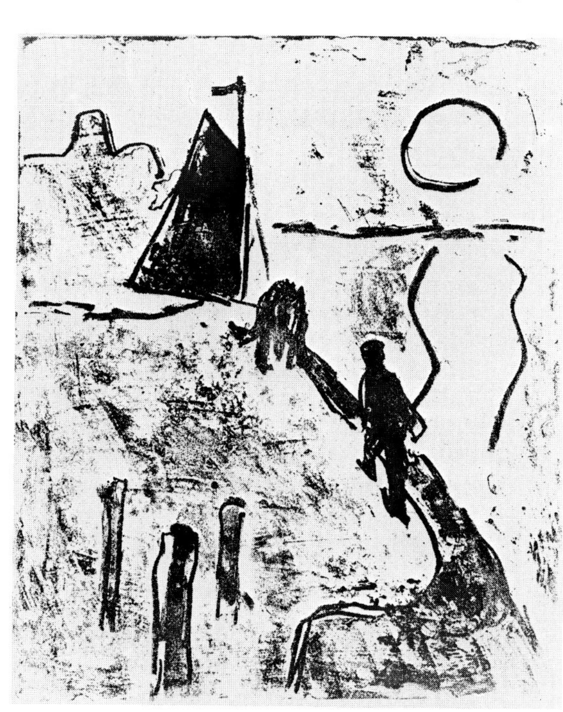

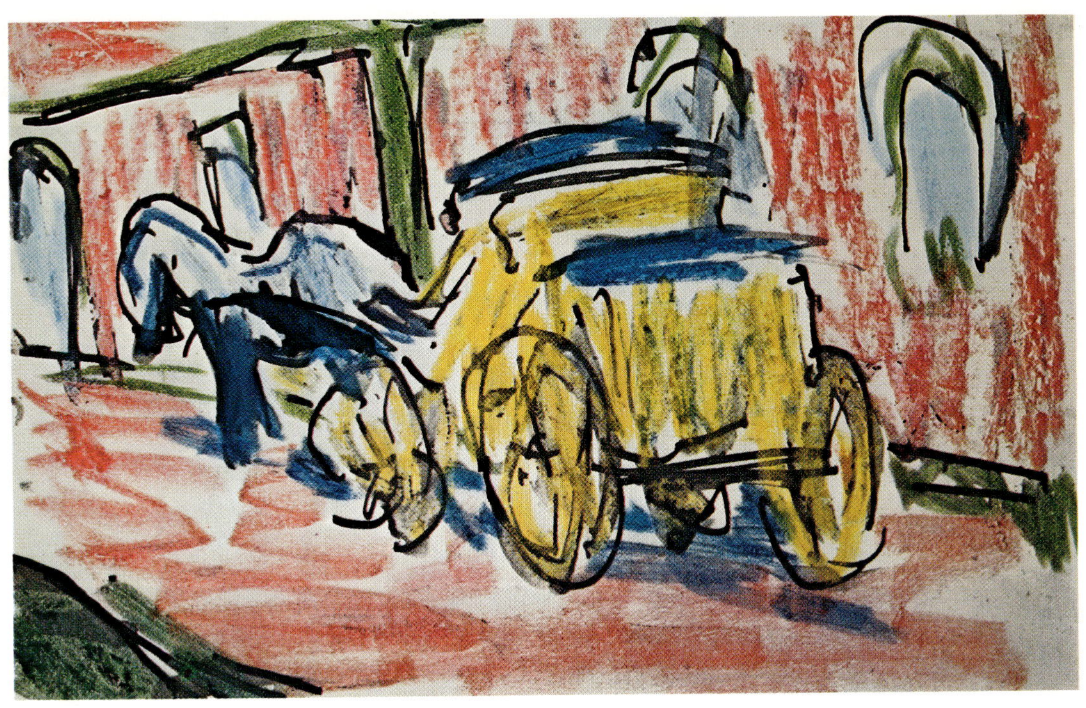

66 **Pferd und Wagen**
Horse and Carriage

1910

Pen, ink and wax crayon 9×14

Sent as a postcard by the artist to: *Dr. Schapire, Hamburg, Osterbeck Str. 43.* Postmarked: *Varel 21.8.10.* Written on reverse: *Heute Brief. Bei Hamburg alles belsebt, lasst sich aber arrangiern* (next word illegible) *danuber, später Post. Am montag zu viel tun, als zu denken, je ne crois point. Herze. Grüss.* (Re – your letter of today. Hamburg all booked up, but could . . . be arranged. More about this later. On Monday too much to do and think at the same time, je ne crois point. Best wishes.)

Bequeathed by Dr. Rosa Schapire 1955.

Lit: Leicester Museum and Art Gallery: *Watercolours and Drawings,* 1963 (281)

20 A 1955

67 **Mädchen mit aufgestemmten Armen**
Girl with outstretched Arm

1911

Woodcut 23·2×31·3

Signed and dated: *S. Rottluff 1911* and titled:
Mädchen mit aufgestemmten Armen

Schapire H 56

Bequeathed by Dr. Rosa Schapire 1955.

93 A 1955

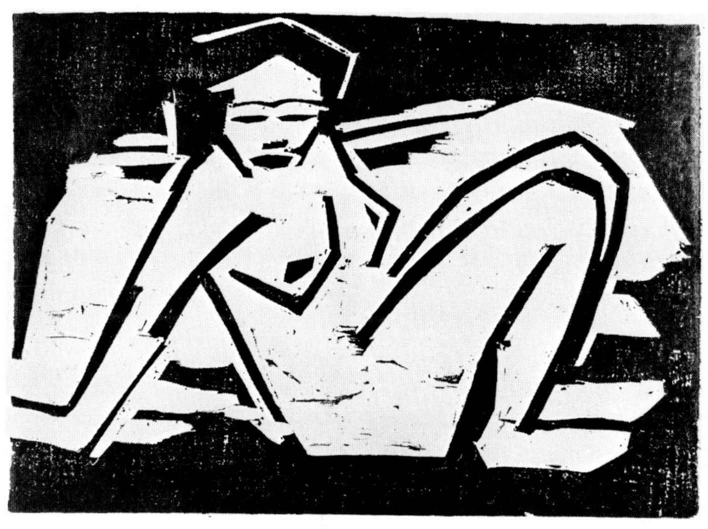

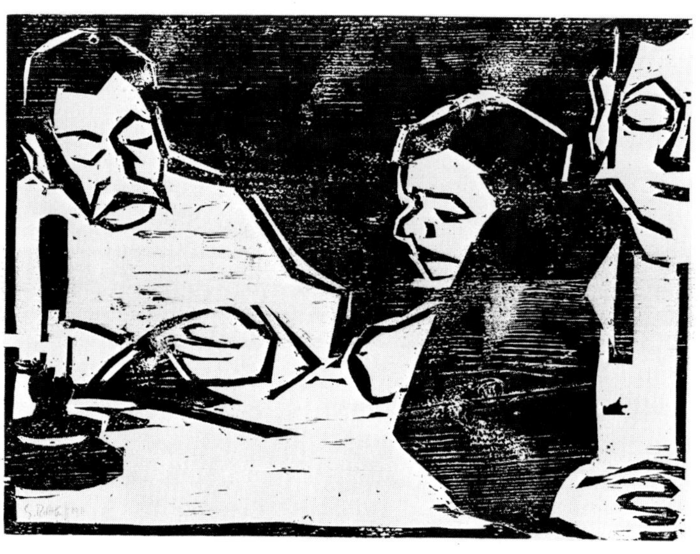

68 **Abendunterhaltung**
Evening Conversation

1911

Woodcut 39·6×50·3

Signed and dated: *S. Rottluff 1911*

Schapire H 65

Bequeathed by Dr. Rosa Schapire 1955.

94 A 1955

69 **Liegendes Mädchen**
Reclining Girl

1911

Lithograph 33·7×40·1

Signed and dated: *S. Rottluff 1911* and titled:
Liegendes Mädchen (the paper has been trimmed for
mounting and the original artist's inscription of the
titled removed and rewritten in another hand). It is
also signed on the stone.

Schapire S 73

Bequeathed by Dr. Rosa Schapire 1955.

88 A 1955

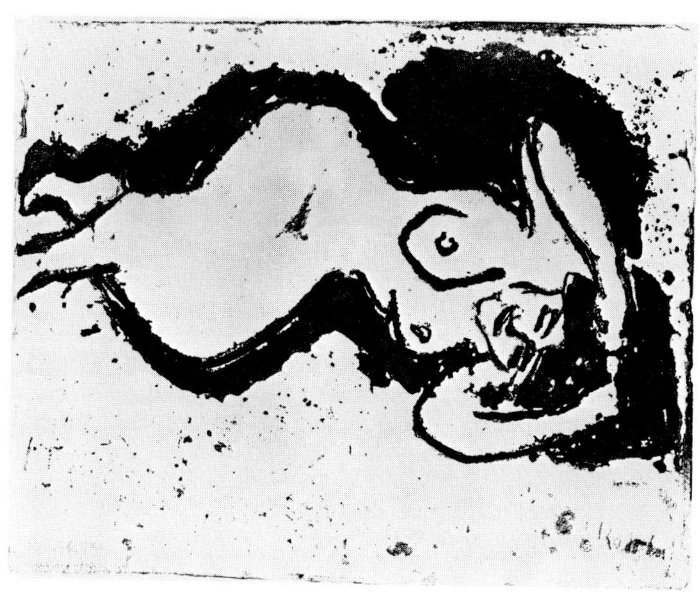

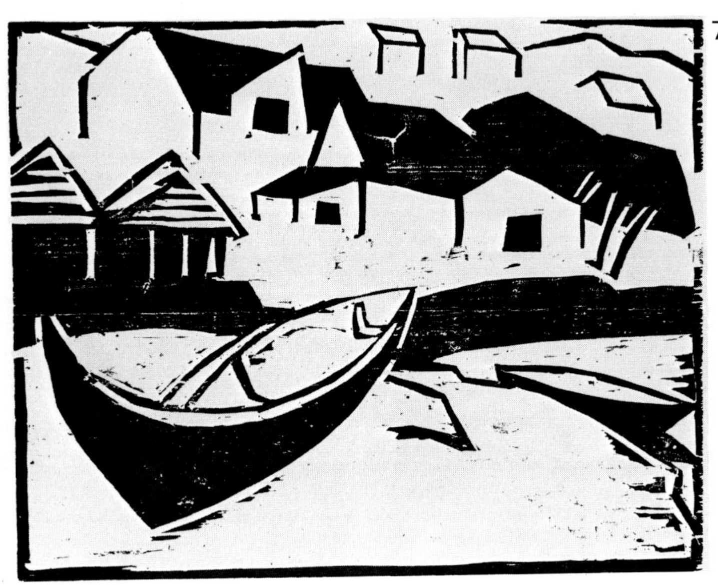

70 **Landschaft aus Norwegen**
Norwegian Landscape

1912

Woodcut 29·6×36

Signed and dated: *S. Rottluff 1912* and titled:
Landschaft aus Norwegen

Schapire H 78

Bequeathed by Dr. Rosa Schapire 1955.

91 A 1955

71 **Sitzende**
Seated Nude

1913

Lithographic postcard 14·5×9·5

Signed and dated on the stone only: *S. Rottluff 1913*

Printed beneath image: SCHMIDT-ROTTLUFF:
AKT/Sonderabdruck aus der AKTION. Printed on
reverse: *'Die Berliner Wochenzeitung DIE AKTION
sei empfohlen, denn sie ist mutig ohne Literaten
Frecheit, leidenschaftlich ohne Phrase und
gebildet ohne Dünkel'. Franz Bleim. Losen Vogel,* and
*DIE AKTION, herausgegeben von Franz Pfemfert,
erscheint jeden Sonnabend. Probenummern 30 Pf.
durch den Verlag Berlin-Wilmersdorf.*

Bequeathed by Dr. Rosa Schapire 1955.

Lit: W. Grohmann: *Schmidt-Rottluff,* 1956, p.35,
repr.

Die Aktion was a Berlin literary and political
magazine for the Expressionist movement. It was
founded in 1913 by Franz Pfemfert who was also its
editor. It was the first German periodical to propose
that revolutionary art and revolutionary politics were
the same. Schmidt-Rottluff contributed many
woodcuts for use as illustrations during the pre- and
post-war years.

23 A 1955

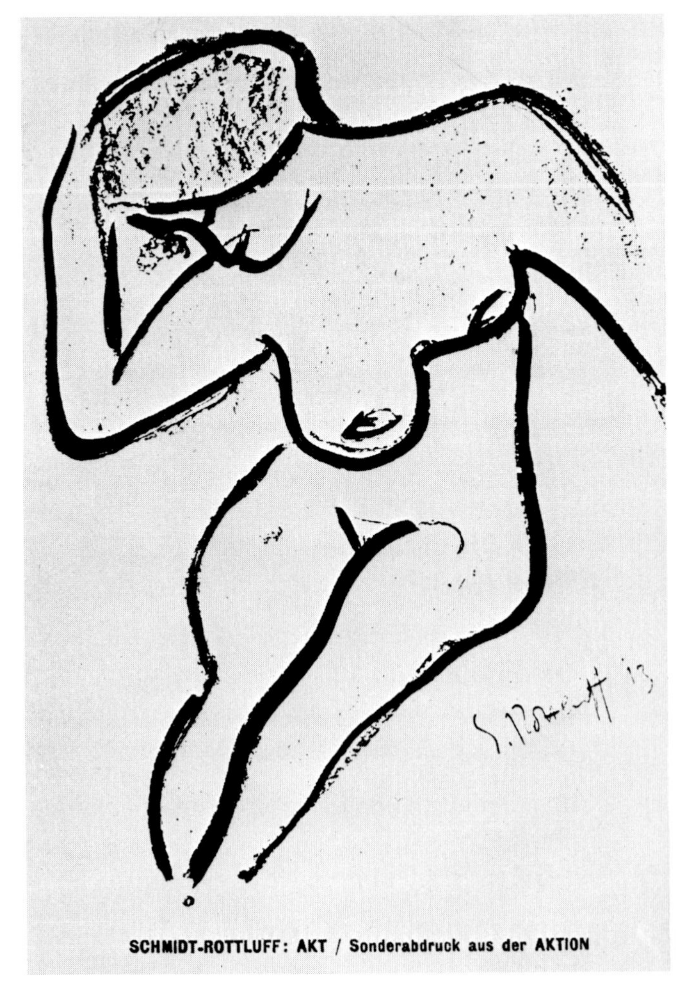

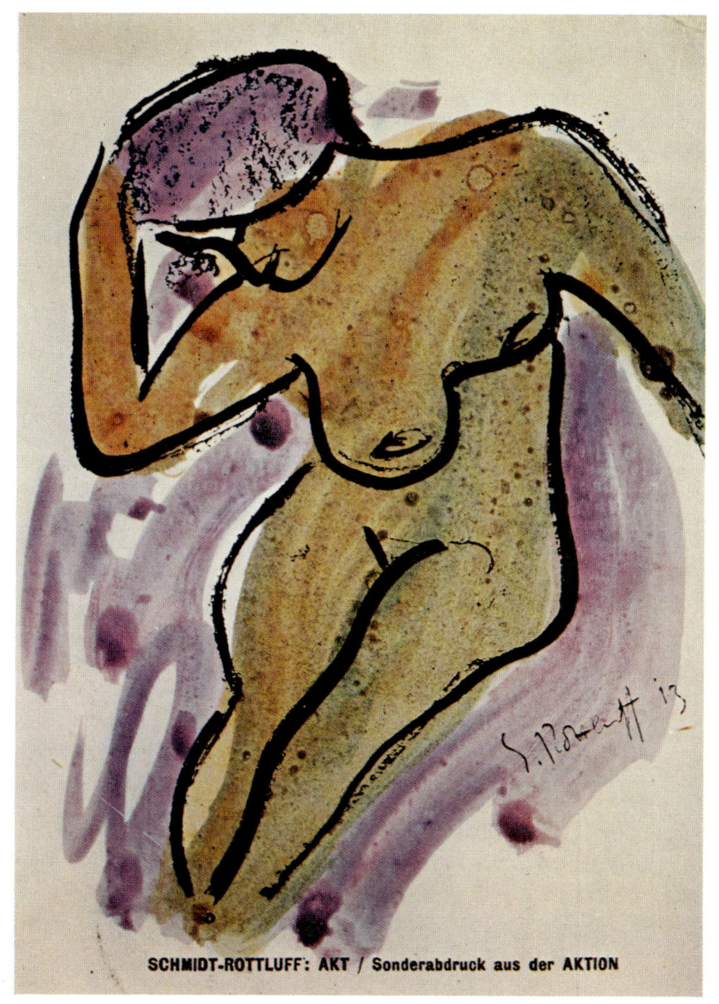

72 Sitzende

Seated Nude

1913

Lithographic postcard with watercolour 14·5 × 9·5

Signed and dated on the stone only: *S. Rottluff 1913*
Printed beneath image: *SCHMIDT-ROTTLUFF: AKT/Sonderabdruck aus der AKTION* etc.

Sent as a postcard by the artist to: *I. H. Frl. Dr. Schapire, Osterbeck Str. 43, Hamburg.* Postmark and date illegible except for: *Lote ....15.* Written on reverse and only partly legible: *Zu den 2 Radierungen möchte ich allerdings jetzt auch wissen ... und woher! Paula Modersohn war ohne Zweifel sehr interessant ... das einzige war von Worpswede ... später interessieren. Grüss!* (I would like to know more about the 2 etchings what and where from! Paula Modersohn was certainly very interesting – the really interesting things came from Worpswede and later. Greetings!)

Bequeathed by Dr. Rosa Schapire 1955.

Lit: Leicester Museum and Art Gallery: *Watercolours and Drawings,* 1963 (289)

27 A 1955

73 Frauenkopf
Female Head

1916

Woodcut on yellow paper 17·5 × 24·1

Signed, dated and numbered: *S. Rottluff 1916 164*

Schapire H 189

Bequeathed by Dr. Rosa Schapire 1955.

Exh: Durham, Sheffield, Leicester: *Germany in Ferment,* 1970 (19)

Lit: W. Grohmann: *Schmidt-Rottluff* 1956, p.76 repr.

89 A 1955

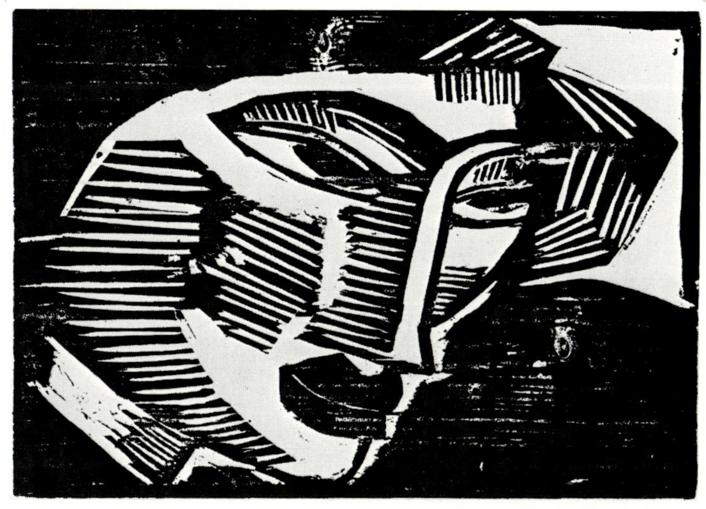

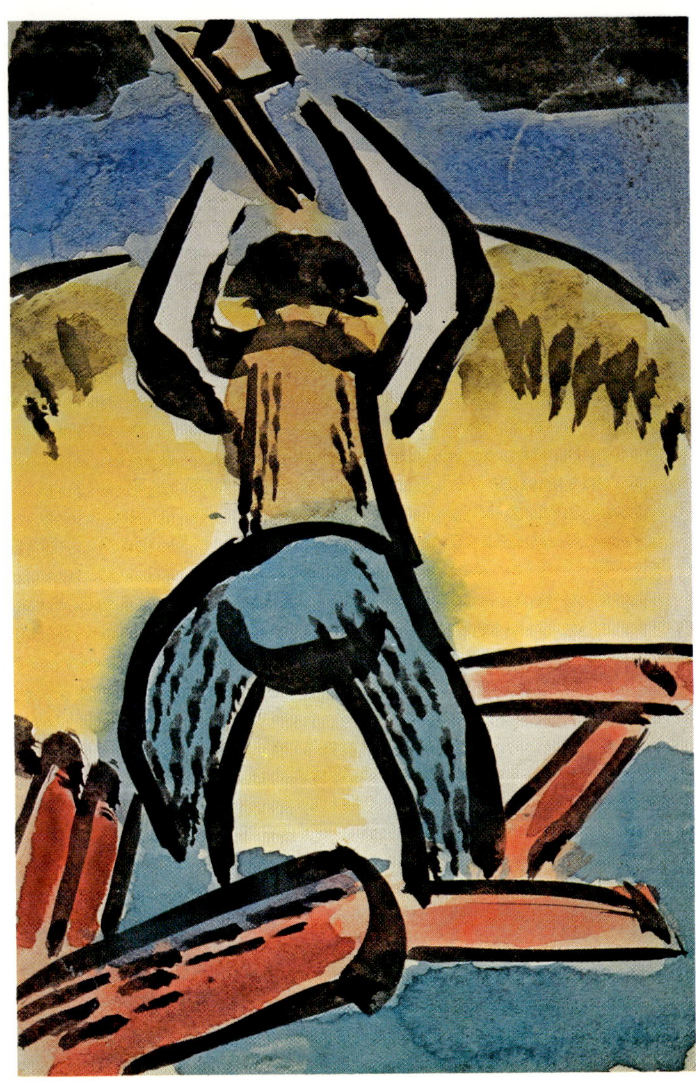

74 Holzhackender Mann
Man chopping Wood

1920

Watercolour and black ink 15·5 × 10·5

Sent as a postcard by the artist to: *I. H. Frl. Dr. Schapire, Hamburg, Osterbeck 43.* Postmarked: *Jershoft 16.7.20* and stamped with the artist's name and address: *Schmidt-Rottluff, Jershoft, Kr. Schlawei Pommern.* Written on reverse: *So-na-ich laufe hier auch andauernd mit schlechtem Gewissen herum – aber was will man machen. Wenn's nicht von selber kommt hat's ja auch keinen Wert. – Hat der Dr. G. aus Essen wenigstens einen brauchbaren Kopf? Schönste Grüsse – auch von Emy-Trude!* (Well, I am always running about with a bad conscience – but what can one do? If it does not come of its own accord, it's useless. Has Dr. G. from Essen at least got a suitable head? Best wishes – also from Emy-Trude!)

Bequeathed by Dr. Rosa Schapire 1955.

Lit: Leicester Museum and Art Gallery: *Watercolours and Drawings,* 1963 (287)

22 A 1955

75 Landschaft mit Baum
Landscape with Tree

1921

Pen, ink and watercolour 15·5×10·2

Sent as a postcard by Emy Frisch, later the artist's wife, to: *Fräulein Dr. R. Schapire, Hamburg, Osterbeck Str. 43.* Postmark illegible. Stamped with the artist's name and address: *Schmidt-Rottluff, Jershoft, Kr. Schlawei, Pommern.* Written on reverse: *Meine liebe Ro. – Tausend Dank für das Päckchen, das glücklich angekommen ist. Sonst brauchen wir Dich erst mal noch um nichts weiter zu bemühen – da wir jetzt dem Böttger, der jede Woche nach der Stadt fährt, all unsere Besorgungen aufgeben, wenigstens die für ihn verständlichen. – Und da geht's erst mal ganz gut. Aber vielen herzlichen Dank noch und alle guten Sonntagsgrüsse. Deine Emy.* (My dear Ro. – Many thanks for the packet which arrived safely. We shall not have to bother you any more at the moment as Böttger, who goes to town every week, has been asked to make our purchases for us, at least those which he can undertake. And so, everything is in order for the moment. Once again many thanks and best Sunday wishes. Your Emy.)

Bequeathed by Dr. Rosa Schapire 1955.

Exh: Durham, Sheffield, Leicester: *Germany in Ferment,* 1970 (15)

Lit: Leicester Museum and Art Gallery: *Watercolours and Drawings,* 1963 (285)

28 A 1955

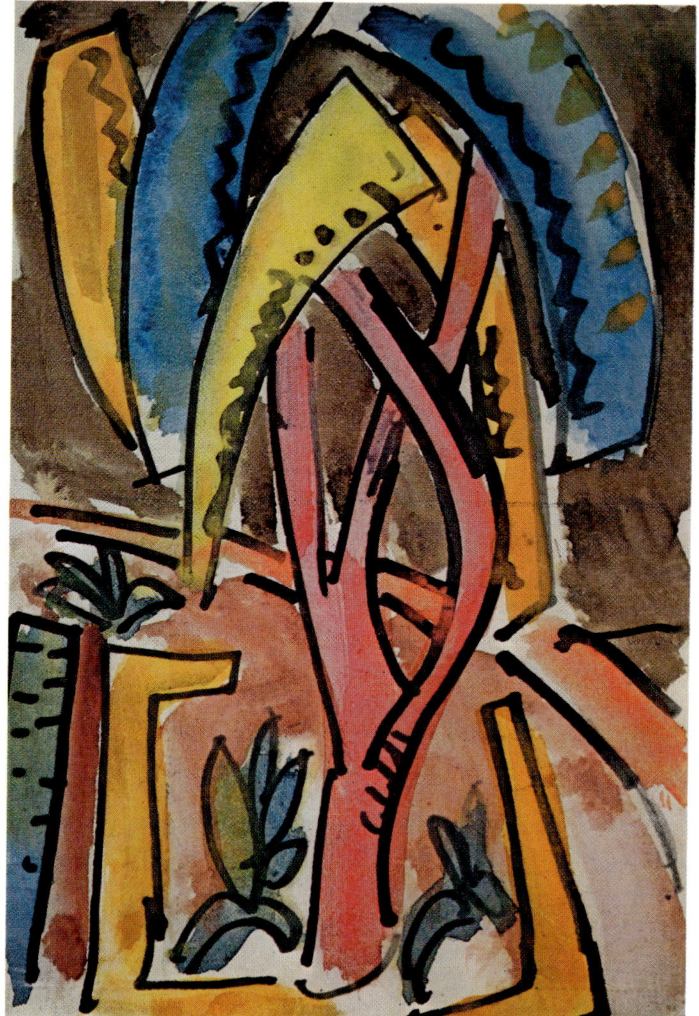

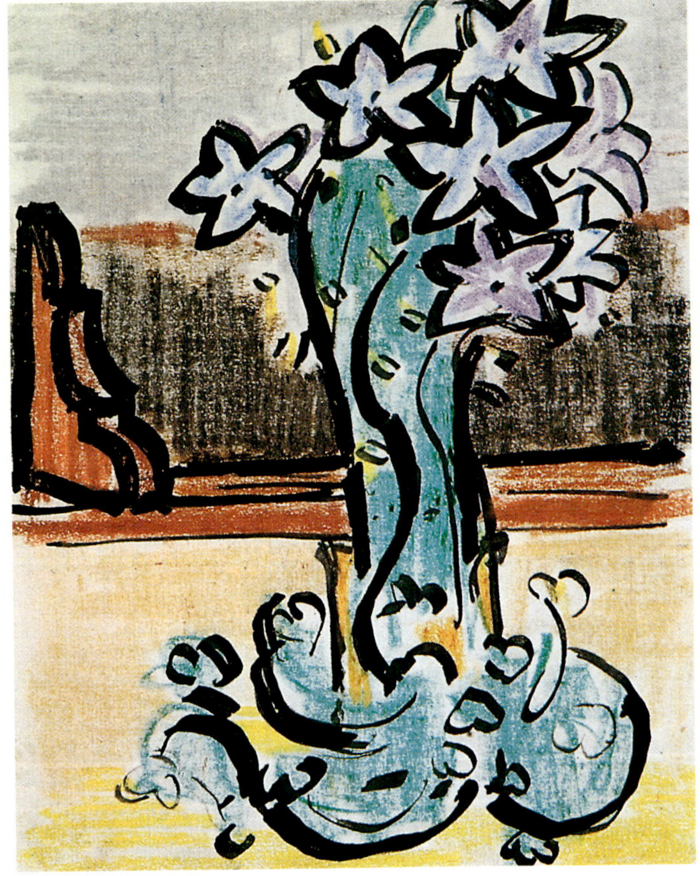

76 Vase mit Blumen
Vase with Flowers

1921

Pen, ink and wax crayon 13·5×10·5

Sent as a postcard by the artist to Dr. Rosa Schapire.
No address, postmark or stamp. Inscribed on reverse
by Dr. Schapire: *Jershoft 17 Aug. 21.* Written on
reverse: *Meine liebe Ro., wir haben bis auf unseren
letzten Brief nichts wieder von Dir gehört und sind
nun völlig im Ungewissen. Roswita ist gestern
abgereist – jetzt wird es erst leerer hier – es war dies
Jahr sehr voll was wirklich nicht sehr erfreulich ist.
Man denkt dann jedesmal ans Auswandern. –
Hoffentlich geht es Dir gut, dass dies nicht der Grund
fürs Ausbleiben einer Nachricht ist. Emy hatte jetzt
auch Fieber und lag zu Bett – heute ist sie wieder
aufgestanden. Noch alle herzlichsten Grüsse und von
Emy . . .* (the last few words are illegible). *D.K.* (My
dear Ro, as we have not heard from you since your
last letter, we are completely in the dark. Roswita left
yesterday – now it will be quite empty – the year has
been very busy which is not particularly appreciated.
One tends to think about emigration. Hope you are
well, that that isn't your reason for not writing. Emy
had a fever and stayed in bed – she got up today.
Best wishes from your Emy . . . Y.K. (your Karl).)

Bequeathed by Dr. Rosa Schapire 1955.

Lit: Leicester Museum and Art Gallery: *Watercolours
and Drawings,* 1963 (290)

25 A 1955

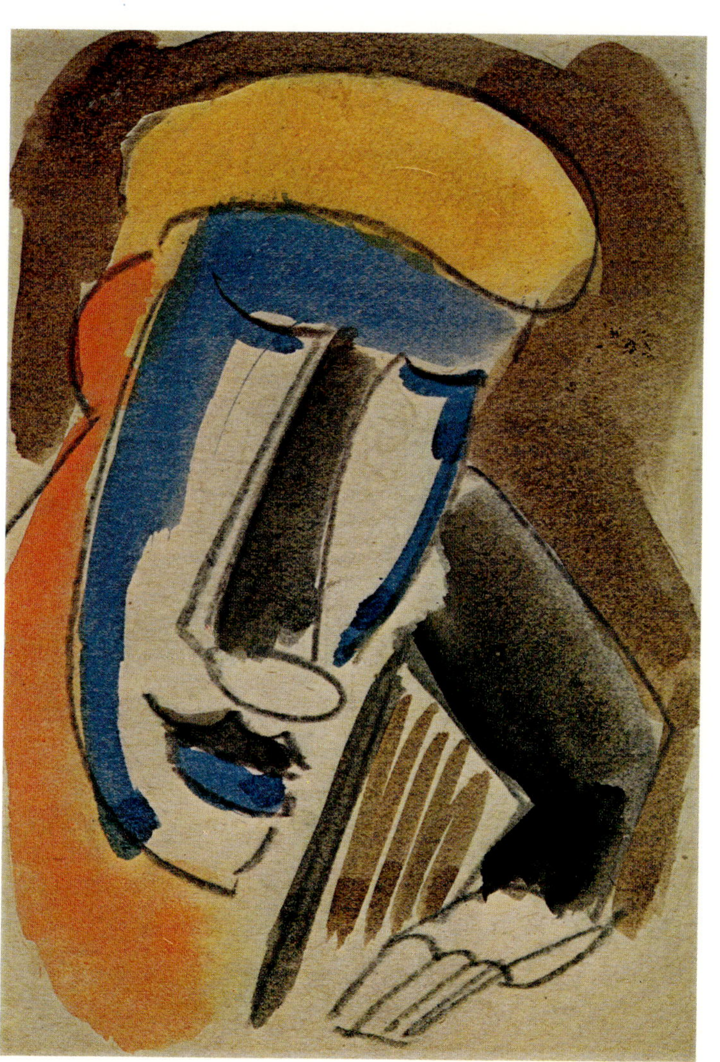

77 Kopf

Head

1921

Watercolour and pencil 15·5 × 10·5

Sent as a New Year's greeting card by the artist to:
Frl. Dr. R. Schapire, Hamburg, Osterbeck Str. 43.
Postmarked: *Chemnitz 30.12.21.* Written on reverse:
Herzlichste Neujahrsgrüsse! K. Emy-Trude, Fritz . . .
(the remaining signatures are illegible). (Heartiest
New Year greetings! K. Emy-Trude, Fritz . . .). Each
person has signed their own name on this greeting.

Bequeathed by Dr. Rosa Schapire 1955.

Exh: Durham, Sheffield, Leicester: *Germany in
Ferment,* 1970 (14)

Lit: Leicester Museum and Art Gallery: *Watercolours
and Drawings,* 1963 (280)

24 A 1955

78 **Männer im Boot**
Men Boating

1924

Pen, ink and wax crayon 15·3 × 10·2

Sent, with the following two cards, as a birthday greeting from the artist to Dr. Schapire who celebrated her 50th birthday on 9th September 1924. Each one carries a single word inscription which when read together form the greeting *Zum Fünfzigsten Geburtstag* (On your 50th Birthday).

Written on reverse: *Zum.* Inscribed on mount by Dr. Schapire: *S-R. Jershöft 9th September 24.*

Bequeathed by Dr. Rosa Schapire 1955.

Lit: Leicester Museum and Art Gallery: *Watercolours and Drawings,* 1963 (288)

26 A 1955

79 **Landschaft**
Landscape

1924

Pen, ink and wax crayon 10·5 × 15·5

Written on reverse: *Fünfzigsten.* Inscribed on mount by Dr. Schapire: *S-R. Jershöft 9th September, 24*

Bequeathed by Dr. Rosa Schapire 1955.

Lit: Leicester Museum and Art Gallery: *Watercolours and Drawings,* 1963 (283)

18 A 1955

80 **Landschaft mit Doppelregenbogen**
Landscape with Double Rainbow

1924

Pen, ink and wax crayon 10·5 × 15·5

Written on reverse: *Geburtstag.* Inscribed on mount by Dr. Schapire: *S-R. Jershöft 9th September, 24*

Bequeathed by Dr. Rosa Schapire 1955.

Lit: Leicester Museum and Art Gallery: *Watercolours and Drawings,* 1963 (284)

19 A 1955

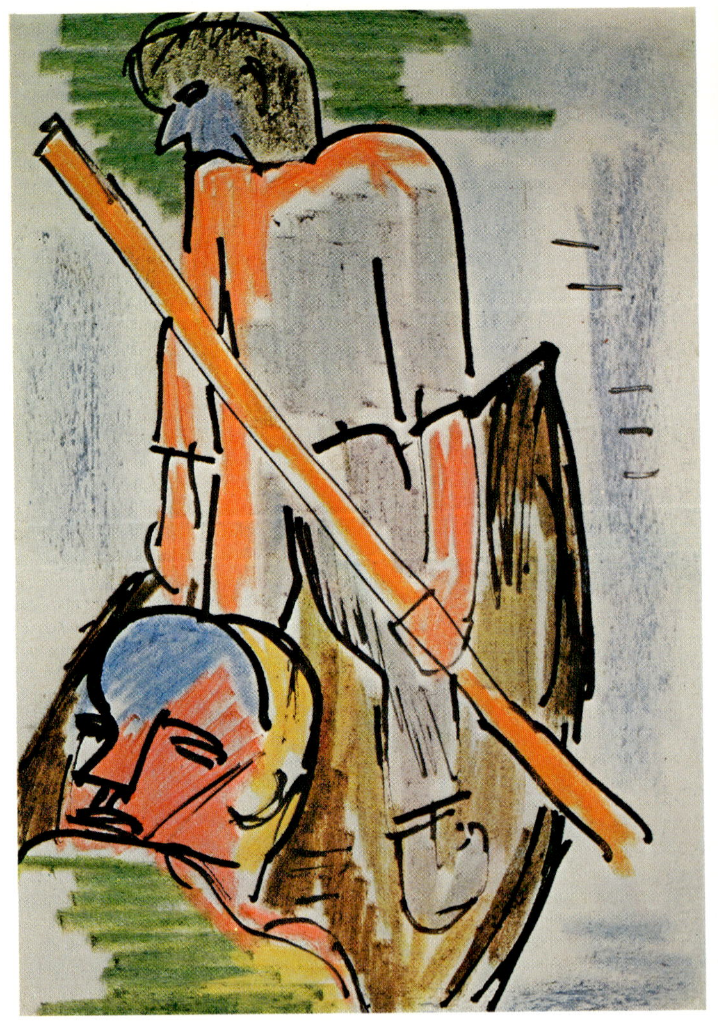

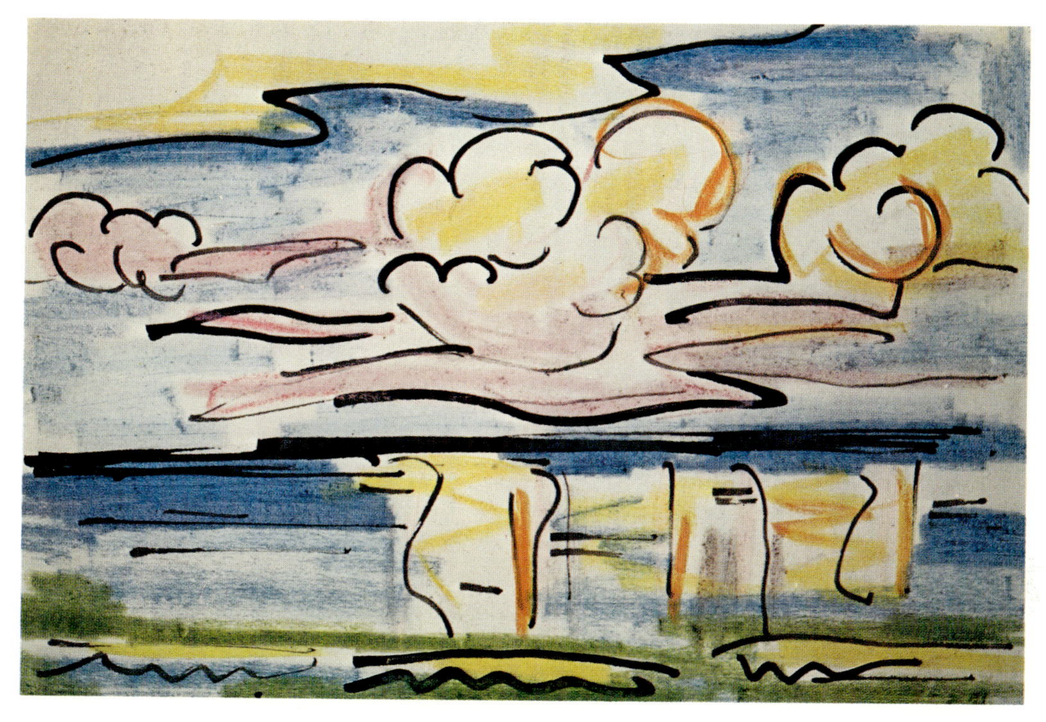

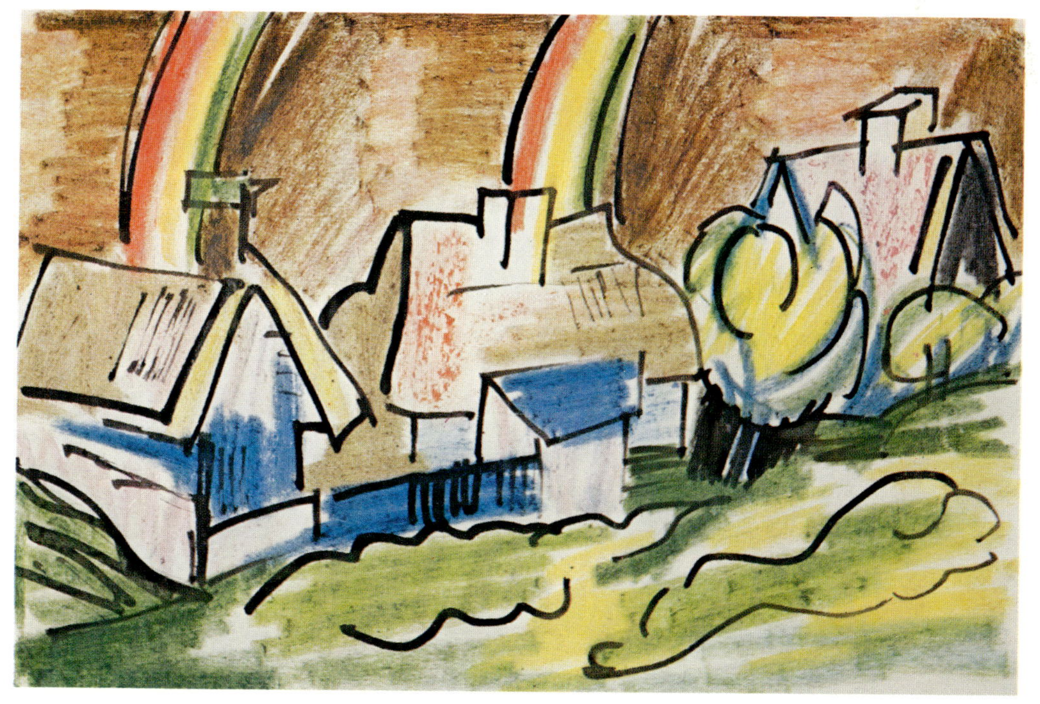

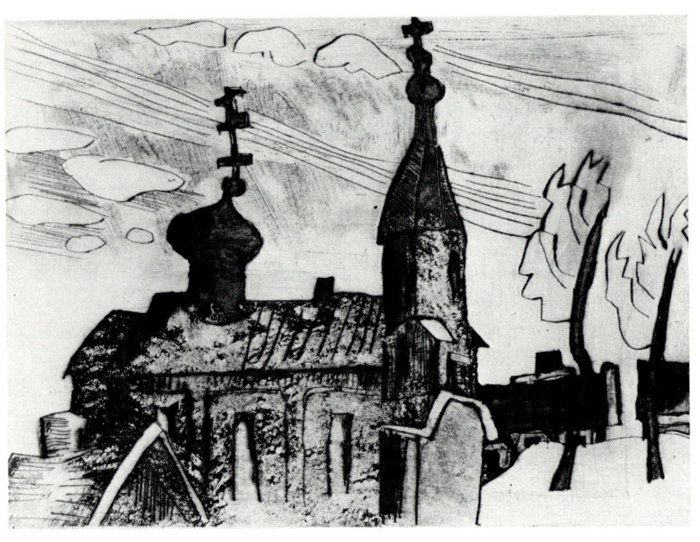

81 **Kirche**
Church

1924

Drypoint and etching 17·7×23·7

Signed, dated and numbered: *245 S. Rottluff*

Rathenau 55

Bequeathed by Dr. Rosa Schapire 1955.

83 A 1955

82 **Landschaft**
Landscape

1938

Watercolour 50×67

Signed and dated: *S. Rottluff Zum 9.9.38*

Bequeathed by Dr. Rosa Schapire 1955.

Exh: Durham, Sheffield, Leicester: *Germany in Ferment,* 1970 (16)

Lit: Leicester Museum and Art Gallery: *Watercolours and Drawings,* 1963 (282)

This large watercolour, probably painted in the region of Lebasee, Pommerania, where the artist lived from 1933, was also a birthday present to Dr. Schapire, this time on the occasion of her 64th birthday.

17 A 1955

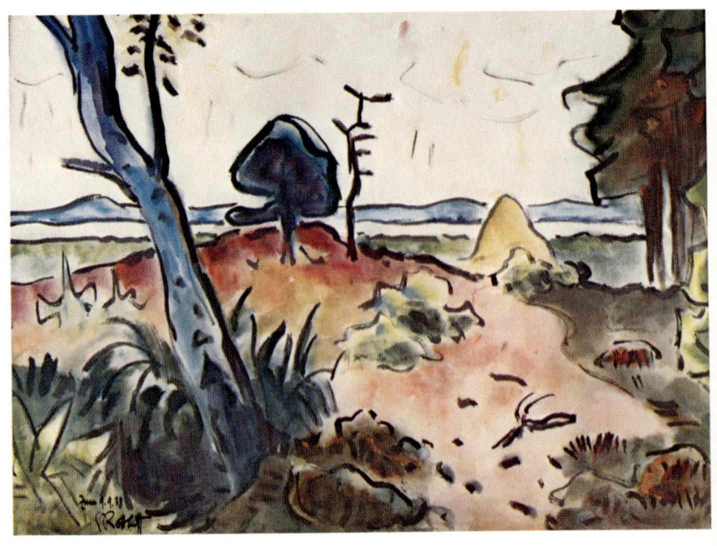

Dr. Rosa Schapire 1874-1954

Art Historian and 'passive' member of Die Brücke

Dr. Rosa Schapire was born in Brody, on the Austrian-Polish border, the daughter of a distinguished Jewish family. She was educated in Zurich and Heidelburg where she trained as an art historian. Alongside her deep concern with Germany's social conditions, she held out great hopes for the new art which was emerging. After further periods of study at Leipzig and Berlin, she graduated in 1904. In 1907 in Hamburg, where she was living, she was introduced by Martha Rauert, a collector, to Emil Nolde and thus began the first of her many friendships with the artists of Die Brücke. Her immediate understanding and enthusiasm for their work led to her becoming an affiliated member of their group in the same year, the first art historian to do so. Although her relationship with Nolde broke down with his departure from the group, her attachment to his former colleagues Kirchner, Heckel and particularly Schmidt-Rottluff intensified. As an associated member of their group, she received a yearly portfolio containing original prints and a specially designed membership card and yearly report.

She was also probably the most important recipient of the famous illustrated postcards sent by Kirchner, Heckel, Schmidt-Rottluff and Pechstein, which remain the best documentation on her relationship with the group (see *Maler der Brücke. Farbige Kartengrüsse an Rosa Schapire von Erich Heckel, Ernst Ludwig Kirchner, Max Pechstein, Karl Schmidt-Rottluff. Mit einem Geleitwort herausgegeben von Gerd Wietek 1958).* Approximately 150 such postcards are known to exist and 11, sent to Dr. Schapire by Schmidt-Rottluff, were bequeathed by her to the Leicestershire permanent collection (see above). Her friendship with Schmidt-Rottluff was very close and lasted longer than her association with other members of Die Brücke. She often visited the summer home which he shared with Heckel at the small Oldenburg coastal town of Dangast. Many of the postcards he sent her were done during the summers he spent with his friends on the coast whilst Rosa remained in Hamburg. Owing to the extrovert character of Schmidt-Rottluff's writing, the messages on the backs of the cards, which in any case often contain abbreviations, are usually kept short and their content limited to rapid exchanges of greeting, question and answer.

Rosa Schapire had her portrait painted three times by Schmidt-Rottluff, in 1911 and 1915 (both estate of the artist) and 1919 (Tate Gallery, London). He also decorated a room in her Hamburg flat for which he designed the furniture and carpets. Will Grohmann, the art historian and author of many definitive works on the German artists of the period, has described how 'when the room still existed you had to conduct yourself as if it were a museum containing a document of the artistic spirit of those times'.

In 1924 she published her definitive catalogue of Schmidt-Rottluff's graphic work up to 1923 and it is on this work that her reputation as an art historian is based. Also during the 1920's she published, with the help of Wilhelm Niemeyer, the newspaper *Die Kündung* in Hamburg which supported the Expressionist movement and its development in Germany. In 1939 she escaped to England and was able to bring with her a large collection of Schmidt-Rottluff's work. In September 1953 she opened the first British exhibition of Schmidt-Rottluff's work at Leicester Museum and Art Gallery. Although this show consisted of graphics and stone carvings only and did not include either paintings or watercolours, Dr. Schapire considered this to be one of the most important events of her life in England.

Arthur Segal
1875-1944

Segal was born in Jassy, Roumania. In 1892 he entered the Berlin Academy and in 1896 moved to Munich to study under Professor Schmidt-Reute and later Professor Hölzel. From 1902-03 he studied in Paris and Italy. In 1904 he settled in Berlin and exhibited with the Berlin Secession and in 1910 helped with the formation of the **Neue Secession** and exhibited with Nolde, Heckel, Kirchner and Schmidt-Rottluff. In 1911 he exhibited with **Der Blaue Reiter** and the **Künstlervereinigung München.** In 1914 he moved to Ascona, Switzerland, where he met and exhibited with Arp and Jawlensky, remaining until 1920 when he returned to Berlin. He became a director of the **Novembergruppe,** exhibiting with them until 1932. In 1925 he refused a teaching post at the **Bauhaus** and exhibited at the Metropolitan Museum of Tokyo. In 1926 he had a one-man exhibition in Rotterdam and in The Hague and the following year he exhibited in the 'Ways and Directions of Abstract Painting in Europe' held at the State Museum of Mannheim. In 1933 he emigrated to Spain and settled in Palma, Majorca. In 1936 he moved to London, where he died.

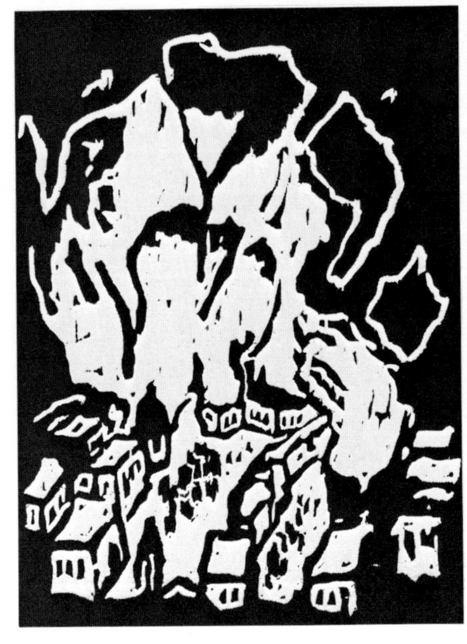

83   **Köpfe über Häusern**

Heads above Houses

1912

Woodcut 35 × 24·5

Signed and dated: *Arthur Segal 1912*

Purchased from Mrs. Margaret Fisher, London 1975.

360'1975

Alois Leopold Seibold
1879-

Seibold was born in Vienna and studied under Jaspar.

84   **Skt. Francis empfängt die Wundmale**
St. Francis receiving the Stigmata

1919

Etching 19·5 × 16

Signed and dated: *Alois Seibold 1919* and on the plate: *A. S. 1919*

Presented by Mrs. Monika Kinley, London 1975.

925'1975

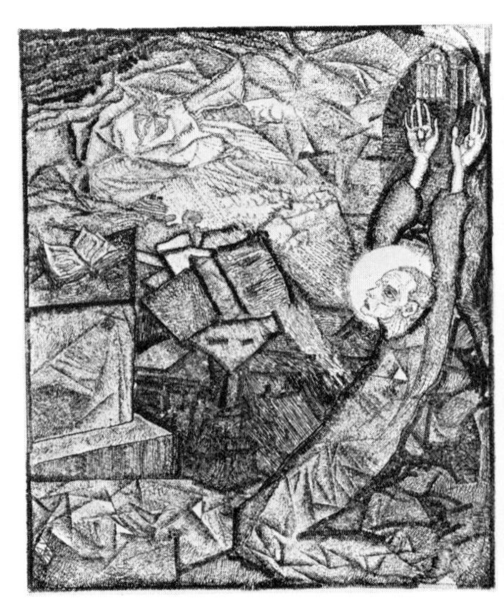

Renée Sintenis

1888-1965

Renée Sintenis was born in Glatz, Silesia. She studied initially at Stuttgart Academy and then from 1908-11 at the School of Arts and Crafts, Berlin. Following her years of study, her work received great support from the poet Rilke and she rapidly gained recognition and financial success. She was greatly influenced by the Impressionists but her work neither changed nor developed greatly and much of it tended towards the academic and sentimental. Her work was essentially small scale and throughout her life concentrated on the depiction of three main subjects: animals, the human form and portraits. After the Second World War she was largely forgotten, although she taught at the Berlin Academy from 1947-55. She died in Berlin.

85 **Selbstbildnis**

Self Portrait

1933

Terracotta 30·5 × 14

Presented by N. Elgar Esq., Woolcombe, near Wellington, Somerset, on behalf of his late wife, through the National Art Collections Fund 1974.

502'1974

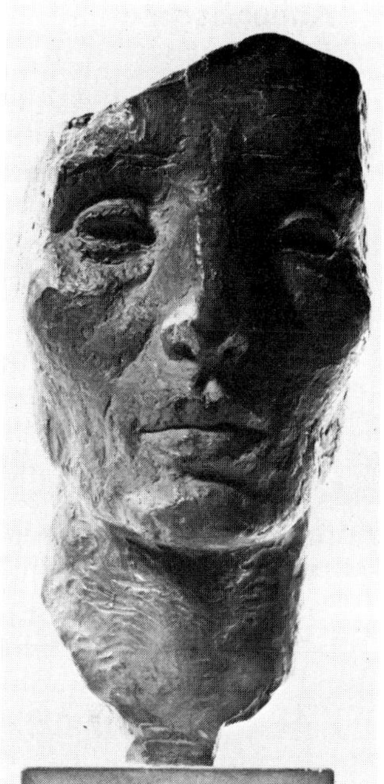

Max Slevogt

1868-1932

Slevogt was born in Landshut. From 1885 to 1889 he studied at the Munich Academy under Herterich and Wilhelm von Diez. In 1889 he visited Paris and studied at the Académie Julian and the following year, on a trip to Italy, met and became friendly with Wilhelm Trubner 1851-1917. In 1891 he moved to Berlin where he became involved with the Secession and particularly with Liebermann and Corinth. In Berlin he came in contact with Impressionism which he readily accepted although, like Corinth and Liebermann, he preferred figure subjects to landscape. Much of his material was taken from the stage, the ballet and cabaret, reproduced as rapid visual impressions. In 1898 he visited Holland to study the work of Rembrandt. In the first decade of the twentieth century he concentrated on theatrical subjects and was deeply influenced by the work of Manet. However, in 1914 he made a trip to Egypt and it was in the landscapes he painted whilst travelling that he came nearest to pure impressionism. Later he returned to his earlier technique which was closer to 'coloured sketching'. In 1917 he became director of a master's studio at the Berlin Academy of Arts and was also made a member of the Academy as well as those of Munich and Dresden. In 1924 he painted murals in Berlin and Neukastel and in 1927 for the Hauff Room in the Bremen Ratskeller. In 1931-32 he painted the Golgotha fresco for the Friedenskirche in Ludwigshafen am Rhein, destroyed during the war. Slevogt died in Neukastel.

86 Gesichte

Visions

1916-17

Portfolio of 21 plates including the title page. Each
plate numbered. In original folder, one of fifty.

Stone, zinc and aluminium plate lithographs, sheet
size 54 × 39

Each plate signed: *Slevogt* in pencil

Rühmann 23

Purchased from Mrs. Monika Kinley, London, with
the assistance of a national grant-in-aid
administered by the Victoria and Albert Museum
1976.

Lit: Dr. J. Plesch: *Janos, the Story of a Doctor,* 1947,
p.382

Printed at Panprefue by R. Hoberg and H. Lulfing in
1917, although some of the plates were produced
the previous year. Slevogt was commissioned as a
war artist but, instead of producing a folio of morale
raising propaganda, he produced a universal
condemnation of war which was confiscated by the
authorities.

Title page

   recto: *Gesichte/21 Stein=u. Zinkdrucke/von/M.
Slevogt/gedruckt in der Panprefue/ – R.
Hoberg – H. Lulfing/1917*

   verso: *Den Frieden kann das Wollen nicht bereiten
Wer alles will, will ich sich vor allen mächtig
Indem er siegt lehrter die Andern streiten
Bedenkend macht er seinen Feind bedächtig
So wachsen Kraft und List nach allen Seiten
Der Weltkreis ruht von Ungeheuern trächtig
Und den Geburten zahlenlohe Plage
Droht jeden Tag als mit dem jüngsten Tage*
                        Goethe

976'1975/1

86a Plate 1

Der Gang ins Ungewisse
The March into the Unknown

1917

Stone lithograph

976'1975/2

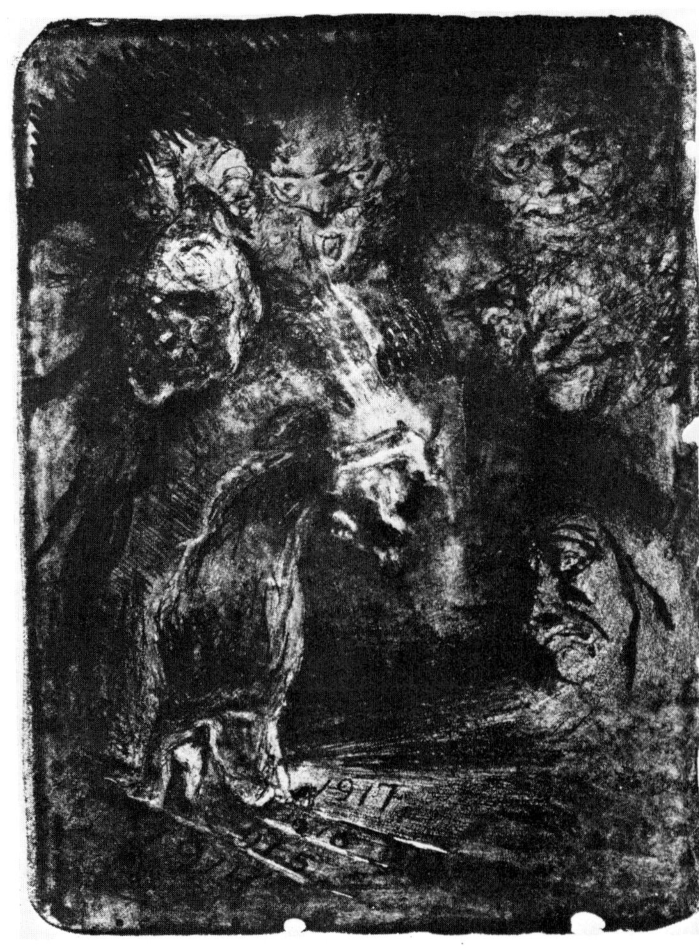

86b   Plate 2
Heulende Hyänen
Howling Hyenas

1917

Stone lithograph

976'1975/3

86c   Plate 3
Drachensaat
Dragonseed

1916

Stone and zinc plate lithograph

The image for this plate comes from *Jason and the Argonauts* where Jason is obliged to perform certain tasks for King Aeëtes in order to obtain the Golden Fleece. One of these tasks, which he completed only with the help of Medea, was to yoke a pair of fire-breathing bulls and with them to plough and sow a field with dragon's teeth from which sprang up armed men with whom Jason was obliged to fight.

976'1975/4

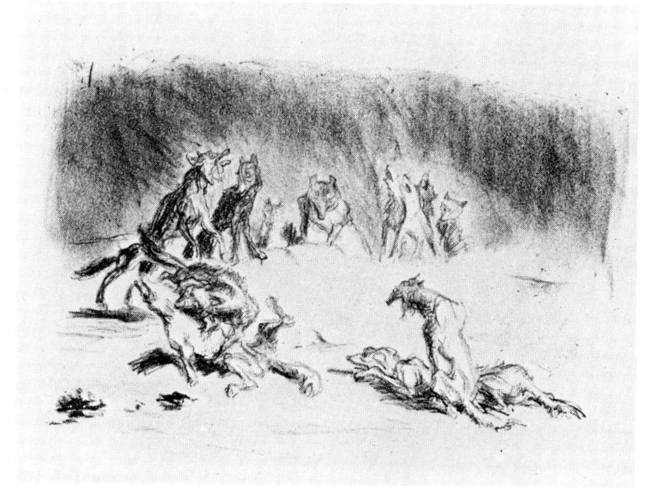

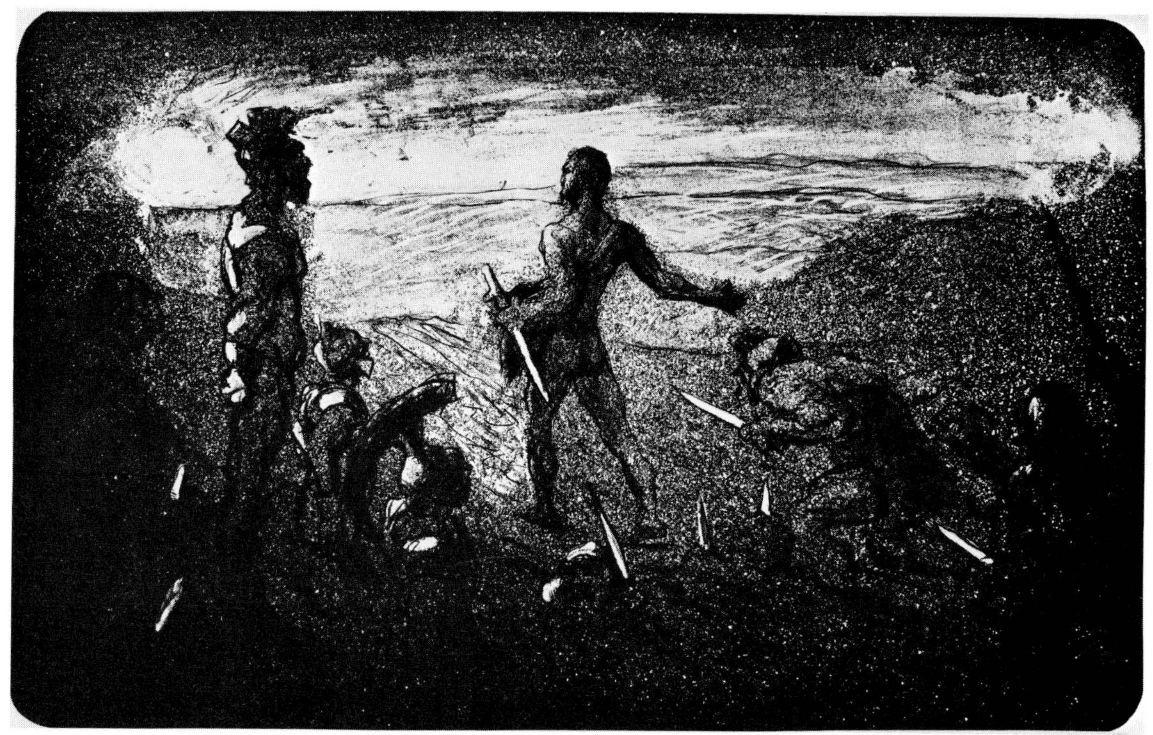

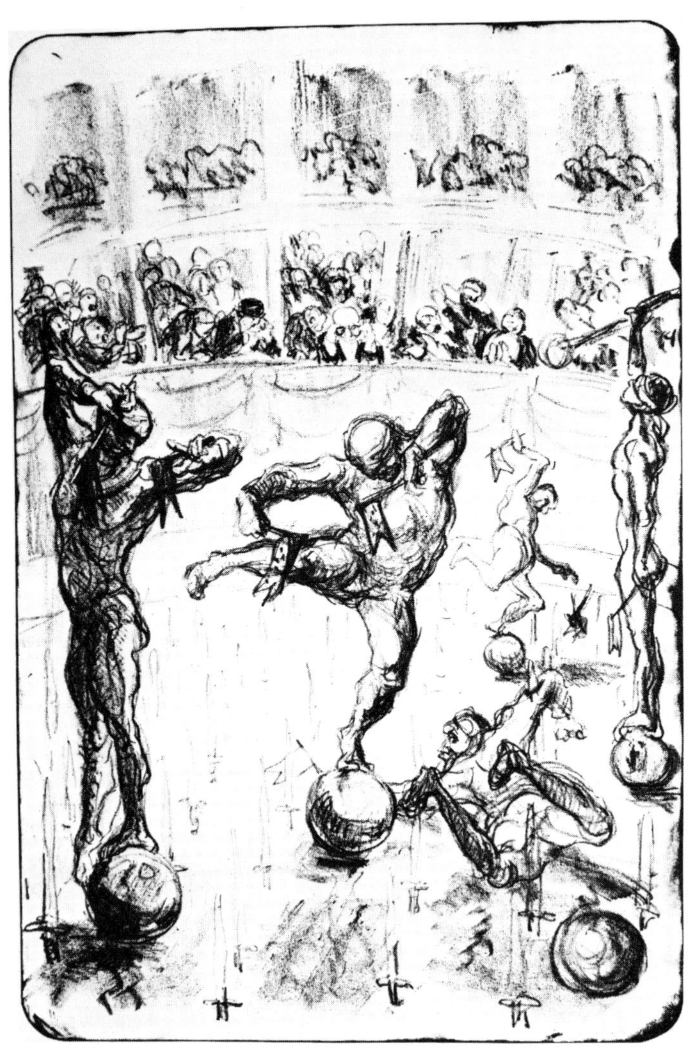

86d   Plate 4
Schwertentanz der Diplomaten
The Diplomats' Sword-dance

1916

Zinc plate lithograph
976'1975/5

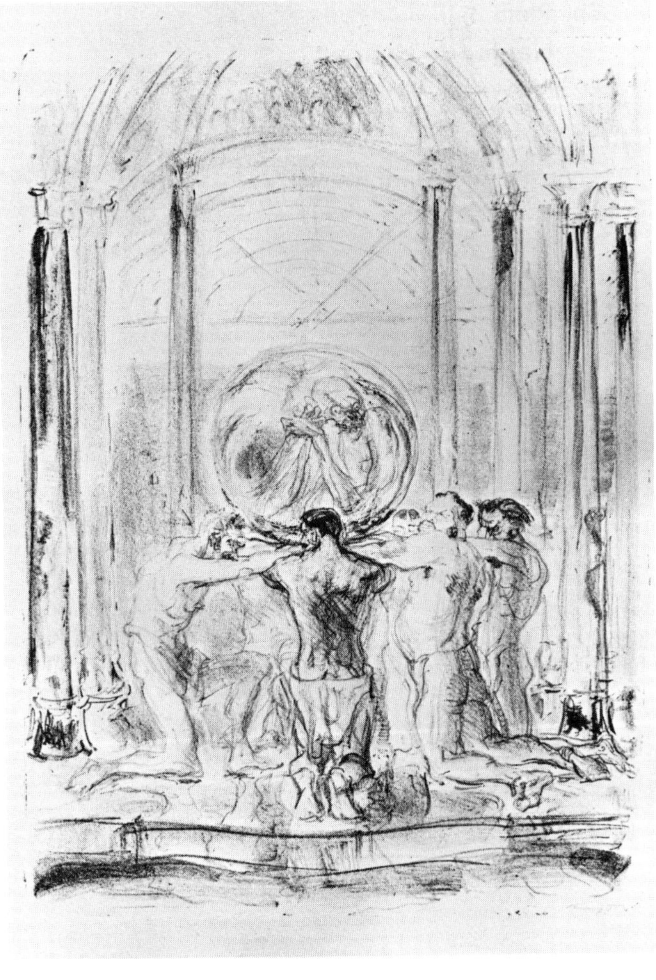

86e   Plate 5
Utopie des Friedens
The Utopia of Peace

1916

Stone lithograph
976'1975/6

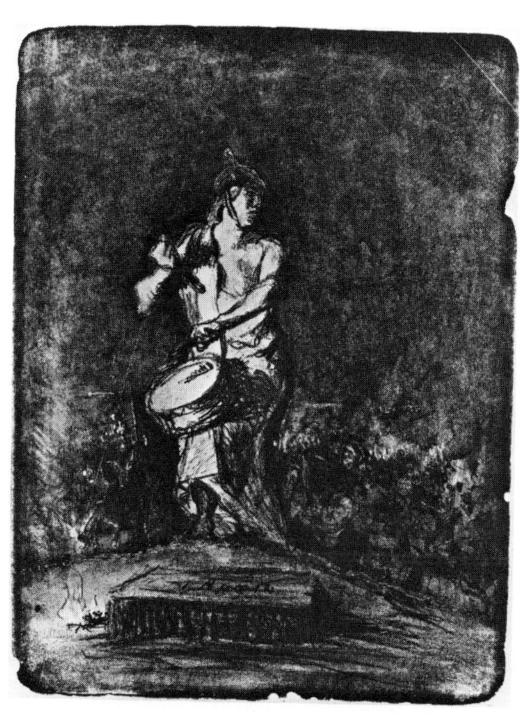

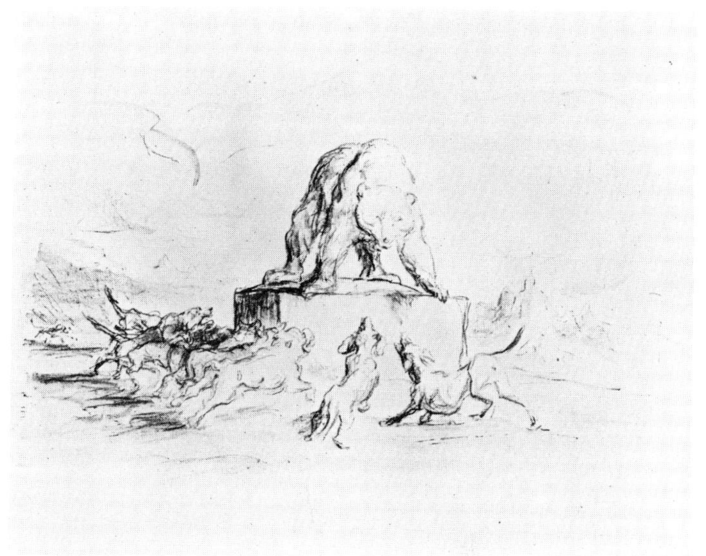

86g   Plate 7

Die Verteidigung (Bär von Hunden umbelt)
The Justification (Bear surrounded by Hounds)

1917

Stone lithograph

976'1975/8

86f   Plate 6

Die Erhebung
The Call to Arms

1916

Stone lithograph

976'1975/7

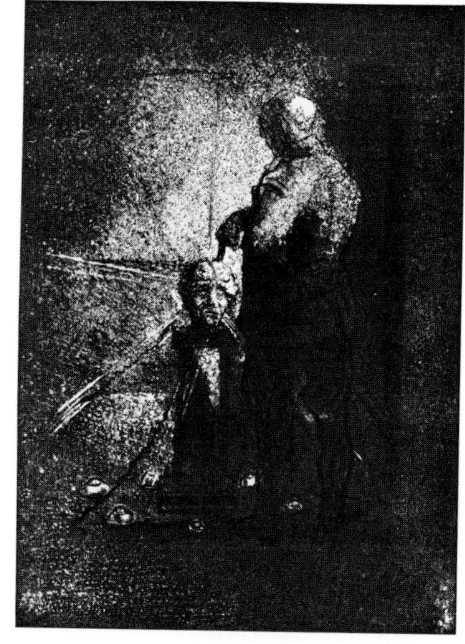

86h   Plate 8

Die oberste Heeresleitung
The Supreme Command

1916

Stone lithograph

976'1975/9

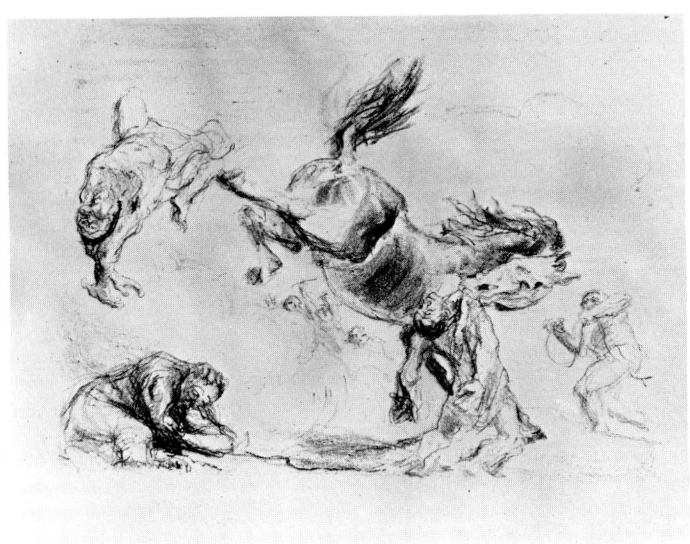

86i   Plate 9

Abwehr (Ein keilendes Pferd)
Defence (A struggling Horse)

1916

Stone lithograph

976'1975/10

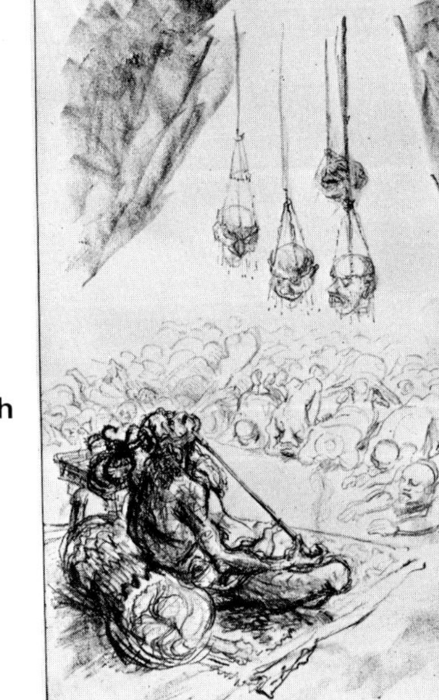

86j   Plate 10

Der Traum des Siegers (Ein Götze der sich anbeten lässt)
The Victor's Dream (An Idol who allows himself to be worshipped)

1916

Zinc plate lithograph

976'1975/11

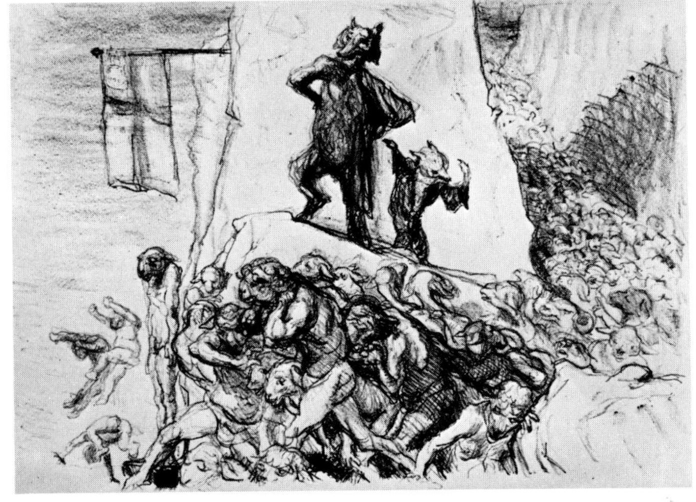

86k   Plate 11

Die grosse Masse (Von einem Fuchs verführte Tiere)
The Masses (Animals misled by a Fox)

1917

Zinc plate lithograph

976'1975/12

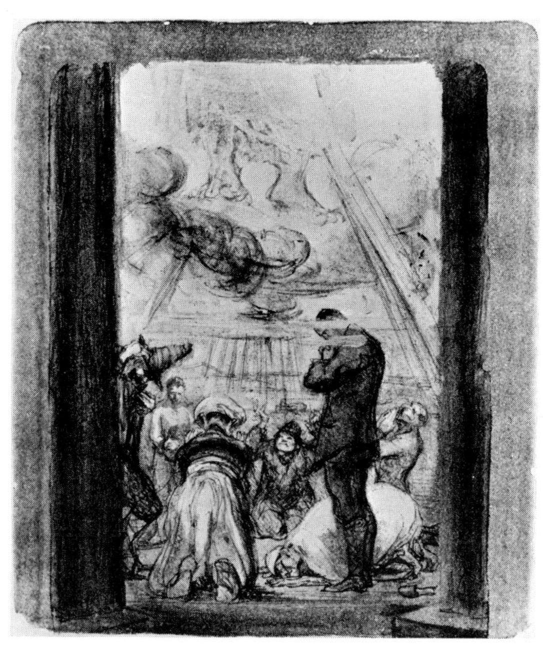

86l   Plate 12

Der grosse Allierte (Drei verschiedene kriegsführende volker im Gebet)
The Great Allies (Three warlike Nations in Prayer)

1916

Stone lithograph

976'1975/13

86m   Plate 13

Pegasus in Kriegsdienst
Pegasus forced into Military Service

1917

Stone lithograph

976'1975/14

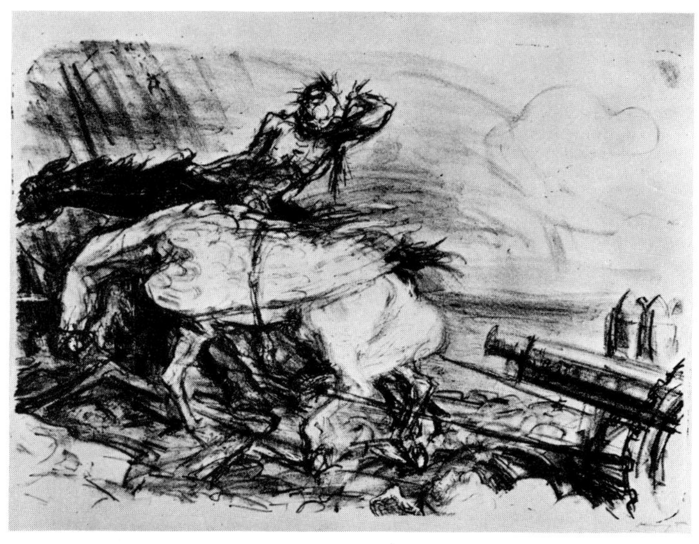

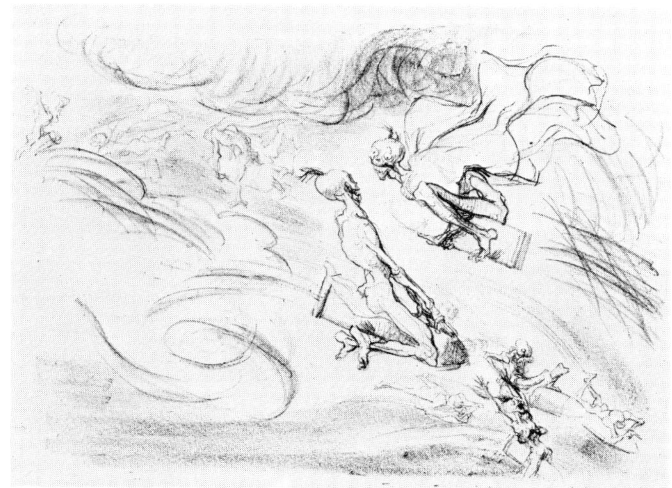

86n   Plate 14

Granatfeuer
Shellfire

1917

Stone lithograph

976'1975/15

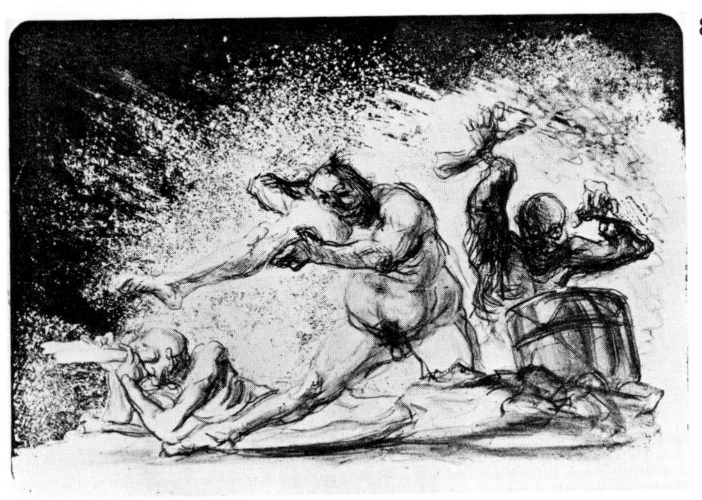

86o Plate 15

Paroxysmus der Vernichtung (Gespenster Kämpfen mit ihren eigenen abgehackten Gliedern)

Paroxysm of Destruction (Spectres fight with their own severed Limbs)

1916

Stone and zinc plate lithograph

976'1975/16

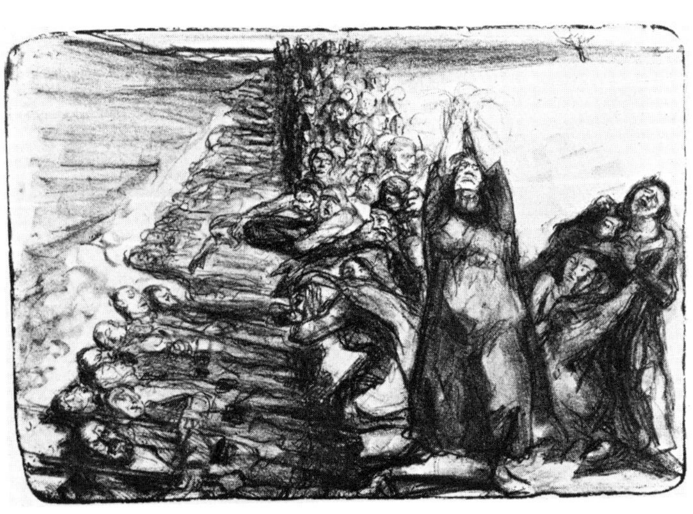

86p Plate 16
Die Mütter
The Mother

1917

Stone lithograph

976'1975/17

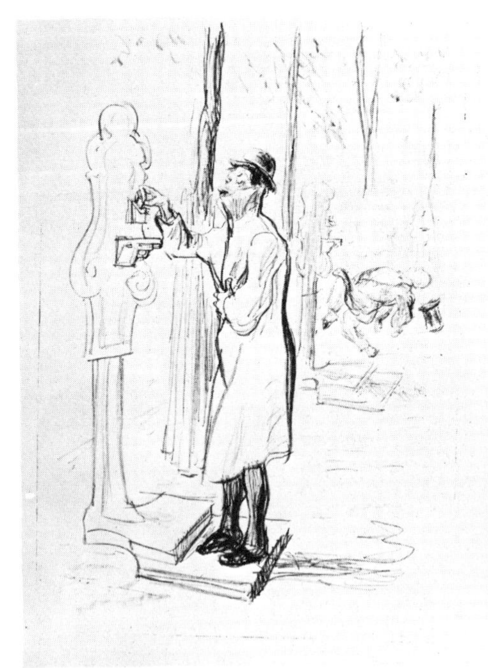

86q Plate 17

Der Selbstmord-Automat
The Suicide-Machine

1917

Zinc plate lithograph

976'1975/18

86r   Plate 18

**Der Flieger, der die Tiere des Sternkreises
abschiesst**
*The Aviator, who shoots the Creatures of the
Zodiac*

1917

Stone lithograph

976'1975/19

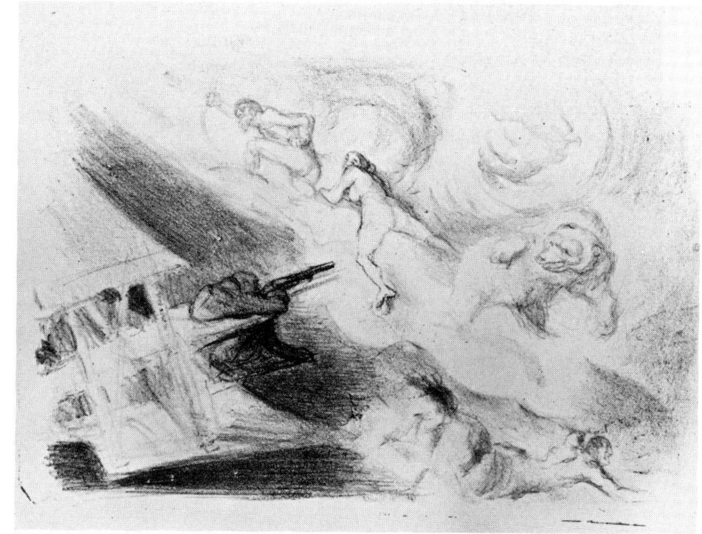

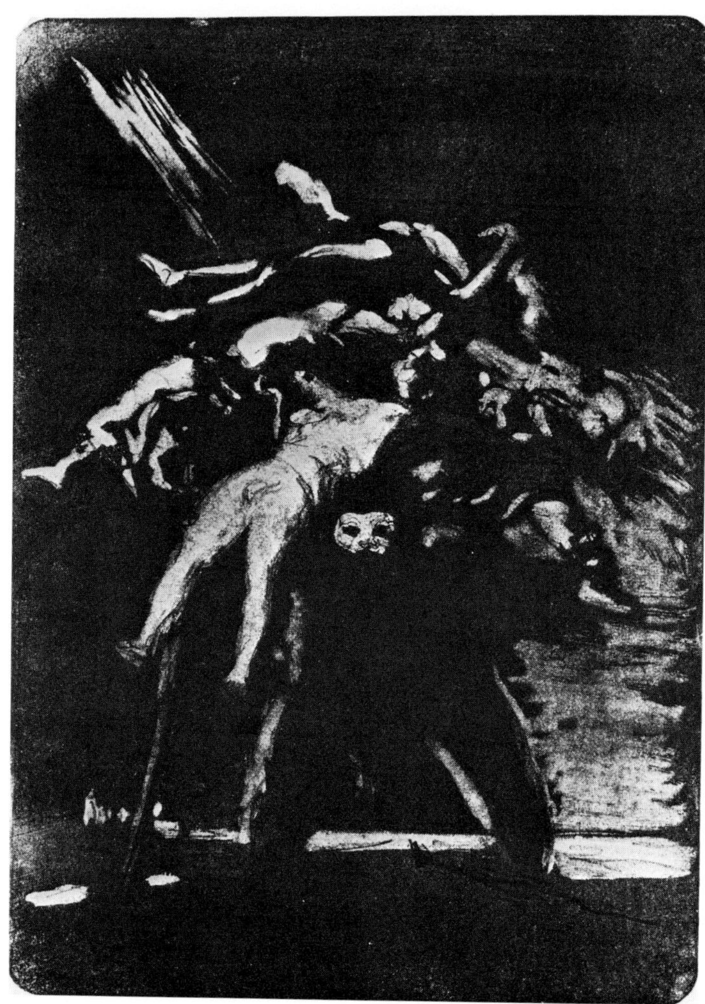

86s   Plate 19

**Der Verantwortliche (Der Unbekannte,
maskiert, watet mit einer Anzahl von Leichen
auf den Rücken durch ein Blutmeer)**
*The Answerable (The Unknown, masked,
wades with Innumerable Corpses on his Back
through a Sea of Blood)*

1917

Stone and aluminium plate lithograph

976'1975/20

86t   Plate 20

Die Vergessenen (Eine Frauengestalt – das Vaterland – deckt die Gefallenen im Massengrabe zu)
The Forgotten (A Female Figure – the Fatherland – covers the Fallen in Mass Graves)

1917

Stone and zinc plate lithograph

976'1975/21

The complete folio has a further plate (21) which is entitled: *Finale. Auf der abgebrochenen Eiche, die von Soldaten gräbern umgeben ist, sitzt der deutsche Adler mit gebrochenen Schwingen. Unten ein Invalide auf Krücken. Specht und Singvogel deuten auf neues Leben.* (Finale. On the broken Standard, surrounded by soldiers' graves, sits the German Eagle with broken wings. Below an Invalid with crutches. Woodpeckers and songbirds signify the renewal of life.)

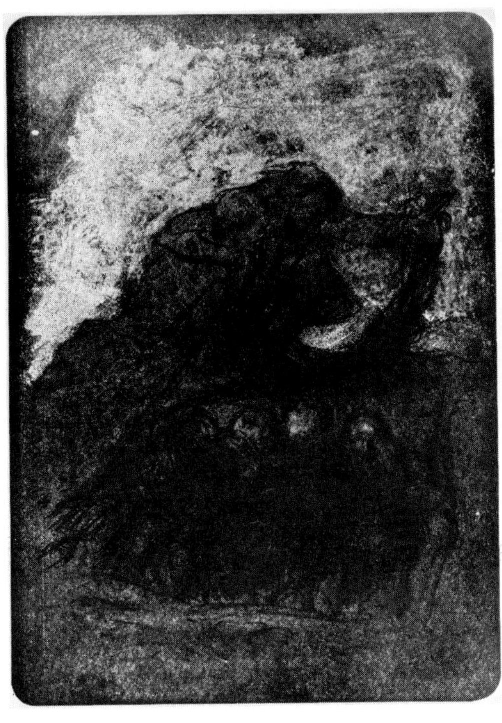

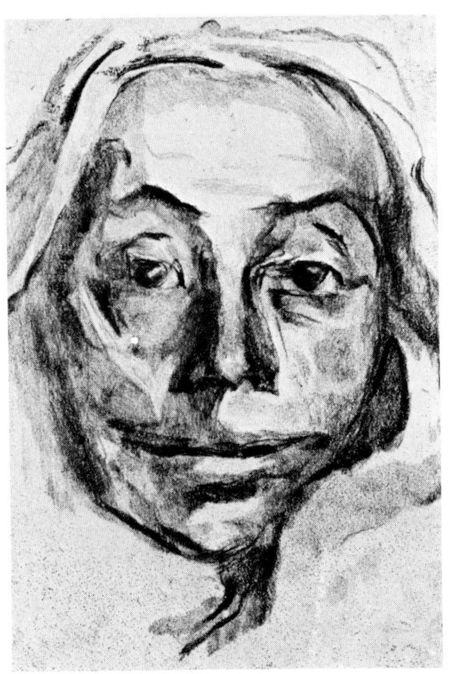

Hedwig Weiss
1860-1923

Hedwig Weiss was born in Königsberg where she later studied under Rudolph Mauer. She also studied in Berlin under Stauffer-Bern and in Munich under Durr. Essentially a landscape painter, she also produced numerous graphic works and some book illustrations. In 1892 she exhibited at the Berlin Academy and in subsequent years with the Berlin Secession. She died in Berlin.

87   **Bildnis Käthe Kollwitz**
Portrait of Käthe Kollwitz

Aquatint, stipple and etching 21 × 14·5

Signed l.r.: *Hedwig Weiss.* Numbered 20/50
Inscribed in pencil: *Käthe Kollwitz*

Purchased from Mrs. Margaret Fisher, London 1971.

15 A 1971

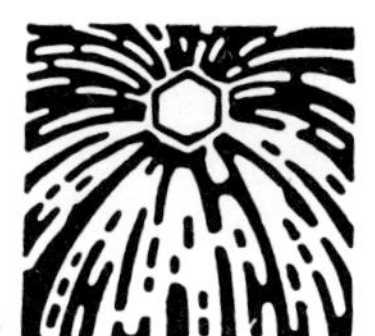

Bibliography

Bayer, Herbert, **Gropius,** Walter and **Gropius,** Ise (ed.)
Bauhaus, Weimar 1919-1925, Dessau 1925-1928 The Museum of Modern Art, New York 1938

Bénézit, E.
Dictionaire des Peintres, Sculpteurs, Dessinateurs et Graveurs (8 vols.), Paris 1966

Berger, John
Marcel Frishman, Oxford 1957

Berlin, Brücke-Museum
Karl Schmidt-Rottluff. Das graphische Werk zum 90 Geburtstag des Künstlers, 1974

Börsch-Supan, Helmut, **Neihardt,** Hans Joachim and **Vaughan,** William
Caspar David Friedrich 1774-1840. Romantic Landscape Painting in Dresden, The Tate Gallery, London 1972. Exhibition Catalogue

Bremen, Kunsthalle
Der Holzschnitt, 1974

Carls, Carl D.
Barlach, London 1969

Durham, Sheffield and **Leicester**
Germany in Ferment, 1970. Exhibition Catalogue

Fechter, Paul
Das Graphische Werk Max Pechsteins, Berlin 1921

Feist, Peter H.
Deutsche Kunst 19./20. Jahrhundert, Staatliche Museen zu Berlin, 1966

Finke, Ulrich
German Painting from Romanticism to Expressionism, London 1974

Glaser, Curt and **Meier-Graefe,** Julius
Max Beckmann, Munich 1924

Goldwater, Robert J.
Primitivism in Modern Painting, New York 1938

Gosebruch, Martin
Nolde Aquarelle und Zeichnungen, Munich 1957

Gay, Peter
Weimar Culture, London 1969

Grohmann, Will
Das Werk Ernst Ludwig Kirchners, Munich 1926

Grohmann, Will
Paul Klee, London 1954

Grohmann, Will
Schmidt-Rottluff, London 1956

Grohmann, Will
Wassily Kandinsky, Cologne 1948

Grohmann, Will
Painters of the Brücke, Tate Gallery, London 1964. Exhibition Catalogue

Hancke, Erich
Max Liebermann, Berlin 1914

Hauser, Arnold
The Social History of Art (Vol. II), London 1941

Hess, Hans
Lyonel Feininger, London 1961

Hess, Hans
George Grosz, London 1974

Hodin, J. P.
Edvard Munch, London 1972

Hoffmann, Edith
Kokoschka, Life and Work, London 1947

Jaworska, Wladyslawa
Gauguin and the Pont Aven School, London 1972

Jensen, Paul
The Cinema of Fritz Lang, New York 1969

Kandinsky, Wassily and **Marc,** Franz (ed.)
Der Blaue Reiter Almanac, Munich 1912, Eng. Trans. London 1974

Klipstein, Dr. August
Käthe Kollwitz Verzeichnis des Graphischen Werkes, Bern 1955.

Kokoschka, Oskar   *My Life,* London 1974

Lang, Lothar   *Expressionist Book Illustration,* London 1976

Lankheit, Klaus   *Franz Marc – Katalog der Werke,* Cologne 1950

Lankheit, Klaus   *Franz Marc,* Berlin 1950

Laquer, Walter   *Weimar, A Cultural History 1918-1933,* London 1974

Lucerne, Galerie Fischer   *Gemälde und Plastiken Moderner Meister aus Deutschen Museen,* 1939

Manvell, Dr. Roger (ed.)   *The International Encyclopaedia of Film.* Section on Germany by Roger Manvell, London 1972

Manvell, Dr. Roger and **Fraenkel,** Heinrich   *The German Cinema,* London 1971

Marc, Franz   *Briefe, Aufzeichnungen und Aphorismen,* 2 vols., Berlin 1920

Marc, Franz   *Briefe aus dem Feld,* Berlin 1940

Müller, Heinrich   *Die Späte Graphik von Lovis Corinth,* Hamburg 1960

Munich, Haus der Deutscher Kunst   *Grosse Deutsche Kunstausstellung,* 1937. Exhibition Catalogue.

Myers, Bernard S.   *Expressionism, A Generation in Revolt,* London 1963

Nagel, Otto   *Käthe Kollwitz,* Dresden 1963, Eng. edit. London 1971

Nolde, Emil   *Jahre der Kämpfe,* 2nd Enlarged Edition, Flensburg 1956

Phaidon Press Ltd.   *Dictionary of Twentieth Century Art,* London and New York 1973

Pforzheim, Kunst – und Kunstgewerberverein   *Emil Nolde, Wilhelm Lehmbruck Meister der Plastik des 20. Jahrhunderts,* 1961. Exhibition Catalogue

Powell, Nicholas   *The Sacred Spring. The Arts in Vienna 1898-1914,* London 1974

Prasse, Leona E.   *Lyonel Feininger das Graphische Werk,* 1972

Rathenau, Ernst   *Karl Schmidt-Rottluff: das graphische Werk seit 1923,* New York 1964

Rewald, John   *The History of Impressionism,* New York 1946 (Revised and enlarged edition 1961)

Rewald, John   *Post-Impressionism – From Van Gogh to Gauguin,* New York 1956

Richter, Hans   *Dada – art and anti-art,* London 1965

Roethel, Hans Konrad   *Gabriele Münter,* Munich 1957

Roethel, Hans Konrad   *Modern German Painting,* London 1958

Roethel, Hans Konrad   *The Blue Rider Group,* Tate Gallery, London 1960. Exhibition Catalogue

Roethel, Hans Konrad   *Kandinsky: the Road to Abstraction,* Marlborough Fine Art, London 1961. Exhibition Catalogue

Roethel, Hans Konrad   *Wassily Kandinsky, Das Graphische Werk,* Cologne 1970

Schapire, Rosa   *Karl Schmidt-Rottluffs Graphische Werk bis 1923,* Berlin 1924

Scheyer, Ernst   *Lyonel Feininger: The Formative Years,* The Detroit Institute of Arts, 1964. Exhibition Catalogue

Schiefler, Gustav — *Das graphische Werk Emil Noldes bis 1910,* Berlin 1911

Schiefler, Gustav — *Max Liebermann: sein graphisches Werk,* Berlin 1923

Schiefler, Gustav — *Das graphische Werk Emil Noldes 1910-1925,* Berlin 1927

Scholes, Percy A. — *The Oxford Companion to Music,* London 1942

Schult, Friedrich — *Ernst Barlach,* Berlin 1950

Schwarz, Karl — *Das graphische Werk von Lovis Corinth,* 1st edit. Berlin 1917, 2nd edit. Berlin 1922

Selz, Peter — *German Expressionist Painting,* London 1957

Sievers, Johannes — *Die Radierungen und Steindrucke von Käthe Kollwitz innerhalb der Jahre 1890-1912,* Dresden 1913

Taylor, A. J. P. — *From Sarajevo to Potsdam,* London 1966

Thieme-Becker — *Allgemeines Lexikon der Bildenden Kunstler*

Thoene, Peter (pseud.) — *Modern German Art,* London 1938

Tietze-Conrat, Erica — *Georg Ehrlich,* London 1956

Vergo, Peter — *Art in Vienna 1898-1918,* London 1975

Werner, Alfred — The Magic World of Alfred Kubin, *The Painter and Sculptor.* Summer 1960, Vol. 3, Number 2

Wietek, Gerd — *Maler der Brücke Farbige Kartengrüsse an Rosa Schapire,* Wiesbaden 1958

Wingler, Hans M. and **Welz,** Friedrich — *Kokoschka. Das druckgraphische Werk,* Berlin 1975

Index

Excluding contents of Chronological Table